RISING SUN OVER BATAAN
MEMOIRS OF WAR

BY

Horacio H. Montoya

✽ ✽ ✽

ISBN: 1-4392-0043-2
ISBN-13: 9781439200438

Visit www.booksurge.com to order additional copies.

ACKNOWLEDGEMENT

I would like to express my sincere gratitude to Robert H. Cowan for the authorization to re-print a number of images from his web site at Bellavista press@comcast.net The images can be found on pages 107-121 inclusively.

Furthermore, I am reminded of the service of his father James H. Cowan, a fellow soldier, who along with thousands of other American GI's valiantly served their country at Bataan.

NOTE

I would like to acknowledge the unselfish efforts of my son F. Carlos Montoya for his assistance in the preparation of my manuscript for publication. Carlos served as a resource in the clarification and confirmation of historical data and in the selection of an acceptable publisher. He also spent innumerable hours sharing in the arduous and ongoing task of editing the manuscript for publication. I am forever indebted to my son for his assistance and support in bringing to fruition my life long dream of the publication of my war time memoirs.

Horacio H. Montoya

PROLOGUE

This book is about my experience as a prisoner of war when I was captured in Bataan by the Japanese in World War II. The people of the world will never fully appreciate the brutality that Japanese soldiers inflicted on their prisoners unless we who experienced it tell our stories.

My brother, Ben, and I were prisoners of the Japanese for forty months. I maintained a forbidden diary until three months before the Japanese surrender in August 1945. Because the Japanese refused to differentiate POW camps from their other military installations, incendiary bombs dropped from American B-29s hit my barracks at Camp 17 in Kyushu, Japan, about thirty-five miles from Nagasaki. The resulting fire destroyed the diary; the memories remain.

In 1940, President Franklin D. Roosevelt mandated that all eligible young men serve their country for two years. By the end of that summer, I had decided to enlist and finish my studies at the University of New Mexico later.

On January 6, 1941, our Taos National Guard unit was inducted into the U.S. Army, and the Taos Armory became our home for two weeks. I was one of the clerks who worked in the Battery B commander's office. I was indebted to Lieutenant Reynaldo Gonzales for this lucky break. Lieutenant Gonzales had been my biology teacher in high school. He had come to Taos from Lemitar, New Mexico. Fifteen months later, on the day of the American surrender to the forces of Imperial Japan, he was executed by a Japanese firing squad for having Japanese money in his possession.

All the enlisted men in Battery H were issued heavy army topcoats. It was very cold in northern New Mexico and there was snow on the ground. On January 18, the entire battery – men and equipment – was loaded on army trucks and left for Fort Bliss, Texas, where we joined other New Mexico batteries, some 1,800 men, to begin basic combat training as the 200th Coast Artillery, Anti-Aircraft Regiment. The 200th was equipped with three-inch guns, 37mm anti-aircraft artillery, and 30 and 50 caliber machine guns. I was the battery clerk working in a makeshift office with First Sergeant John Vickery and the battery commander, Captain Anthony George. Captain George was a perfectionist, a tyrant, and not well-liked by the men. Because I knew shorthand, I was selected as a one-time court reporter in the court martial of a young soldier from Santa Fe, who was accused of assaulting a commissioned officer in the regiment. Not long after this, Captain George sent me to the Fort Bliss Army Headquarters special school for regimental clerks at the El Paso Technical Institute. Here I learned advanced shorthand, how to prepare army payrolls, and other related subjects. After completion of the course of study, I was placed on temporary detached duty from Battery H and sent to the army headquarters at Fort Bliss.

On August 17, 1941, the War Department notified the 200th Coast Artillery that it had been selected for assignment overseas but didn't tell us where. The 200th was named "the best anti-aircraft unit in the Armed Forces of the United States," and we were to be assigned to areas of critical importance. Colonel Charles G. Sage, our regimental commander, was proud of us.

By the third week in August, we knew that we were going to the Philippines by way of San Francisco. On August 31, the 900 men of the Second Battalion boarded a military train in El Paso, Texas – a memorable scene. Every soldier was dressed in a freshly pressed khaki uniform. I vividly recall the crease in my trousers, the razor-edge fold on my shirt sleeves, and the spit shine on my brown Army shoes. I was dashing! Our regimental band, conducted by First Lieutenant Jim McCahon, was at the train depot to see us off.

We arrived in San Francisco the following day and were quickly rushed from the train depot to Angel Island, the clearing center and point of debarkation for the Far East. We spent our free time waiting in long lines to be inoculated against tropical diseases. The inoculation against cholera was particularly painful.

On September 9, we boarded the U.S.S. *President Coolidge*, bound for Manila. The *President Coolidge* was a luxury ship turned troop ship just prior to the war. A few days out of Honolulu, we ran into a typhoon. The ship was rocked with a steady downpour of rain, fierce winds, and forty to fifty foot waves. It was a terrifying experience. It also made us several days late.

We reached Manila twenty-two days after leaving San Francisco. Our equipment was unloaded almost immediately. Trucks, 37mm cannons, and three-inch guns looked like toys as they dangled in the air as the crane operator lowered them slowly to the dock.

In a matter of hours, we were in a mile-long convoy driving on the "wrong side" of a narrow, two-lane highway. It was a typical hot and humid tropical day. The locals lined up alongside the highway to wave and greet us in Tagalog and Spanish. At the end of the road was Fort Stotsenberg in the province of Pampanga, sixty miles south of Manila and within a stone's throw of Clark Field, the U.S. Army base for B-17 heavy bombers and P-40 fighter planes.

Our responsibility was to protect Clark Field from enemy aircraft, so we were ordered to move out into the surrounding fields and simulate combat living conditions – "bivouac," as we called it. We were in complete blackout every night, and every day we would target practice with live ammunition. Morale was sky-high.

By the end of November, war clouds over the Far East had thickened. The young New Mexicans surrounding Clark Field were ready to fight. It was just a matter of time.

DEDICATION

I am dedicating this book to the men of The 200th and 515th (AA) Coast Artillery Regiments of the New Mexico National Guard who gave their lives in the battles of Bataan and Corregidor, and in the prisoner of war camps in the Philippines and the southwest Pacific.

These young men represented the United States with honor and courage. They were truly the standard-bearers of freedom, and their legacy will be remembered for years to come.

CONTENTS

SIGNIFICANT DATES

1941

6 January: Taos, New Mexico, National Guard Unit inducted into the U.S. Army at Taos Armory

Summer: War department drafts 200th Regiment from Fort Bliss, Texas, for a Far East deployment

9 September: 200th Regiment ships overseas from Angel Island, California, aboard USS *President Coolidge*

10 December: 11 a.m., fifty-four Japanese bombers attack Clark Field

24 December: Midnight, Allied retreat to Bataan Peninsula begins as Japanese tanks invade Clark Field

31 December: Midnight, Battery H, 200th Regiment crosses Pampanga River via Calumpet Bridge into Bataan

1942

9 April: American forces surrender to Japanese at Mariveles

10 April: "Bataan Death March" begins as Japanese commander orders American POWs to march north to Camp O'Donnell

1945

August: 500 Americans transferred from Camp Cabanatuan to Fukuoka Camp #17, Omuta, Japan, to work in a coal mine

6 August: *Enola Gay* drops "Little Boy" on Hiroshima

9 August: *Bock's Car* drops "Fat Man" on Nagasaki

15 August: Japan surrenders

18 September: Camp #17 evacuated; POWs turned over to U.S. Army authority in Nagasaki

25 September: Liberated Americans leave Nagasaki for Manila

Honolulu Star-Bulletin 1st EXTRA

6 PAGES—HONOLULU, TERRITORY OF HAWAII, U.S.A., SUNDAY, DECEMBER 7, 1941—6 PAGES ★ PRICE FIVE CENTS

WAR!

(Associated Press by Transpacific Telephone)

SAN FRANCISCO, Dec. 7.—President Roosevelt announced this morning that Japanese planes had attacked Manila and Pearl Harbor.

OAHU BOMBED BY JAPANESE PLANES

CHAPTER 1

✵ ✵ ✵

PEARL HARBOR BOMBED

I looked at my wristwatch. It was 8:05. I had spent the night on an Army issue shelter half under the truck we used to tow our cannon. As I slipped into my boots to join the rest of my squad, I could hear the chow truck approaching our gun position with breakfast.

"Have you guys heard the news?" Sergeant Paul Trujillo blared out from the passenger side of the chow truck. "Pearl Harbor has been attacked by hundreds of Jap planes." I knew that Clark Field would be next.

Our main source of news in the field was homemade radios. Don Bell, the announcer at KMZH in Manila, was already hoarse. "Honolulu bombed," he repeated on the air over and over again. Some of our radio operators had intercepted radio news reports from San Francisco that verified the attack.

To the north of the Philippine Archipelago was Formosa, a source of worry and frustration to our generals. The Japanese government had an important air base within a stone's throw of Clark Field. General Lewis H. Brereton from the Far East Air Force Headquarters was begging for permission to bomb Formosa. He was also concerned over reports of Japanese bombers over Lingayen Gulf north of Manila. A heavy fog was reported over Formosa.

Our base commander made sure that Clark Field was well protected from a surprise enemy attack. Our P-40 pursuit planes hovered overhead continuously. Platoon Sergeant Luther Ragsdale and Platoon Corporal Ben Montoya supervised the dispersal of our 37mm and 50 caliber ammo into fox holes at a workable distance from our area of operation. Private First Class Lolo Montoya and Private Fernando Concha were acutely concerned. They were our ammunition handlers and did not relish the idea of having to carry the ammo very far. Fernando was nicknamed Fred. He was from the Taos Pueblo, about five feet five inches tall, stocky, and as strong as an ox. We were very good friends. On occasion, he enjoyed teasing me in a kind way. There was a popular song that I used to sing and hum, and Fred happened to be around to hear me sing, "I Wonder Who's Kissing Her Now?" He assured me that she still loved me and that she would wait for me, no matter what. The fact that I could never convince Fred that I had no steady girl used to irk me to no end.

This Monday morning was particularly stressful. It was about 10:30, and I was exhausted. My green denim fatigue top was drenched with sweat. The squad opted to "take five." As I sat down on an ammunition box, I turned my head to take a good look at the runway. The planes were landing every few minutes. At the end of the field they would make a U-turn and taxi back to the hangar close to where we were.

The pilots would deplane in a hurry and head for the officers' dining room for a quick lunch. A few hours later, enemy bombers scored a direct hit on the dining room.

The probability of war with Japan was on everybody's mind, civilian and military alike. During our five-minute break, we talked about the many unlicensed ham radio operators near Clark Field. American reconnaissance planes reported a gigantic Japanese buildup on Formosa, and there was a Japanese task force steaming down the China Sea.

"Chow time," someone yelled in the background. I looked over my left shoulder. I could see our battery Army truck in a cloud of dust heading toward our second platoon position. The KPs were standing precariously in the back end of the vehicle ready and eager to start serving chunks of beef in hot brown gravy.

Lieutenant Ashby reminded us to dip our mess kits into the container of boiling water provided by Sergeant Trujillo. The lieutenant was twenty-eight years old, six feet tall, and weighed 170 pounds. I had a lot of respect for him.

It was a few minutes before 11 o'clock. The planes on the runway were the only reassurance of American power. I remember the glint from the surface of the silver-colored wings of our massive B-17s, the pride of the U.S. Army Air Corps. The rays from the 100-degree tropical sun beat down on forty to fifty aircraft sitting on the vast expanse of the field. They were sitting ducks.

I had just glanced at my wristwatch; it was 11:55. I've always been a slave to time. I was queasy; lunch wasn't sitting well. As I gathered my mess equipment to wash it and put it away, I heard someone say, "Planes approaching from the north." Someone else said, "They seem to be our own U.S. Navy planes." I looked up north toward Manila. What I saw was a perfect V-formation of fifty-four gray, twin-engine bombers. They were loud and impressive. They weren't ours.

I was suddenly chilled. I looked around to see that my brother Ben was safe. Through our field glasses, we saw a Rising Sun on the underside of the wings. The Fifth Column had done a superb job, for not one iota of forewarning had been received by any of our anti-aircraft units. Our lines of communication had been sabotaged!

We ran to our positions ahead of Lieutenant Ashby's command. I took the position as lateral gun pointer; Ben was the vertical gun pointer and trigger operator. Fred Concha, Lolo Montoya, and Sam Romero were in charge of the 37mm ammunition. They would supply it and load it as needed.

I tilted my Army hat to get a good view at the skies. The fifty-four-plane formation was almost overhead. A few seconds later, I looked up again. They were now directly overhead with their bomb-bay doors open. I saw cylindrical metal objects glistening in the bright tropical sun. For a moment they appeared to be leaflets. They weren't.

Five hundred yards behind us, 500 and 600 pound bombs were exploding in the midst of our P-40 and P-36 fighters. Our beloved four-engine B-17s were ripped apart by shrapnel unleashed by the explosives in the bombs.

Not more than a year earlier back in the States, I had watched a *Movietone News* feature preceding a movie. It portrayed a Japanese ship leaving a port in San Francisco loaded with scrap iron. In the end, it showed a loose piece of metal in the stern flapping in the wind as though it was saying goodbye. The closing words of the commentator were, "Goodbye, I'll be seeing you."

My mind snapped back to reality; the bomb explosions were coming closer and closer to my gun position. *Will the next piece of shrapnel have my name on it?* My hands were wet with perspiration as I positioned them on the two small wheels right in front of me to start rotating the canon laterally. Ben, sitting to my left with his eyes fixed on the range finder in front of him, looked young and restless...the qualifications for a good soldier.

The command, "Commence Firing," was barely audible in the midst of the sound of explosions and the drone of bombers flying overhead. By now, Ben had depressed his right foot on the trigger to fire our first volley. He and I had maneuvered the ten-foot cannon straight up, but our projectiles were exploding thousands of feet below the target. We discovered that the bombers were flying at about 30,000 feet, far beyond the range of our 37mm gun pieces. The three-inch guns positioned farther out had a range of 27,000 feet, but they were ineffective as well.

The skies were full of puffs of black smoke coming from the explosions of our projectiles and those of the three-inch guns. There were clouds of dust coming from the bomb concussions at the base. Fires with flames shooting hundreds of feet up in the air were visible at Clark Field and our barracks area. The enemy had scored direct hits on the officers' dining room during their noon meal. The planes had also scored direct hits on an ammunition dump. The billows of black smoke rising up in the air indicated that they had bombarded a gasoline dump. Even the dry grass and vegetation between our position and the airfield were on fire. The runway was littered with shrapnel-riddled fighter planes and bombers.

As the formation flew overhead, I heard a swarm of Zeros as they strafed our gun positions all around the base. We could see the Rising Sun under their wings as they zoomed over our heads at tree-top level. We could see the faces of the pilots through their side windows. They were smiling. Their, machine-gun fire was rapid and deadly. The atmosphere was filled with the heavy drone of fighter plane engines and the sound of explosions from our 37mm shells. The slugs from the Zeros' machine guns were landing all around us. I could see puffs of dirt not more than ten feet away. Our gun crew was too busy to notice these near misses. We were, later, to brag and laugh about this experience.

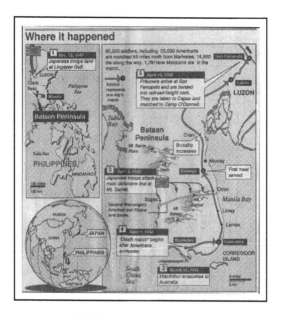

Where it happened

CHAPTER 2

✷ ✷ ✷

ESCAPE FROM CLARK FIELD

The month of December slipped by quickly. There were numerous reports of Japanese tanks approaching Clark Field from the north. We were preparing to evacuate. By eleven o'clock on Christmas Eve, our platoon was loaded up and ready to go. Our 37mm gun was in tow behind us. I could see the other trucks drive by as we waited for our turn to join the 100-truck convoy. There were officers on jeeps directing the operation. Finally, Joe Medina shifted into a slow cruising speed and we headed south to Bataan.

The 200th was to travel all night to San Fernando. We were to protect the Calumpet bridges, to the south, from attacking planes the next day.

The back section of our truck was loaded to capacity. Ben and I, along with the rest of the squad, were cramped among ammunition boxes and duffle bags. Everyone had his rifle in hand. We could not hang our legs out and over the tailgate. Our uniforms were moist with perspiration. Everyone was wearing an ammunition belt around his waist. The belt was designed to carry twelve metal ammo clips with 30-caliber ammunition. The metal clips around our waists made it exceedingly difficult to sit comfortably in a cramped position.

Someone up front yelled, "You guys, pass the cold beer up this way, I'm thirsty." There was no cold beer and the joke fell flat. Everyone was preoccupied with his own thoughts about home and family and Christmas. The roar of a small army of enemy tanks as they prepared to occupy Clark Field replaced Christmas carols.

The sound of their approach was intimidating. There was no way to estimate the distance between them and us. Then there was an explosion and I could see streaks of fire shooting hundreds of feet into the sky. The field had been mined with dynamite before we left. Mission accomplished.

Our convoy was traveling in nighttime blackout mode, with headlights off. The front parking lights were on but were directed toward the ground. The tail lights were similarly positioned. The blackout restrictions were so strict that we could not even light up a cigarette. Captain George, our battery commander, had threatened us with a court-martial in the event we disobeyed the order.

The highway was deserted. Suspicious persons in the vicinity of the Army convoy were apprehended and turned over to our intelligence officer for questioning. During wartime, nothing is left to chance. The Japanese Army had spies all over the island documenting movements of U.S. Army forces from one area to another.

We had just passed the little town of Sambambatum, "Sloppy Bottom," and were approaching Angeles. Ben edged himself towards the tailgate. He raised his rifle up in the air to change hands, but it slipped from his grip, fell to the road, and discharged. No one got hurt. I turned around to pat my brother on the back.

"Don't worry, Ben, Sergeant Harris will issue you a new one at our next stop."

Earl Harris was our supply sergeant. Harris was a likeable fellow in his twenties from Taos. He and his assistant, Jake Padilla, were in charge of issuing supplies that included rifles, ammunition, uniforms, shoes, work-detail clothing, and green under shorts and undershirts. Their working day was long and tedious. Taking inventory seemed to take up most of their time. Their job in this convoy was to make sure the supplies moved with the troops. Private Jake Padilla was a unique GI. He was just over five feet tall and slightly built. He was also cold and unfriendly. I remember him issuing clothing two sizes too big or too long. He was not sympathetic to pleas for a better fit. Nonetheless, he was a dedicated soldier.

I tried to catch some sleep and ignore the roar of engines and grinding of gears. Most of our vehicles were Army prime movers. They were towing searchlights and three-inch cannons.

Our truck was towing a 37mm anti-aircraft gun mounted on a four-wheel steel platform.

Except for occasional pit stops, the guys in the back end of the truck slept through the trip. I felt for Joe Medina having to drive while the rest of us slept.

I was awakened by a loud metallic noise. Joe Medina had just stepped off the cab of the truck and slammed the door. We had arrived at the Calumpet Bridge site. I glanced at my watch. It was 3:30 A.M. There was a cool breeze blowing from the wooded area that surrounded the open space selected for our gun emplacement. I could hear heavy truck traffic as the rest of the regiment scouted around for suitable sites.

As I jumped off the back of the truck, Fred Concha patted my back.

"Merry Christmas."

"*Feliz Navidad*, Fred."

A sense of sadness came over me momentarily. I looked out and across the open space selected for our gun position. I could see Ben talking to Sergeant Ragsdale, our platoon leader. I knew they were discussing the placement of our military equipment in preparation for the battle. The planes would begin bombing at daybreak. We had to be ready to retaliate. Our gun position was strategically located on the top of a knoll. We had to have a good view of the approaching enemy planes. This beautiful view would also make us more visible to the enemy pilots in the air. We expected that the bridges would be more appealing than our gun positions.

I walked away from the truck and crossed a fifty-yard area of high, tough, tropical grass to reach Ben. There was more light now as we waited for sunrise. I could feel a light mist in the air that was typical of the thick tropical jungle.

"¿Que pasa?"

"Not much", said Ben. "We're going to have to start burying the boxes of 37mm ammo right away to keep them out of sight of the damn Jap bombers."

I knew I'd have to start digging holes with the rest of the squad before long.

I walked up close to Ben and nudged him in the ribs. "Merry Christmas, Brother."

"This is one hell of a Christmas Day, isn't it?"

I looked at him momentarily as I placed my right hand firmly on his shoulder. He just tapped my hand as I walked away. Ben and I were very close, but we had a lot of work to do. I joined the rest of our squad in unloading ammunition. The boxes of 37mm shells were heavy. We had to bury the ammunition a safe distance away and make sure that it was well camouflaged from the air. We would take turns digging an eight-by-twelve-by-three-foot hole for the 37mm cannon. The work had to be completed before sunup. Then perhaps we could get a little shuteye before the enemy bombers arrived.

Lieutenant Ashby told us to take five. That was good news. We were through with the detail. Now we could rest. I could see Joe Medina getting into the cab of the truck. Ben and I got under the chassis. The rest of the squad selected other hiding places. The idea was to hide from the sun. Everybody had the same thought: sleep. We covered our faces with our helmets as we lay on the ground and fell asleep.

I was awakened by the roar of the Army vehicles heading south into Bataan, the area that was to become the haven of General Douglas A. MacArthur's troops. There were military vehicles and personnel and Filipino civilians of all ages. Old men walked with their belongings slung across their backs. Some were leading carabaos. Old and young women, some pregnant, trudged along in their bare feet. No doubt their babies would be born somewhere in the jungle or, if lucky, in an Army field hospital. Army trucks, tanks, and half-tracks found it difficult to maneuver through all this chaos. Civilian Pambusco buses inched their way in the bumper-to-bumper traffic honking incessantly. In peacetime, these buses belonged to the Pampanga Bus Company. Pampanga is a Philippines province where Clark Field and Fort Stotsenberg were located. The buses were painted bright yellow or orange. These colors were not good camouflage against enemy air attack. Surprisingly, the Japanese warplanes did not take advantage of the situation.

It was still before sunrise as I looked around. I saw the rest of the squad fast asleep under a shrub or under a shelter-half. I lay back on the ground under my truck and fell asleep again. The traffic would continue to cross the Calumpet Bridge for the next few days. My regiment would be there to protect them. San Fernando, a strategic railroad station, was located just south of us. It was used by the U.S. Army before the war and later by the Japanese army.

About seven o'clock on this Christmas Day, I was awakened from a deep sleep by a command from our platoon officer.

"Enemy planes approaching from the north! Man your guns on the double!"

I rolled out from under the truck after lying face-up on the ground, asleep, for two hours. The sun shining directly in my eyes roused me completely. My hair, dampened with perspiration, was matted with dirt. On my way to the field piece, I stumbled over Lolo, who was sitting on the ground tying his shoes.

Ben and I reached the gun at the same time. I jumped on my seat on a rotating platform. After maneuvering the gun barrel in the direction of the incoming planes, Ben stepped on the foot trigger and we started firing. The skies above us were filled with an array of black puffs of gunpowder from the exploding anti-aircraft shells. We could see, vividly, the Rising Sun emblazoned on the wings as the planes went into a steep dive toward the bridge.

We were witnessing this attack from a distance of about 400 yards, a quarter-mile. They were dropping 1,000-pound bombs. I could feel the concussions in my chest. We fired several rounds without a hit. Diving planes are incredibly difficult to hit because they travel at such a high rate of speed in their descent. We saw planes pull up from the dive missing the target as the bombs exploded in the dry riverbed, one-hundred feet below the steel span.

We provided air cover for our retreating forces for two days, while the last men crossed the bridge spanning the Culo River. Then intelligence reports indicated that the Japanese army was advancing and hot on our trail. We were warned by our senior officer to be prepared to fight off any Japanese infantry fire as we prepared to cross the Calumpet Bridge only 500 yards away. Our best protection was the 30-caliber machine gun that we had welded onto the back of the truck passenger cab.

My battery was the last one in the convoy to cross the bridge. A regimental staff officer was following us in his jeep.

The convoy ahead of us extended for a mile. The air was filled with a thick cloud of dust and gasoline exhaust fumes from the hundred military trucks ahead of us. We were in full retreat. General MacArthur later characterized the retreat as a "strategic withdrawal."

There was only a small amount of small-arms fire from the enemy as we reached the Promised Land, the other side of the bridge. Within a few minutes, we heard and felt an enormous explosion behind us. Steel crashed into the Culo River below, courtesy of the U.S. Army demolition forces. Japanese army engineers had a tremendous job to do if they wanted their artillery and tanks to cross that river. We thumbed our noses at the enemy as we breathed a sigh of relief. Our destination was Bataan Field, midway down the peninsula, where there was a small airfield for the remaining five P-40 Thunderbird fighter planes. My platoon was assigned to protect Bataan Field with our 37mm ack-acks. We were to spend three months in that assignment. Japan would use that time to transfer men and equipment into the Philippines. As a result, we had a short lull in the fighting as they amassed 600,000 troops on the island of Luzon for the invasion of Bataan and Corregidor.

The retreating convoy of the 200th left the Calumpet Bridge area at nightfall. My platoon, along with our 37mm guns, would have to travel twenty miles toward Mariveles. We would be going south, under cover of darkness. This was essential to protect the troops from air bombing and strafing by the Zeros. We would have been sitting ducks for their pursuit planes.

Colonel Sage ordered the troops to bivouac for the night. It was close to midnight. The trucks pulled over by the side of the road and each soldier had to improvise his own bed. Security was established around the perimeter of our troops.

I picked out my bed on what seemed to be a comfortable bush. A few minutes into my sleep, I was awakened by a prickly, burning sensation all over my lower body. I was on an ant hill. My next move was a "strategic withdrawal" from the hill, and then I disrobed down to my socks and shoes. The only parts of my body not invaded by the tropical ants were my head and neck. I discovered that the ants had no respect for privacy. The bites were so numerous and so painful that I had to borrow some water from the kitchen truck to swab my body with a damp, cold wash rag. After an hour of fretting and cursing, I moved my lodging to an ant-free place. I managed to get two or three hours of sleep that night. I was the laughing-stock of the platoon the next day. Some of my buddies, jokingly, felt I was entitled to a Purple Heart.

CHAPTER 3

✧ ✧ ✧

THE ENEMY IS UPON US

I woke up on Wednesday morning, April 8, 1942, to the threatening sound of a Japanese plane flying over our gun position. I laid low in my foxhole waiting for an explosion. There was none. This maneuver was not uncommon. The enemy would fly in over the treetops to avoid being shot at by our artillery. They were free to pull these stunts, since we had no planes left to defend our air space. Our ground forces immediately to the north were incapable of maintaining a line of defense anymore. In the last week, we had witnessed enemy planes strafing our tanks as they retreated south not more than a mile away from our position. We were on the side of a hill about 800 yards north of Bataan Field and about 500 yards west of the main highway. Bataan Field was located in a shallow canyon, and the runway extended from the west end to the east end and out into Manila Bay. On a clear day, we could see the bombs fall on the field. I knew the terrain well. On occasion, Joe Medina and I would walk down the narrow road from our position to the highway and then to a shallow creek at the bottom of the canyon.

This day, I had the feeling the world was coming to an end. I felt a heavy weight in my chest. I could not see how we could hold our positions very much longer. Our lines of defense were non-existent. The highway was full of civilians and Philippine army soldiers running south. By midday, I could hear machine gun fire right behind our gun positions. From our vantage point, we could see enemy planes swooping down to strafe the endless columns of army tanks and artillery on the highway below us. The air was humid and choked with dirt. The smell and taste of gunpowder was everywhere. I kept drinking lukewarm water from my metal canteen to wash it away. At midday, our squad was summoned to meet with Lieutenant Ashby. Everyone sensed the urgency of the meeting.

The lieutenant said that he had been ordered to leave this area as soon as possible and go to Cabcaben Field to await further instructions.

Sergeant Ragsdale asked if it were true that our regiment might be converted into an infantry unit.

It was. In the meantime, we were to start destroying our weapons, shoot out the tires in the 37mm gun carriage, damage the gun bore and the internal parts, and hide and bury the ammunition away from the vicinity of the field piece.

Fred Concha, Lolo, and I took turns firing our Enfield rifles at the field piece. We punctured the tires. We shot holes through the gun's firing mechanism and the traversing and rotating wheels responsible for directing the fire against the enemy aircraft. We removed the breechblock from the firing box. The breechblock was a solid piece of steel measuring three-by-two-by-two inches. The cannon was totally inoperable without this part. I took it and put it into my field bag. Later that evening, as we were establishing the last line of defense at Mariveles, I disposed of it in the jungle.

By the time we finished our chores, it was late afternoon. Everyone in our platoon was packed and ready to run. Every item worth carrying was loaded into the truck. My field bag, a small green Army tote bag, was packed with my personal hygiene articles Additionally, I had clean under shorts, my prayer book, and my Pony camera securely packed in the bag. I was particularly proud of the segments of undeveloped film in my camera depicting the ultimate reality of war. I had shots of enemy Zeros hitting the defenseless dining room on the first day of the war at Clark Field. Other pictures were just as gruesome. I hoped that someday I would be able to record them in my Memoirs of War. As I was resting on a rock, before reporting to my platoon sergeant, I heard someone calling me. I turned around to Lolo standing on higher ground and waving his arm at me.

I went over to him, and he pointed out an area on the ground not more that 200 yards away. As we lowered our voices, I witnessed a squad of five enemy soldiers driving stakes into the ground. They were setting up an artillery gun just behind us. We were silent as we tramped back to our squad.

We jumped aboard the Army truck and escaped south to Mariveles. Lieutenant Ashby was riding in front with Joe Medina. Sergeant Ragsdale, our second in command, was riding in the back of the truck with us, chain smoking.

For a brief moment, I felt relieved as I rode down the narrow, winding road toward the main highway. I looked around to assure myself that my brother, Ben, was okay. He was. The breeze from the speeding vehicle felt good on my sweaty face and neck.

I could see some of the trucks from the other batteries of the 200th as we reached the highway. The sun was setting over the jungle behind us. In the air, enemy pursuit planes were strafing and bombing the mass of humanity on the road – civilians. We could see some of the casualties by the side of the road. There were also carcasses of dead cavalry horses and disabled jeeps and tanks along the side of the highway. There were scores of human casualties. Invariably, some Good Samaritan in a vehicle would stop and the body or the injured person would be loaded on the vehicle, which then continued south.

Suddenly, we heard our platoon leader cry out, "Get down and take cover!" We all jumped off the truck and lay down on the ground by it. We saw an enemy plane fly over us with its machine gun firing. The puffs of dirt from the slugs as they hit the ground were visible as we lay prostrate on the ground.

The sun had set. I could barely see our convoy of trucks behind me. We were moving at no more than five miles per hour. It was getting dark. The air was filled with dust and exhaust fumes. There was machine-gun fire on our right and left. We were warned that the enemy troops chasing us were seasoned soldiers who were moved into Luzon from other military strongholds. It was rumored that these troops were the *crème de la crème* of the Imperial Japanese fighting men. It was very demoralizing to hear this.

Superior Japanese infantry forces, supported by tanks and artillery, had attacked our northern line on Bataan earlier in the day. The enemy had flown fresh reserves into the fight. Our forces had sustained heavy losses. Japanese dive-bombers assisted in the attack. They dropped bombs and machine-gunned our front-line soldiers.

On this moonless night, our platoon forged on toward the southern tip of the Bataan peninsula.

There was no way our forces, numbering about 35,000, could stop the Imperial Japanese Army of 500,000-plus seasoned troops. Our tanks and heavy artillery were non-existent. Brigadier General Edward P. King, the commander of the American Forces, ordered Colonel Charles Sage to establish a line of defense across the southern tip of the peninsula.

Back on the road, I could see that the Army MPs were unable to control the traffic. To intensify the fear and confusion, artillery from Corregidor across the bay started to fire their

12-inch guns over our heads. The heavy artillery batteries from Fort Hearns and Fort Smith each fired eight rounds an hour. We glanced up at the black sky as the artillery pieces fired their salvos. I could feel the concussion in my chest as the monstrous shells split the hot tropical air. It was frightening but it did something to lift our morale. The rumor immediately spread among the troops that the shells were covering a landing of U.S. reinforcements. But that is all it was, a rumor.

Nevertheless, good rumors in the last days of Bataan helped to maintain a healthy morale among the American and Filipino soldiers. Army engineers maintained a landing dock at Mariveles to facilitate any landing efforts by our military. The sad truth was that this never happened.

Mariveles, a point just south of Cabcaben Field, was filled with combat soldiers representing every military service on the island. Joe Medina and I took turns identifying shoulder patches from the 31st Infantry, the Quartermaster Corps, the U.S. Army Air Corps, and others.

General King's orders to Colonel Sage included converting the 200th and the 515th anti-aircraft units into infantry units. The 200th was to form on the right of the road and be linked with the 515th on the left. The line of defense was to run along the lateral south edge of the airstrip. The airstrip was situated from left to right across the breadth of the Bataan peninsula.

A lot of the men from our New Mexico unit were missing. Some were lost in the retreat, while others were in the hills fleeing for safety. On April 7, Battery F from Gallup, New Mexico, was caught in a bombing raid by Japanese planes. They lost three 37mm guns and three trucks, and three soldiers were killed.

I noticed that Sergeant Ragsdale was hustling the men of our second platoon into a private area in the jungle. It was pitch dark. Voice recognition was the only way to tell one man from another. Shortly thereafter, Ashby muscled his way into the group. His voice came out of the darkness loud and clear.

"This platoon will join forces with friendly units to the west. Our destination is the south ridge of Cabcaben Field. Good luck."

On the way to the ridge, we heard the voice of Captain Anthony R. George, our Battery Commander.

"Men! I'm your senior officer in charge of this infantry operation. We will not retreat anymore. Anyone seen retreating or faltering in any way will be shot to death by me."

Our nocturnal trek through the jungle continued through the six-foot-high blades of Cogon grass. Cogon grass is used in the Philippines for fodder and thatching. The vast majority of the grass shacks of the poor were roofed by layers and layers of this sturdy grass.

On the trail to my left was Sam Romero, the Native American wise guy in our squad. I yelled, "What time is it?" He answered, "I don't know. Why don't you look at your watch?" By this time of night, tempers were short. I could see he was lighting a match to look at his wristwatch. "It's four o'clock, my friend."

By now we had walked for eight hours. We had nothing to eat and very little to drink. We had water in our canteens, but it was hot. To conserve water we would simply wet our lips and tongue every time we reached for a drink. Tantalizing thoughts of cold beer tortured me throughout the night. I was very tired by that time. My khaki shirt was drenched with perspiration. I was even getting cold in the early-morning jungle breeze. We had to contend constantly with large ants and chiggers getting onto our necks and under our socks. The perspiration from our bodies exacerbated the bites and raw skin and made them burn more intensely.

We were between two extinct volcanoes, Mount Natib to the north and Mount Bataan and the Mariveles Mountains to the south. Most of the area was solid jungle. We trudged through valleys and peaks. Our GI-issue shoes were wet from crossing small streams. An Army shoe is very heavy when wet.

If we listened carefully, we could hear frightened cries and curses in different dialects: English, Spanish, and Tagalog, the Philippine language. The 12-inch field pieces of the Hearn and Smith Batteries from Corregidor across the bay kept up their barrage over our heads throughout the night. It was the only activity that night that was able to sustain my morale.

By five o'clock the morning of April 9, 1942, we reached the southern Cabcaben Line. This is where we would dig in and wait. The Japanese had moved their heavy artillery up close from their positions in San Fernando. We could see their tanks lined up on the opposite side of Bataan Field facing us. The words of Captain George earlier kept ringing in my ears: "We shall fight to the last man." It was difficult to be optimistic, but I couldn't afford to be overwhelmed with fear. I had a solution for all my faculties at that moment: I was chain-smoking. The cigarettes would become saturated with the nervous perspiration running down my face. I would discard the wet cigarette and light up another one. I couldn't sit still for fear of shaking.

Upon reaching the designated line of defense, at the top of the ridge, we all breathed a sigh of relief. I followed the example of the rest of the squad and took off my shirt and spread it out on a nearby bush. I had chigger bites on my back. The itching was so intense that I went to the nearest tree to rub my back against the bark. It helped. I laid my equipment on the ground to relieve the pressure of the weight on my legs. I was so tired that I threw myself on the ground. The twigs and stones pressed against my bare back, but I didn't care.

For a second, I contemplated my fate on this day. I could not afford to die. I had to help my brother, Ben, survive. Death was not an option. I got up immediately to start digging my foxhole.

I slipped into my shirt in a hurry without bothering to tuck it in. I picked up my army bayonet to start digging. The spot I selected was just behind a stout tree with a trunk that was ten to twelve inches in diameter. I felt that it would protect me from any sniper fire from across the ravine.

I walked over to Ben's area. As I approached him, I threw my arm around his shoulders, and I noticed his khaki shirt was still wet with perspiration. Then I sat down on a rock by him. I saw the weariness in his eyes.

I put my hand on his bent knee and said, "How are you taking all this, Corporal?"

He forced a smile. "You know, Brother, I have a feeling that you and I will survive all this. I think that sometime soon, we will be relieved by our own forces when they land on the Luzon peninsula."

Wishful thinking.

I returned to my foxhole. I always thought that Ben was a brave soldier. He was known for his toughness on the defensive line for his high school football team. During one of his games he suffered a shoulder dislocation. He did not receive adequate medical treatment at the time. The result was that, during combat, his shoulder would pop out of place from time to time. I was the only one around who knew how to reset it. In the field, it was not unusual for me to be picked up in a jeep and driven to Ben.

As I walked back to my foxhole, I turned my head to my right to look across Cabcaben Field. I was about fifty feet above the level of the field. It looked very peaceful. About 200 yards across was the Japanese army. At six o'clock in the morning, I could see wisps of smoke rising from the jungle brush. The enemy soldiers were cooking their dehydrated steamed rice for breakfast. The soldiers simply poured the dehydrated rice into boiling water for a hot rice dish. This rice was carried in small cloth pouches attached to their cartridge belts.

By this early hour, the U.S. Navy had finished destroying its materiel and munitions dumps at the Mariveles dock and was sinking their small war ships.

The *Dewey Drydock* sank after the crew detonated six 155mm scuttling charges. The minesweeper *Bittern* went under. The *Taiping,* loaded with bombs, blew up. All Navy personnel were ordered to Corregidor for beach defense. During the night, the Navy had moved 80,000 gallons of fuel oil, 130 tons of diesel, over a million rounds of 30caliber ammunition, and forty-five tons of food to Corregidor.

Those of us not fortunate enough to escape to Corregidor were left behind to defend the peninsula. We were left holding the bag.

"Yea, though I walk through the valley of the shadow of death, I will fear no evil..."

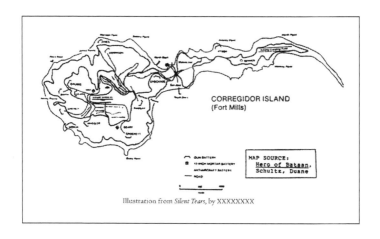

CORREGIDOR ISLAND
(Fort Mills)

MAP SOURCE:
Hero of Bataan,
Schultz, Duane

Illustration from *Silent Tears*, by XXXXXXXX

CHAPTER 4

☆ ☆ ☆

BATAAN FALLS

By 8 o'clock on Thursday morning, April 9, 1942, U.S. Army troops had settled down to repulse the Imperial Japanese 14th Army. Their artillery pieces had had all night to dig in. Their air force was actively bombing and strafing anything that moved on our side of the line of defense. On their strafing runs, they flew so close to the ground that we could see the pilots' faces inside their cockpits. We were very tense as we waited to engage their infantry and artillery on the ground.

Suddenly, I saw Lieutenant Ashby motioning everybody to gather around him. I laid my rifle against the tree and walked up to him. He waited until the whole squad was gathered around him.

"Men, I have been informed by Captain George that we are not to fire on the enemy unless fired upon. This is an order issued by General King, our commanding general."

This information caused real concern for the men. Does it mean we are surrendering? If we let them shoot first, we might not be around to return the fire. I thought that this was the beginning of the end. Would it not be more humane to fight to the last man than to surrender to the enemy? These points were being debated by my buddies around me.

Lieutenant Ashby was not certain that we understood the gravity of the command. As he took his sunglasses off, he said, "Captain George made it quite clear to me that we are not supposed to question the intent of the order. My feeling is that we are undergoing some very serious discussions with the enemy. They are crucial to our welfare. Get back to your positions."

We all went back to our foxholes. Approximately two hours later, the latest order from General King was circulated down the line: Do not fire even if fired upon. This order was more devastating than the one before. We were told to get rid of our ammunition, but to keep our rifles. I buried the shells from my two bandoliers and cartridge belt. In the event that we had any Japanese money or souvenirs, we were told to destroy them or bury them. We were particularly warned to destroy any object or literature that would reveal to the enemy the military unit to which we were attached. These were words of wisdom that would, perhaps, save our lives later in the day.

By midmorning, the rumor spread out among the troops that three Army officers were seen in a jeep going north toward San Fernando. They were carrying a bamboo pole with a white flag at the end. This news was very demoralizing. The thought of capitulation was alien to the minds of the troops on Bataan. We were trained to fight the enemy, not to surrender.

At eleven o'clock the night before, General King had decided to surrender his troops. His choice was one of launching a counterattack, as ordered by General Jonathan M. Wainwright, and having his men slaughtered, or he could, against orders, surrender. General King decided on the latter. At six o'clock, when General Wainwright learned of King's decision, he told Lieutenant Colonel Jesse T. Traywick, an assistant operations officer on Corregidor, "Go back and tell him not to do it." But it was too late. General King had made his decision at 2:30 that morning.

At six o'clock, General Wainwright radioed the bad news to General MacArthur. General King's decision to surrender would haunt him for the duration of the war. He expected to be court-martialed upon returning to the United States.

At 3:30, General King had dispatched two of his staff officers to contact the enemy in the north. Colonel Everett McWilliams and Major Marshall H. Hurt left King's headquarters in a reconnaissance car with a motorcycle escort. When they reached the Lamas River, they met an American delay force with a few tanks and self-propelled 75mm guns heading south. By daylight, the three men carrying General King's message were driving north into Japanese territory.

Back at the Cabcaben line, the American troops had gone into a state of total disarray. The order had come from the highest level of command to prepare to surrender to the Japanese Imperial Forces. Our officers made sure that a series of guidelines were followed in the course of capitulating to the enemy. We were to ascertain that all ammunition was destroyed. We were to remove any symbol of rank from our shirtsleeves and collars. Military documents, maps, and Army literature were to be burned. In brief, it was a crash course in the art of surrendering to the enemy.

As we lined up in single file to march down the hill to surrender, Lieutenant Ashby spoke. "We are to surrender to the Japanese artillery officer down at the airfield at eleven o'clock. Make damn sure you take the bolt assembly from your rifle. You hold the bolt assembly in your left hand as you walk down. Tie a white cloth to the bore of your rifle, and carry your rifle upside down at right-shoulder arms. Salute the

Japanese officer as you surrender your weapon and follow instructions from him. Good luck and let's go."

Lieutenant Ashby led his platoon down the hill with Sergeant Ragsdale right behind him. We all walked in silence down the dusty trail, everyone with his own thoughts. We were all tired from the long walk the night before. We had not had anything to eat for almost seventy-two hours. But I did not hear any complaints. On occasion, I could hear the mumbling of prayers or the repetitive sound of a rosary.

My thoughts were that, by some quirk of fate, I would be recaptured by our forces. The thought of escaping into the jungle was also in my mind. I thought about a lot of things as I followed Ben down the trail.

I looked at my watch. It was close to eleven o'clock. There was sporadic shooting by some Japanese units as they took advantage of the helpless American or Philippine units. I could hear dive bombers gunning their engines as they zoomed into the last vestiges of resistance by American or Philippine soldiers.

Ironically, the weather in this second week of April was beautiful. The tropical sun was typically hot. There wasn't a single cloud in the sky. As we trudged down the hill, the runway of Cabcaben Field came into view. What seemed to be 2,000 or more men were sitting on the dirt runway facing Manila Bay.

All the men were American soldiers. They had been summoned by the enemy to come down from the jungle to surrender. The soldiers were unkempt. Their faces were unshaven. Their uniforms were dirty and wet with perspiration. One could tell that their uniforms had not been washed in weeks. The stench of sweat and gunpowder was pervasive. On the opposite side of the field was a phalanx of Japanese light army tanks. The tanks were facing the American POWs with their cannons lowered, ready to fire. There were enemy soldiers standing at both sides of each tank. Some of the tank drivers even had their motors running so that they could react to any eventuality. There were hundreds of soldiers patrolling the area. Each one had a rifle with a fixed bayonet in his right hand. The bayonets glistened in the sunlight.

My platoon was prepared to meet the enemy as we reached the bottom of the trail. On our way down, we had to step over the bodies of Philippine soldiers who had been shot in the last hours of our retreat. The flies were all over the dead. Some had their eyes open with dirt in their eyeballs. Others had half of their faces blown off and copious amounts of dry blood on their army shirts.

I could see Sam Romero ahead of me as he was reporting to the enemy soldier. To my left was a pile of U.S. Army weapons. There were rifles, .45 caliber pistols, Browning Automatic Rifles (BARs), and even mess kits and field bags. There was a lot of dust in the immediate vicinity. I could see that the enemy soldier was also reaching for pens, watches, and billfolds as the American soldiers approached him. He was issuing commands in Japanese. They were loud and threatening.

"Kochi koy, Amerika. Amerika dahme. Kura, Amerika. Kochi koy, Amerika."

Kochi koy translates into "Come here."

On occasion, an officer would appear from somewhere to translate. He spoke English without an accent and, unlike his compatriots, he was civil.

The Japanese soldier was dressed in a shabby, two-piece light-green uniform. The common soldier wore black, high-cut tennis shoes with a split toe. The officers wore heavy leather army shoes, and a saber hung from their belts. The size of the saber determined rank. It was not unusual to see a major dragging the saber as he walked. The average height of a Japanese fighting soldier was perhaps five-foot-three. They wore olive-green caps that had a little star above the bill and flaps that came down over their ears and around their necks. They swaggered around with rifles with mounted bayonets. The bayonets were about twelve to fifteen inches long and razor-sharp.

After walking down the hill through the brush and cogon grass with my rifle upside down on my right shoulder, I braced myself to report to the Japanese officer...to surrender my weapon. I saw Sam Romero being escorted away after surrendering his gun. Judging from the way they barked orders, I thought the two soldiers were going to bayonet him.

I walked up to the officer in charge as he motioned me to throw my rifle and trigger assembly into the pile of weapons on my left. All the while the officer kept screaming out forceful commands in Japanese.

"Kura, Amerika! Amerika dahme!"

Not knowing what to do, I stood at attention. He came forward with the rifle up in the air as if to bring it down on my head. I cringed as I stood still just waiting to have my head split in two. At that moment, he stopped as a Japanese interpreter stepped forward, seemingly from out of nowhere.

"The officer is ordering you to surrender your field bag as well." I quickly took the bag from my shoulder and tossed it in with the rest of my belongings. It broke my heart to part with that field bag and the camera, film, and clean clothing it contained.

It was close to midday, which I could tell by the intensity of the sun's rays beating down the back of my neck. I was not wearing a wide-brimmed hat. My khaki shirt was sweaty and dirty. I had never perspired so much in my life. And I was terrified. I saw an enemy soldier beating a defenseless American with the butt of his rifle. The American was bleeding from his mouth and his ears. The young GI had simply misunderstood a command issued in Japanese. The soldier turned the rifle and started to use the bayonet. By this time, the GI was barely able to stand up straight. The soldier was bellowing out the same command: *"Kioski! Kioski!"* At the time, we did not know that *Kioski* meant "Attention."

The poor GI was repeatedly kicked as he lay on the ground. He was ultimately bayoneted to death. I said a short prayer.

I gathered my wits as I continued walking. I turned around to make sure my brother was nearby. Ben and I, and the rest of the squad, were pushed and shoved at the end of a rifle butt to join the rest of the prisoners of war on Cabcaben Field. We flopped ourselves on the soft dirt and crossed our legs. We were now facing Corregidor across the Manila Bay.

I looked around and recognized some of our boys from Batteries D and G. Immediately behind me and to my left were members from Battery C from Santa Fe. We were surrounded by hundreds of Japanese infantry troops and by small Japanese tanks. Every enemy soldier was carrying a rifle with a sharp and shiny bayonet at the end of the barrel. And we were but a fraction of the 75,000 troops under General King's command.

This number included 12,000 Americans. We were all prisoners of the Japanese General Homma and his 14th Army. We would not see an American flag for four more years. The thought was difficult to bear without becoming emotional.

Despite the jungle growth of trees and vines surrounding Cabcaben Field, the tropical sun above us was merciless. We had no drinking water. Some of our troops had even surrendered their canteens. The U.S. Army water containers were nowhere around. We dared not ask our captors for water.

The cloud of dust created by the human traffic around us reminded me of dust clouds created by stampeding cattle back on the ranch in my hometown. My face and my neck were raw from wiping off an accumulation of dust and perspiration.

Before surrendering, General King had made provisions to save enough vehicles to evacuate his army to any point on Luzon designated by the Japanese. On this day, I did not see any efforts on the part of the enemy to begin moving anyone from this congestion. The number of their troops increased by the hour.

The enemy artillery used horses to transport some of their artillery pieces. Ben, sitting behind me, nudged me.

"Look, Bro, look what's coming up the road. The Japs seem to be getting ready to put up an artillery piece behind us."

As I looked up, I saw three horses being led by some soldiers. One horse was carrying the barrel from the artillery piece on its back. The other two horses were each carrying a wheel. The rest of the disassembled pieces of the gun were hung around the necks of the soldiers. It was difficult to grasp the fact that an army with such primitive mobility was winning the war in the Philippines.

The artillery crew that had just arrived began to set up their piece not more than a hundred feet behind us. I could see them driving the stakes that could anchor the cannon to the ground. An artillery duel would not be good for the American POWs.

The Japanese were getting ready to fire on Corregidor. The shells would be flying over our heads towards that island across the bay. An uncanny silence settled over the captive troops. We were all stricken with fear. Corregidor would definitely return the fire. Their 14-inch shells could obliterate this area. And in attempting to run for cover, we would be shot to death by the troops surrounding us.

Meanwhile, near the Lamas River bridge, General King agreed to surrender unconditionally his Luzon Force of more than 75,000 soldiers to the Japanese Imperial Forces. The surrender was made in the presence of Colonel Nakayama, senior operations officer for the Japanese 4th Army. Later, General King and his aides would be transported to Balanga for more questioning and fine-tuning the surrender terms. Balanga was about fifteen miles north of Cabcaben Field.

The American troops, having sat on the ground for more than four hours, were tired and getting very impatient at the guards patrolling around us.

"Goddamn Japs, get us out of this hell!" yelled someone from behind.

"Get us some drinking water, you slant-eyed SOBs," said someone else.

It was a good thing the enemy did not understand English.

The language barrier was giving the enemy soldiers an excuse to be cruel and sadistic – not that they needed one. So many of our boys were literally kicked to death simply because they did not comprehend *Kioski*. Once the victim fell to the ground and was unable to stand up on his own, he would be bayoneted to death. The enemy soldiers would kick and stab a defenseless body even in the last moments of life.

I can still hear Sam Romero cursing, "You yellow-bellied cowards! Give me a bayonet and I will fight you!" With Sam's experience with hunting knives, he was tough enough to make good his threat. He was an experienced hunter in the mountains of northern New Mexico.

As I stood up from my sitting position in the dirt at Cabcaben Field, I looked around and saw a sea of faces of American GIs around me. Their faces were haggard and red from the direct rays of a tropical sun in hundred-plus-degree heat. I must have looked the same way. We were dehydrated from lack of drinking water. Young soldiers are not content to sit around doing nothing, and some GIs were ready to risk their lives for a change of pace. The enemy soldiers around us were getting fidgety, too. Some were cocking the triggers of their rifles. Others were leveling their bayonets as though they were ready to initiate a charge. A riot or an insurrection by unarmed American troops could result in a massacre.

All of a sudden, the air above and around us was filled with the sound of a booming explosion. We instinctively hit the ground. I could feel the heat from the artillery projectile over my head as it sliced through the air towards Corregidor. The concussion knocked us down on the ground. The artillery crew behind us had fired a volley at The Rock. After a few minutes, the second volley followed. Then a third. They kept on firing.

It was a lesson in Japanese military discipline to witness the soldiers as they followed the commands of their officers. The soldiers, being short in stature, moved exquisitely fast as they prepared to fire. As I watched, I was reminded of a puppet show back home. The officer in front of the cannon barked out commands as he stood at attention, slicing the air with his saber to accentuate his authority. The puppets would move about, mechanically and obediently. Then they would take cover on the sides of the artillery emplacements. The firing of the cannon would follow with a thunderous explosion and flash of fire from the bore that created an enormous cloud. The air smelled of gunpowder.

The artillery fire behind me continued. It was early afternoon by now. Some of us were lucky enough to have earplugs. I was only twenty-five feet from the gun. The action attracted more and more Japanese troops to our area. They were even coming down in trucks. Our American troops must have been outnumbered seven to one. Suddenly, the predictable happened. Our Navy began to return the fire. We discovered that our gunboats were patrolling the bay. They were the fast, sleek, maneuverable gunboats that Joe Medina and I used to see from the hills of Bataan. Joe and I would take our binoculars and watch from a high rise whenever the Japanese pursuit airplanes would chase a gunboat, trying to machine-gun it. The gunboats would outmaneuver the enemy plane every time. Japanese pilots were never successful in sinking or even severely damaging one.

After the third calibration attempt by our gunboats, they scored a direct hit on the Japanese artillery piece behind us. The ensuing explosion was so powerful that it hurled bodies and metal parts a hundred feet into the air. Both Japanese and American soldiers perished in the massive explosion. Jimmy Smith from C Battery, who was sitting closer than I was, later said that his face was splattered with human blood that day. The area was littered with body parts.

Amid the commotion following the explosion, there was a mad rush to escape into the brush around us. A group of American GIs, including me, made a dead run for safety by heading across the highway and into the jungle. Our destination was Corregidor. It was a bold and calculated risk. We hoped that we could blend into the thick jungle and eventually get across the bay. It was a field day for the soldiers guarding us. They immediately opened fire.

I could hear the soldiers yelling, *"Kura Amerika! Kura America! Kochi Koy!"*

I could hear the bullets buzzing. Some of my buddies were being hit and killed right in front of me. I could see and smell the blood as some of our GIs fell on the ground to die. Some were a bloody sight as they bled from the head or from a gaping hole in the neck. Neck wounds bleed profusely. Several times I would look back to see an enemy soldier kill an American who simply fell or was unable to get up from a leg injury. There was a lot of screaming coming from the enemy as they attempted to control the mass escape.

Suddenly, I realized that Ben was nowhere around. I stopped momentarily. I looked around. I couldn't see my brother. "Ben!" I screamed at the top of my voice. "Where are you?" He was nowhere to be seen. I screamed again, "Ben, aren't you with us?" I decided then that Ben had stayed behind. He had not joined us in our escape. I was determined to go back across the road and get him. I might die attempting to save him, but I was determined.

I dropped down on my stomach in a shallow gulley to avoid detection. By this time, the shooting had subsided a little. The gulley would eventually lead me back to the highway.

Once I was back on the road, I ran back to the area where Ben was still sitting. I grabbed him by the hand and jerked him towards me. We started to run back across the highway to join the other GIs. We could hear a barrage of gunshots aimed at us. They would make a peculiar "zing" as the bullets went past our heads. When Ben and I caught up with the others, I saw that we were surrounded by what seemed to be an army of Japanese infantry soldiers. There must have been a hundred or more of us who had been re-captured just a few hundred yards from the beach. Conquerors, historically, punish an escaping prisoner of war by executing him.

"Kura, Amerika" and "Go." We were being brutally pushed and jostled at the end of a bayonet or a rifle butt. Those Americans who lost their balance or were knocked off their feet were kicked mercilessly. If they were unable to get back on their feet, the soldiers would bayonet them to death. The Japanese infantry was notorious for its inhumane bayonet attacks in the field.

After what seemed like an eternity, we finally reached a place suitable to the Japanese leaders. A third of the original force of Americans that had tried to escape into the jungle were shot or bayoneted to death. The path was littered with bodies. Some of them were disemboweled as a result of repeated thrusts from Japanese bayonets. Still more gruesome were the corpses that lay decapitated from a kneeling position. The prisoner of war was forced to kneel down on the ground. A Japanese officer would stand at attention in front of the victim. From a standing position, he would bellow out a command as he withdrew his Samurai sword from its scabbard. He swung the sword from right to left, leveling it across the neck of the victim. The detached head would fall to the ground as the torso in a khaki uniform toppled to the ground. The head would roll around briefly on the ground.

There were many cases of decapitations of American POWs by Japanese soldiers later on in the war. Some of our GIs witnessed incidents in which the severed head bounced up and down.

By the end of the afternoon, our group of escapees was pushed and punched into a private patio of a home belonging to a Filipino citizen. It was an attractive hacienda-type home sitting on a knoll about 300 yards from the main military highway running north and south. Due north were the towns of Limao, Limay, Orion, and Pilar. The jungle trees and brush had been meticulously cleared around the whitewashed, one-story building. It presumably belonged to a rich banana plantation owner.

On the west side facing the main highway, the owner had built an eight-foot-high fence out of ten-inch-wide pieces of lumber. It was, perhaps, a means of maintaining a degree of privacy from the traffic and noise coming from the highway below. This fence would serve as a backdrop for Japanese army war propaganda pictures later on in the afternoon. These pictures would appear on thousands of newspapers on the Japanese mainland.

Following the picture-taking sessions we were re-grouped into single files with our backs to the fence, with the tallest GIs in the back row. The Americans in the middle row were shoved and butted into kneeling down on the ground. The language problem was beginning to bring about serious consequences. I was hit in the head with a rifle butt because I didn't understand the command to kneel down. I could feel warm blood running down my back from a cut behind my right ear. In the front row were the shorter soldiers. They had to sit down on the ground with their legs folded in front of their chests. It was a painful and uncomfortable position.

CHAPTER 5

✧ ✧ ✧

A STAY OF EXECUTION

During the interval, word of our dilemma reached our high-ranking Army officers who were still detained on the landing strip across the road from us. At the risk of their lives, they begged for permission to intervene on our behalf. A general in the Quartermaster Corps, we were told, had been informed that my group of a hundred men, who had tried to escape into the jungle earlier, were at risk of being executed for trying to escape.

The U.S. Army officer immediately sought help. Through an interpreter, he confronted the Japanese senior officers to plead and perhaps suggest alternatives to the outright mass execution of a group of a hundred American POWs who had run into the jungle earlier in the day.

Ahead of me, I could see the highway packed with Japanese infantrymen, artillery, and tanks going south. The enemy was, presumably, amassing troops for the invasion of Corregidor later on in the week. Emaciated-looking horses were pulling some of the artillery pieces on wheels. I could also see American POWs being forced to walk in the opposite direction. The Americans were being pushed and shoved to walk faster and faster. This was the beginning of the Bataan Death March.

By now I had realized that life was worth fighting for. I knew my loved ones were praying for Ben and me back home.

Yea, though I walk through the valley of the shadow of death, I will fear no evil. For Thou art with me. Thy rod and Thy staff, they comfort me...

My faith would sustain me for the duration of the war.

We were tired and dehydrated. There was no letup from the direct rays of the hot tropical sun. Although it was late in the afternoon, the heat was intense. Our bodies were beginning to feel the tension from standing, kneeling, or sitting in one position for two hours. Our chances of survival were very slim.

Suddenly, the Japanese began assembling 30-caliber machine guns. They positioned them right in front of us. They started to calibrate the machine guns by firing round after round of bullets just inches over our heads. It was a chilling experience. Instinctively, I started to touch my body to see if I had been hit. I turned around to see if Ben was safe. We were uninjured. The bullets had simply whizzed over our heads. We were certain the next rounds would be leveled at us.

In our hearts we knew the end had come and that we were going to be massacred. I hoped that my death would be instantaneous.

My buddies around me were either cursing our captors or quietly praying.

All of a sudden, a Japanese officer to the right of us raised his right arm and issued a loud command in Japanese as he faced the guards around us. The guards immediately abandoned their machine guns and stood erect at attention. At that moment, we could see a U.S. Army general and his aides being escorted towards the Japanese officer.

We could tell that the deliberation was about the fate of our group. In the meantime, the Japanese Army was accelerating the evacuation of Americans POWs from Cabcaben Field. We could see from our vantage point the exodus of our young men who were being forced to walk towards Camp O'Donnell, sixty miles north. Perhaps half of them would make it. The rest would fall by the wayside to be bayoneted to death.

These were the loyal GIs who had fought to the last on Bataan, waiting for the American fleet to arrive and rescue them. The sad truth is that the Philippine Islands had been written off by the War Department. The Japanese naval blockade around the islands was considered impregnable. Our supplies were, instead, being shipped to the European Theater.

The discussion between American and Japanese officers went on for about an hour. I could see the Japanese officer waving a saber to make his point. The American general was a brave man.

From the top of the knoll where we had been sitting for four hours, I looked across the Bataan Peninsula at the setting sun. The rays were playing hide-and-seek behind the jungle trees. The sun was ready to sink into the China Sea to draw to a close on this awful day.

The tension decreased slightly. At least the soldiers around us were not at a constant bayonet charge stance. One of my buddies whispered, "I don't think they're going to hurt us anymore."

Without any warning the Japanese officer in charge turned abruptly, faced our group, and roared, "Kioski!"

That meant that we were to stand at attention. We had learned the translation during the day as we were being beaten for misunderstanding orders. By the time we left the area that day, the Japanese had come up with an interpreter. This young Japanese soldier had attended the University of Southern California. His command of English was excellent. Furthermore, he was well-mannered. We immediately nicknamed him "Southern Cal" when we talked about him. Later on in our experiences as prisoners of war in the various camps, we would come up with nicknames such as "Air Raid," "Black Shirt," "Blinky," "The Bull," and "La Putita."

As the sun was setting, we were marched down a hillside toward the main highway by two platoons of Japanese soldiers. I could see their bayonets glisten as we were forced to double-step down the hill. A string of trucks was waiting for us at the road. We were loaded into the trucks and taken off in a northerly direction. Manila Bay was on our right.

Elements of General Homma's 14th Army were traveling south in preparation for the invasion of Corregidor.

On the other half of the highway, going north, were the defeated warriors of the Philippine-American Army. These men were the lead of the Death March. Only half of them would complete it.

As Ben and I traveled north in the dilapidated truck, we shook hands and prayed for a second or two in thankfulness. We knew someone was praying for us back home.

CHAPTER 6

✩ ✩ ✩

FAREWELL TO BATAAN

There were between twelve and fifteen GIs in my truck. The vehicle was a typical Japanese military truck. It was olive green and the deterioration of its body was incredible.

As we traveled at the rate of ten to fifteen miles per hour, it seemed that at the next bump in the road we would become separated from the cab in front. The truck had seen better days. The road to Limao, Limay, and Orion

was a rough one. This is the road that eventually would take us to our first concentration
camp.

Ever since we had surrendered earlier in
the day, I shook every time I came close to a
Japanese soldier, afraid that I would misunder-
stand a direct command and suffer the consequences.

As the convoy inched along the road to-
ward Limao, I turned around to see how many
of my original squad were riding in my truck.
Ben was standing right beside me. Corpo-
ral Joe Medina was also aboard. Lieutenant
Ashby, Sergeant Ragsdale, Fred Concha, Lolo
Montoya, and Sam Romero were not with us.
They were on the Death March.

"Kura, Amerika Dahme!" Japanese infantry
soldiers yelled at us as they walked south towards Mariveles. Our boys standing inside the
truck by the rails were viciously beaten with rifle butts as they stood upright. Their faces were
a bloody mess by the time the driver moved
away from that spot.

We all pooled our resources to help the injured. One of the boys had a deep cut in his
right forehead.

"I have a piece of adhesive tape that I've hidden in my back pocket," I said, as I passed the tape to a bloody hand behind me.

The victim was a sergeant from a tank outfit from Oklahoma. A young man came forward to share some valuable water from his canteen to wash off the blood from the GI's hands and forehead. We patched up our injured as best as we could with our meager resources.

We considered ourselves fortunate beyond words to be riding. The brutal and barbaric mind of the Japanese soldier was evident all around us this day. It seemed as though the Japanese High Command had recruited the most demented minds in the Japanese infantry to escort the Americans POWs to the various camps.

Any POW who showed the slightest indication of non-compliance with an order was summarily beaten mercilessly. The Japanese soldier would start out by kicking the POW in the genitals, while the subject was still able to stand. The enemy would follow through by kicking him in the face as he lay on the ground. Ultimately, the *coup de grâce* would come with a forceful bayonet thrust into the chest or an execution-style shot to the head.

I felt a deep sense of guilt for riding an army truck as I witnessed these inhuman deeds committed by the Japanese.

As we drove on, someone shouted, "Look at that bayonet fight between seven Jap soldiers and four Filipino Scouts."

We all looked to an opening in the jungle on our left. There was a cloud of dust as the bayonet duel continued. In a matter of a few seconds, a single Filipino soldier had killed two Japanese soldiers. In the next few moments, we saw an enemy soldier creep up from behind and land a lethal bolo punch to the back of the head of one of the Filipinos as he was engaged in a bayonet-thrusting battle with two other Japanese. The Filipino's legs buckled as he fell to the ground. He was then repeatedly bayoneted in his neck, chest, and stomach. It was a game of numbers. The Filipinos were outnumbered, and they were defeated.

My buddies and I were viewing the most brutal level of fighting in modern warfare. In battle, it is one thing to terminate the life of an enemy soldier by shooting him in the head or the chest. In a bayonet encounter, the victim dies from ruthless and savage stab wounds to the neck, to the stomach, and to the heart area. Death is painfully slow.

The bodies of the dead combatants were left on the side of the road. The bodies of the Japanese would be gathered by the Japanese army before dawn and would be stacked up like cordwood for cremation. The bodies of the brave Filipinos would be left on the ground to rot in the sun. Later on, we saw Japanese army trucks and artillery pieces driving over dead American and Filipino bodies.

Our convoy inched slowly up the military highway, and we began to feel the cool breezes from Manila Bay. The breezes from the jungle were not as cool but were welcome, nonetheless. Our shirts were just now beginning to feel dry. Everyone was unusually quiet. We were all tired and hungry.

We had reached Limao on the way to San Fernando.

I could hear the sighs and laments of my buddies as they trudged ahead at the point of a bayonet. A lot of them were suffering from dysentery or malaria.

I removed my helmet from my perspiring head for a few seconds as the truck picked up speed. The cool night air was soothing. My hair was wet and matted from the combination of sweat and dust. The hunger pangs in my stomach were intense. *How much of this can I take?* I wondered.

Suddenly, the truck accelerated and we noticed the wheels were going over what appeared to be speed bumps. Sam Romero came up to the front of the truck excited and incensed.

"You know what guys...this goddam Jap is driving the truck over dead American bodies lying on the road." "Lower your voice, Sam. Don't let the driver hear you. "Slant-eyed bastards." "Sam!"

He was driving on the shoulder of the highway to get around some of the mangled trucks, tanks, and scores of other military debris left behind by American and Japanese forces. Fallen trees that were split by artillery shrapnel littered the terrain. The smell of rotting flesh permeated the night air. Being among the dead at night was horrifying.

It was 10 o'clock. We were between Orion and Lima, fifteen miles north of Cabcaben Field, where a heavy battle had taken place on April 7-8. The American and Filipino forces had fought gallantly in order to retreat to their reserve battle stations. The degree of fighting varied from artillery duels to infantry skirmishes. At times, it had deteriorated to hand-to-hand combat and bayonet encounters.

The American soldier was not properly instructed in the art of bayonet defense or offense. The Filipino solder, however, had the agility and determination to excel with the bayonet as a lethal weapon. Self-defense with a knife or a sword is ingrained in the mind of an Asian.

As we crossed a railroad track, Joe Medina, our regimental driver, said, "We're in San Fernando. I've crossed these tracks a jillion times. I know where I am." He was right; it was San Fernando.

Before the surrender of General King's forces, Japan's General Homma and his staff had developed a plan to get the U.S. forces out of Bataan as quickly as possible. The captives would walk out of Bataan as far as San Fernando. From there they would be shipped by rail to prison camps in central Luzon. San Fernando was sixty miles from Cabcaben.

That night, we slept in a barbed-wire enclosure in which the conditions were nearly indescribable. During the night we were forced to relieve ourselves by the fence. Those with dysentery had to answer Nature's call right where they were sitting or standing. The smell was terrible. We had nothing to eat that night, but the absence of food was not as critical as the lack of water.

A few men in our group had water in their canteens. This water was priceless. Anyone borrowing a drink was limited to two swallows.

We knew we were by the highway from the sounds of trucks, artillery pieces, and tanks going south toward Corregidor.

By 8 o'clock the following morning, April 10, we were ordered to vacate the compound. Everyone was eager to leave. Those who were unable to walk due to attacks of malaria and dysentery were left behind. We knew we would never see them again.

CHAPTER 7

✫ ✫ ✫

"YEA, THOUGH I WALK..."

It was approaching mid-morning. Our group was marched across the dusty highway from the barbed-wire enclosure to a spot not too far from some railroad cars. The railroad office was located about a block away, alongside the narrow-gauge railroad tracks. The railroad office down the street was an eight-foot-square building with a peaked roof painted red.

The sun was bearing down on us. The tropical vegetation around us was making the air humid. The cloud of dust generated by the vehicles going south made breathing difficult. The Japanese army objective was the eventual conquest of Corregidor. Hundreds of GIs would perish in defense of that strategic island at the mouth of Manila Bay.

Corregidor was only two miles square in area. It was approximately five miles from the southern tip of the Bataan peninsula. Its arsenal of artillery pieces included 14- and 16-inch guns anchored in solid concrete foundations. A projectile from the 16-inch gun created the most intimidating noises as it traveled through the air.

As we marched in formation toward the railroad boxcars, a GI commented, "Who knows, we could be going to Manila to be traded for Jap POWs!"

The young man was from the 194th Tank Battalion. Prisoner exchange is possible. The thought gave us a momentary morale boost.

I was walking alongside Ben, and all of a sudden I had a psychic experience, in which I could hear my mother reciting the Twenty-third Psalm.

Ben interrupted my thought. "'I'll tell you, Brother, wherever we're going, I wish we could get something to eat. I think these Japs intend to starve us to death before too long."

"I have been eating bits of toothpaste to suppress my hunger," I said, reaching into my back pocket and pulling out my tube of Pepsodent. I offered it to him. "No thanks, Horace, I couldn't stomach that stuff."

I didn't blame Ben for refusing my offer. Toothpaste tasted sweet and chalky. It caused a nauseating aftertaste. And now after not having eaten for the last three days, I was hungry day and night. I was also losing weight, and I didn't have any to spare.

We were approaching the San Fernando railroad station. Our spirits rose a little. We were going to ride on the train instead of marching. Little did we know the nightmare that was waiting for us once we were aboard. The Filipino boxcars are two-thirds the size of the ones in the states. They are not as wide since they run on a narrow-gauge track.

"*Stopo!*" yelled a Japanese officer as he flashed his sword in the air. We understood it to mean, "stop" so we came to a quick halt.

Behind us were the boxcars. We looked inside some of the cars and noticed that they were littered with dry cow dung. The cars had sat in the hot tropical sun with the doors closed.

The soldiers around us were mistreating everyone in the formation. They slammed my lower back with a rifle butt for being out of line. They were kicking some of the boys in the shins for the same reason. They became agitated because we did not understand their orders or commands in Japanese. Some of our boys were bleeding from blows to the face and the head.

We were ready to board the train. We were divided into groups of fifty men. My group was ordered to load up. One guard was assigned to each car. The guard opened the door and motioned for us to get in. The heat from inside hit us in the face. Some of us paused for a moment, but the guard leveled his bayonet and threatened us. We jammed in. There was standing room only.

Inside of the car was like an oven, at least 120 degrees. We were packed so tight that it was impossible to squat down. Protests were ignored. When our captors closed the doors, the heat and the smell inside were indescrib-able. There didn't seem to be enough oxygen. I looked around for Ben. He was at the other end fighting for space.

After the train started to move, everyone started yelling, screaming, and gasping for air. Those against the wall would look for a crack or a hole to press their mouths against for fresh air. Some of the men fainted but had no place to fall. Those with dysentery were re-lieving themselves against their friends. Those in better health, not having anywhere else to go, were relieving their bladders in their trou-sers.

As the train chugged and swayed ahead I noticed that the floor was two inches deep in feces, urine, and vomit. An advanced case of dysentery induces a severe case of nausea. How much more of this could we endure?

I recall that the enemy would stop the train once or twice to unload the gravely ill POWs from the boxcars. We would have to carry them to the shade of the nearest tree and lay them on the ground. Their bodies were immediately bombarded by a host of blow flies the size of bees. I bent down for a moment to clean the mouth of one of my buddies only to be hit with a rifle butt and kicked by a Jap guard.

"Hy-yako, Amerika!" screamed a guard behind me as he pointed his bayonet towards the boxcars. *Hy-yako* was the word for "hurry." We all rushed back into the boxcar as fast as we could. They didn't waste any time slamming the door shut behind us. With the absence of the bodies of the men we unloaded just moments earlier, there was a little more room inside. Some of the boys had been able to kick some of the slush and debris off the floor. The train started rolling towards Camp O'Donnell again.

The conditions in the car were just as bad as before. Phobia and the lack of fresh air were causing some of the boys to lose their senses. Some were becoming violent.

"God-damned Japs, turn me loose!" cried a 31st Infantry private at the top of his voice.

We could tell he had gone mad. He was sweating profusely. His face was flushed and sweaty. He had malaria.

"I say, let's kill these guards. We'll take their weapons. We'll shoot 'em and escape into the jungle."

The *rickety-tickety-rickety* reverberated in my ears as the train picked up momentum. It was mesmerizing; I fell into a hypnotic sleep. I had not slept for several days. After all, this was Friday afternoon. All of us had been on our feet, without food, since Wednesday morning, the day before we surrendered. My brother interrupted my slumber.

"Horace! Wake up. You're falling asleep on your feet. The last thing you want to do is fall face down on this filthy floor."

Ben was right. I thought I had only closed my eyes for a split-second, but I had fallen into a deep sleep. My brother shook my head with both hands to clear the cobwebs. I was amazed at the brief length of time it took me to fall asleep. I remembered closing my eyes for a second. The fact is that every single one of us riding this boxcar was in the same exhausted condition. We had to get some rest soon.

The train came to a sudden stop. We had arrived at the small town of Capas, five or six miles from Camp O'Donnell. We had missed Clark Field by less than a mile on our way up. We were on the island of Luzon now, approximately sixty miles north of Cabcaben Field.

When Joe Medina and I rode this same Manila Railroad to Manila on our weekends off, we were more dignified passengers. I remember that Joe and I would wear our neatly pressed khaki uniforms. We would walk from the base to the railroad station at Sambambatum just a few blocks from our barracks.

Today, when we were ordered off the train, we were met by an army of infantry soldiers. We had already experienced the cruelness of the enemy's infantry forces. They would follow a command with the thrust of a bayonet. They would not hesitate to bayonet you to death for the slightest infraction.

"Hy-yako, Amerika, Hy-yako."

We lined up to be counted. By this time, the men from the boxcar behind us had joined with our group. We were all a part of the original 100 who had left Cabcaben aboard trucks. The number had dwindled down to about eighty men. The other twenty men were the unfortunate ones. Some had been dumped off the train because they were sick with dysentery or malaria. They were left to die under the hot tropical sun by the railroad tracks – with a little help from a Japanese bayonet.

"Bango!"

We had been instructed by this time that *Bango* meant "count off."

We finished the count-off of eighty-one men. We were immediately told to line up in a column of twos on the road and to start marching the last five or six miles to Camp O'Donnell. Some of our boys who knew the area said that the camp was originally a partially completed American airfield. It was surrounded by a nearly treeless plain. Tall cogon grass was the only vegetation next to the stockade.

The camp consisted of nipa-roofed barracks. Many of the roofs were still unfinished when we arrived there. Nipa is a tropical palm that grows in Southeast Asia. The feathery leaves are used for weaving and thatching. The nipa roofs were able to withstand the tropical sun and the rainy season when it rains for fifteen consecutive days.

It was two o'clock when we had started the march at Capas. The highway was a dirt road. The heat from the sun and the stamping of Army boots on the dry dirt caused a light, dry cloud of dust that was getting into our noses and eyes. We were marching at a fairly fast clip by the time we had been on the road for a half-hour.

"Hy-yako, Amerika, Hy-yako!"

The comprehension of that particular word was to save brutal beatings or even death later on. We Americans had to learn the Japanese language to survive.

After almost two hours of constant, hurried walking, we arrived at Camp O'Donnell. It was a dilapidated place. Surrounding it was a seven-foot-high, barbed-wire fence and 25-foot-high wooden gun towers.

Beyond the fences was the five-foot-tall cogon grass. The grass was a grim reminder of the night we spent establishing the last line of defense at the Cabcaben Field. Our hands were slashed and bleeding as we made our way in the dark.

Past the cogon grass and beyond the open field was the brown, nearly treeless plain. The geography around the camp was vastly different from that of Bataan. On Bataan, it was jungle country. At O'Donnell, the land was flat and arid. We discovered that there was a creek alongside the north end of the camp. Before the war, there had been a dam at one end, but it was destroyed during the retreat of the

American forces. Later on in the internment of the thousands of men, water from the creek was used by the Americans for cooking rice. There was a water pump in the camp with only one spigot. This was the only source of drinking water for the whole camp. Our captors used water restriction as additional punishment and torture. It was effective.

My group of eighty-one arrived at O'Donnell totally exhausted. We were still hungry and thirsty. All any of us wanted to do was fall on the ground and sleep. I was elated beyond words when I realized that the sergeant had commanded us to stop walking. The guards' brutality intensified since there were two squads of them. Some of the boys who decided to sit on the ground were severely beaten in the head and back with rifle butts, and kicked. The reign of terror continued.

As we were waiting in formation right in front of the camp, a dirty and dilapidated U.S. Army jeep came out of the camp in a cloud of dust and stopped directly in front of us. It was driven by a Japanese army corporal wearing thick eyeglasses. His passenger was a beady-eyed major.

"Kioski!"

We came to attention immediately.

The officer dismounted, swaggered to the front of the jeep, and climbed up on the hood. He turned around to face the formation. He held his sword in his right hand. As he began to speak, he started to work himself into a frenzy, stomping his right boot on the faded green metal. I admired his ability to keep his balance. His face became red, and by now the enemy had found the same young interpreter. Southern Cal was comparatively civil to us.

The speaker told us in a high, squeaky voice that the Japanese had not signed the Geneva Convention, which regulated prisoner of war treatment by an enemy nation. He also told us that Americans were dogs, that they had always been dogs, and that they were going to be treated like dogs. He became hysterical when he accused the Caucasians of being enemies of the Asian for a hundred years.

The officer ranted and raved for about half an hour while we stood at attention. He continued to stomp his feet on the hood of the jeep. His height of five-feet, three-inches made him look like a puppet.

His threats began to hit home when he said that he was going to be the commander of Camp O'Donnell. We knew what was in store for us.

"Be brave, Brother," I said to Ben as we entered the gates of the compound.

"You, too."

We would survive.

And so began the lives of the Battling Bastards of Bataan in Camp O'Donnell. Some of my buddies here would later become some of the 6,000 to 7,000 American soldiers to die in captivity.

Deaths from starvation and execution were standard at Camp O'Donnell from day one. There was nowhere to turn for food. Our own soldiers set up kitchens to cook steamed rice twice a day for the able-bodied. Burial details had to be recruited. Ben and I were among the few fit enough to volunteer to canvass the premises every day for dead Americans.

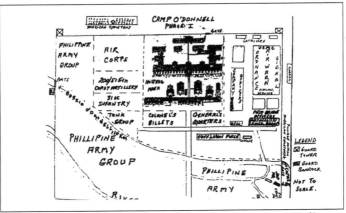

Segments of U.S. Army and Philippine Army Units

CHAPTER 8

✫ ✫ ✫

CAMP O'DONNELL

This brigade of captured American soldiers was simply the vanguard of 9,300 Americans and 48,000 Filipinos to arrive at Camp O'Donnell after the capitulation of Bataan. The Japanese were in a hurry to clear out the American forces from the peninsula so that their job of blasting the island of Corregidor would be easier. The order was given to evacuate the Americans as soon as possible no matter what the cost.

The road from Capas, for us, had been hot and dusty in the glaring light. My buddies and I were numb with fatigue. We burned with fever and were gaunt from hunger and loss of sleep. The harsh commands of our captors rang in our ears. My mind was not as sharp as it had been. Momentary lapses of memory and perception would lead me to not hear clearly the commands issued by a soldier. Ignoring a command by the enemy could be fatal.

Since we were the first bunch of arriving prisoners, we were assigned the grubby nipa-roofed barracks. The floor was dirt. There were two-tiered bunks against the length of the bamboo walls. There were no doors at the entrances. Except for the roof, there was no protection from the elements, although the roof at least protected us from the unrelenting tropical sun. There were no bathroom facilities because there was no running water. There was evidence of a futile attempt to install the water connections for bathroom facilities. I thought of the necessity of latrines. The more I looked around, the sadder I became. I don't think that Ben saw me cry.

"Chow time, bring your mess kits with you, guys!"

The announcement came from the make-shift American kitchen fifty yards away from us. The kitchen was located across the street from the guardhouse. Those within hearing distance rushed towards the kitchen. Our eating utensils varied from one man to another. Some had managed to keep their original Army regulation mess kits. Others, including me, had to make do with bamboo bowls, tin cans, empty C-ration containers, and even helmets. Forks were a rarity. Using chopsticks properly is a lot harder than it looks. But we wanted to eat, so we learned.

Ben and I, along with thirty or forty other prisoners, ran from the *buhai* to the dining room to line up for chow. *Buhai* is the Filipino word for house or barracks.

Everybody was so tired, so weak, and so sleepy that it was torturous to stand in line. Our legs were wobbly and weak. We just wanted to lie down and sleep and lose consciousness. But we were very hungry as well.

Ben, Joe Medina, and I had been in line for no more that fifteen minutes when Joe fell to the ground. We all looked at him as we helped him back on his feet. I looked at him closely. His eyelids were half open. I held his head between my hands and shook it gently to stimulate the blood in his brain. He opened his eyes wider and was able to stand up again on his own.

We were all relieved that he was OK. We joined the chow line eager to enjoy our first meal in four days. All they were serving was a half ration of steamed rice. That was our first meal as POWs.

The sun was getting pretty low on the horizon by the time we finished "dinner." The new cooks had not yet developed the recipe for steamed rice, so the first batch came out soupy, something like oatmeal. The Filipinos had a name for it, *lugaow*. It would have been delicious with cream and sugar, but that was not in the stars for us.

I was constantly haunted by pleasant memories of homemade meals, and by the love in my mother's home with the rest of my brothers and sisters. The fact that Ben and I were here for each other made us both feel better. Later on in our captivity, many times we would get together in an isolated corner of a barracks. Ben and I would kneel down, bow our heads in reverence to God, and pray together. I could feel the presence of my mother during those brief sessions. I was unmarried and my mother, Zoraida, was my spiritual touchstone.

By the end of the first day at Camp O'Donnell, some men were coming down with dysentery and malaria. The time finally came that first day to find a place to sleep. Our barracks was filling up with many seriously ill men. There were no medical services available.

I had been recruited earlier in the afternoon to dig a trench at the far end of our barracks to serve as a latrine. The next day it was invaded by swarms of blowflies. The flies back home were like midgets compared to these tropical specimens. Blowflies are about one-half inch long and their green-tinged belly is just as big around. As disease spreaders, they were responsible for hundreds of POW deaths.

We slept on the path in front of our barracks. Ben, Joe Medina, and I pooled our miscellaneous bits of blankets and shelter halves to cover the hard ground. We used our shoes as pillows. Tropical nights in the Philippines were not meant for sleeping outside without covers. The ground seemed to "sweat" at night. Our clothing would absorb that moisture throughout the night. It did not take us long to find out that moist clothing was not conducive to a restful sleep. As a consequence, we had to rise at five o'clock in the morning to walk and to dry our shirts in the morning breeze.

I fell asleep that night as I lay on my back next to Ben. I was lying on the hard ground gazing at the star-studded sky and hoping for the sandman to drop by soon.

I was abruptly awakened shortly before midnight by a familiar voice. "Horace, wake up. May I join your group for tonight?"

When I recognized the voice I said, "Hell yes, Conrado, why not."

Conrado Vigil was a member of my Battery H. He was from Lemitar, New Mexico, a little village just south of Belen. He was really OK. Before captivity he was inclined to be a loner. He was a devotee of the Virgin Mary and a devout Catholic. He would recite the rosary at the drop of a hat in a crisis. This was not always a good thing to do. In combat, there is a time to fight and a time to pray.

I lay back down on the ground and began to fall sleep as Conrado knelt beside us, clasped his hands together in front of his chest, and began to pray the rosary.

The daytime temperature in the Philippines in April and during the dry season is very hot. The nights are warm until about two or three o'clock in the morning. After that, the early-morning hours are cool and somewhat humid. The dew would collect on objects sitting on the ground.

Nightlife at Camp O'Donnell turned out to be very hectic, which made it exceedingly difficult to rest. The Japanese army changed their guard around the fence and at the watchtowers every two hours. With the Japanese guardhouse at the main entrance of the camp, the relieving squad of ten soldiers would begin their march at the guardhouse and head for the fence and towers. As they marched through the camp, the NCO would literally scream the commands at the top of his voice. This would interfere with the sleep of prisoners within hearing distance.

The soldiers marched in full battle gear and precise formation. Every soldier had an infantry rifle on his shoulder with a fixed bayonet. We had to stand at attention and salute if we were awake and in the immediate vicinity. Failure to obey this rule meant a severe beating or even death.

There were all kinds of interruptions throughout the night. I discovered early that a diet of rice and soup did something to your urinary system. It made me urinate so often that it would ruin a good night's sleep. Survival in this hellhole was not going to be easy. We had to learn to cope with the interruptions by the prisoners sick with amoebic dysentery, malaria, or dengue fever as they tossed around. Shots from the sentries on the towers would ring out during the night. A trigger-happy sentry would shoot at POWs on the ground, sometimes wounding or killing Americans. The Japanese command was hypersensitive to the possibility of escape.

There was no infraction more serious in a POW camp than an escape. The escapee would be captured and brought back to camp. In the presence of fellow POWs, the prisoner would be kicked, shoved, and forced to stand at attention in front of the guardhouse. All this was done in the presence of the Japanese camp commander, as he stood at parade rest with his left hand on the handle of his saber as it hung from his waist.

One of the early American escapees from Camp O'Donnell was a young commissioned officer. There was a small stream that bisected a corner of the camp. The intersection of the wire fence and the small stream created a hole big enough to crawl through. The guards, in their obsession to monitor the prisoners' activities in the camp, had failed to seal the hole between the water and the barbed wire.

The young officer attempted his escape in the wee hours of the morning. He hid under the bamboo barracks closest to the fence. Then he crawled on his stomach towards the hole at the same time the guard detail was changing. Unfortunately, he fell into the water and created a loud splash. He would have made it otherwise. The night was dark and moonless.

The next day, the young lieutenant, wearing only his under shorts, was marched down the main street to the guardhouse at the camp entrance by a squad of enemy soldiers. In the presence of the camp commander, the guards took turns beating the young American in the head, spine, and face with a heavy club. He was forced to stand at attention during the entire beating. The fact that he was unable to stand erect at the command of *Kioski!* was an indication to the guards that he was disobeying an order.

He withstood this mistreatment for two days. At the end of the second day, without food and water, the young and courageous U.S. Army Air Corps officer died on a makeshift platform. His body was removed to a nearby barracks for burial the next day.

As we walked with the body on our shoulders, we prayed in silence to honor our buddy. Unbeknownst to the guards, we would usually have a Jewish or Christian chaplain with us. The chaplain would walk alongside us whispering prayers. This activity was strictly forbidden early in our internment.

The Lord is my shepherd. I shall not want. He maketh me to lie down in green pastures...

On the night of the escape and capture of our young officer, the commander of Camp O'Donnell placed the camp on a strict alert in retaliation.

He was driven aboard an army jeep up and down the main street in the camp. Every few yards he would gesture to his driver to stop. He would slice the air with his sword in his right hand, his interpreter at his side. The translator had trouble keeping up.

"Escaping from this camp is punishable by death! Effective today this camp's prisoners of war will be broken up into groups of ten men."

The commander placed the sword in the scabbard as he continued to spew epithets and belch out insults and threats at the defeated and sick Americans surrounding him. The men he was addressing had already been overwhelmed and beaten by hunger and malnutrition, by malaria and dengue fever, and bouts of dizziness and nausea.

The commander stopped his jeep one more time on his way to headquarters. He spoke briefly and somewhat more rationally.

"In the future, the population of this camp will be broken down into squads of ten blood brothers. In the event of an escape or getaway of a blood brother, the remaining nine blood brothers will be shot to death." Our chances of survival looked increasingly bleak.

By the end of April there were 5,000 to 6,000 American prisoners of war in Camp O'Donnell. The population would grow to 9,300 by mid-May. Across the road, the Philippine camp would house as many as 48,000 Philippine prisoners of war. A good number of those would eventually be re-indoctrinated and released by the Imperial Japanese Army. They would be the lucky ones. The rest would die from dysentery, malaria, and malnutrition.

There were days ahead in which I would see the Filipinos carry their dead down the road that separated the camps. The corpses were carried in blankets strung over a pole. The pole was carried on the shoulders of the litter bearers. They carried as many as 400 bodies a day 8,000 yards down the road to the cemetery.

Camp O'Donnell was an abode of the damned and a hell dominated by the sun and the bayonets of the ruthless Japanese guards.

A party of Americans shown along the route of the Death March. This picture was taken on the outskirts of Lubao early in the morning of what was probably the fourth or fifth day of march for these exhausted men.

Allied signers of the Japanese surrender document - above; Japanese signing the surrender document - below. (courtesy of Roger Mansell).

Americans at Camp O'Donnell turn out with their mess gear. This picture was taken in April. 1942. (TK)

Assembly point of POWs after capture. Note the American tied to the pole in the foreground (National Archives).

Cabanatuan hut constructed of bamboo and nipa. More than 120 POWs were forced to crowd into these buildings built for 40 (US Army Photo, Vince Tayler)

Captured Americans were lined up at Mariveles
Point on Bataan. They were first searched and all
worldly goods taken, then lined up and began the
march out of bataan. (Samuel B. Moody)

Defeated Americans on the Death March. This
captured photo shows the start of the March at
Mariveles Point. (Notice the photographer on
the far right) (National Archives, Robert Conroy)

Dejection of Bataan's defenders was caught by the
Japanese photographer when he pictured GI's in
the above group (TK)

General King and his staff discuss surrender of
Bataan with Japanese Colonel Motoo Nakayama,
General Homma's Chief of Operations.
(Signal Corps)

Mouths covered because of choking dust and carrying their comrades. Death March survivors approach O'Donnell. (National Archives) (Some authors say that this picture shows the burial detail at O'Donnell because of the masks, poles and blankets)

(Editor's Note: This photograph has been verified as the burial detail at Camp O'Donnell)

Original boxcar on siding in San Fernando in which were packed Death March survivors on their iethal trip to Capas. The Japenese forced as many 100 prisoners at bayonet point into these 40 x 8 metal sided boxcars

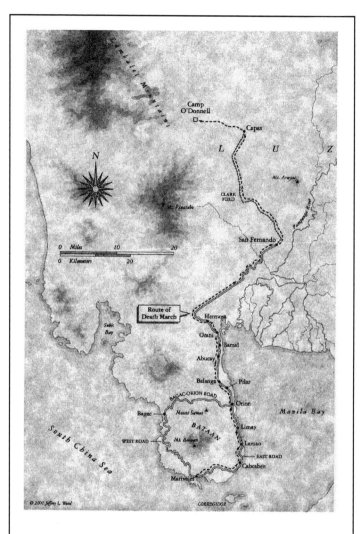

Route of the bataan Death March - from the book
Ghost Soldiers by Hampton Sides

Some prisoners had their hands tied behind their backs with wire and were slapped around a lot (above). Some were even killed on the spot. It just depended on the particular group a man was with and the soldiers guarding them. (Robert Conroy)

Surrending Officers on Bataan. These are Commanding General, Major General Edward P. King, Jr. and (from left) Colonel Everett C. Williams, Major Wade Cothran, and Major Achille C. Tisdale. (TK)

The Death March stretched for 55 miles. The guards were changed every three hours to keep them fresh was no rest for the weary and exhausted POWs (Samuet Moody)

The men who were able carried their weary and exhausted comrades. To leave a man behind meant death. (US National Archives)

The prisoners were spearated into groups and made to sit in the hot sun for many hours before finally being herded onto the "Death March"
(National Archives)

The man who surrendered numbered almost three times the 25,000 the Japanese had expected. Marching to the rear they passed Japanese infantry moving on still resisting Corregidor. They were searched over and over again by Japanese soldiers. (TK)

This is another view of the boxcars that were used to transport the POWs from San Fernando to Camp O'Donnell. Many suffocated to death in the hirrobly cramped quarters. (photo by Vince Taylor)

Soldiers take cover in a trench as a Japanese shell explodes nearby. This was a typical defense fortification on Bataan. (Signal Corps)

Two defenders of Bataan who were taken prisoner
in savage jungle fighting stand with hands raised to
be searched by a Japanese soldier. If meant death
if a soldier had something that said "Made in Japan"
on it or had Japanese money. The Japanese soldiers
thought that they had stolen it from dead Japanese
soldiers. (TK)

Unknown Americans at Camp O'Donnell. Prisoners just marked time, sitting or standing still, very lethargic. Many were mentally depressed and psychologically stressed from the horrors of the Death March (US Army Photo E. Bartlett Kerr)

US and Filipino soldiers on Bataan surrender to the Japanese on April 9, 1942. This was a posed picture for the photographer.

Watched by Japanese soldiers American prisoners sit down for a brief rest along the route to prison camp. To add to the torment, the enemy forced the captives to go bareheaded. Any faltering prisoner was shot or bayoneted. (Donald King)

CHAPTER 9

✦ ✦ ✦

THE GHOST OF DEATH

On the American side of the camp, we were losing from eighty to one-hundred, fifty prisoners per day, mostly to amoebic dysentery. Due to the scarcity of water in the camp, it was difficult to keep these patients clean. Since we could not wash their soiled clothing, we buried it.

The separate wards for dysentery and malaria were nothing more than huge emergency rooms without decent medical facilities. Moral support and hope were the only things we could offer to the ill and dying.

We had volunteer corpsmen from the different services manning the designated wards. They were foul places to work in. The human waste on the floor mats caused a fetid odor. The corpsmen working there were worthy of a special medal for the performance of a mission far beyond the call of duty.

Every day throughout April and the early part of May, thousands of American stragglers from the Death March trickled into Camp O'Donnell. There were joyful reunions of buddies in the Army, the Navy, and the Marine Corps. We would greet them and embrace them as they entered the main gate. Some of our buddies had been listed as dead. Some of the meetings were emotional and, at times, tearful.

During the month of May, life around the camp deteriorated significantly. Malnutrition began to take its toll. We were fed only twice a day and then only one small bowl of white rice per meal. There were no vegetables or meat in the watery rice. Some men would supplement their rations with leftovers from the very sick or the dying. This was one way to expose oneself to a deadly disease. The primary transmission of disease was left up to the black blowflies that swarmed the camp from sunup to sundown. They would descend in black waves on the human excrement at the latrine and return to light on our food if we let them. We had no mess hall in the camp, so we had our meals in an open barracks or in the shade of a building anywhere on the camp. We had to shoo the flies away from our mess kits.

To help control the rampant fly situation, the American officers in charge of the kitchen started a plan to reward with extra food anyone bringing twenty-five to thirty dead flies to them.

Work details varied from gathering wood from alongside the river outside the camp to hauling water in fifty-gallon barrels for our kitchen. There were also graves to dig for the burial of the dead. By May 1942, we had to bury from 150 to 250 Americans a day.

Ben and I had joined the burial details. We were rewarded with an additional half portion of rice a day for the days we worked. By five o'clock every morning the burial details were up gathering corpses from around the camp. We were broken up into groups of four and assigned to a single litter with one body. The most unpleasant chore was gathering corpses. The dead were young, good-looking men in their early twenties; their Army dog tags hung from their necks or were wound around their ankles. Some of them had tattoos of their girl friends' initials on their arms or their chests.

I would get choked up as I loaded my comrades onto the litter for the mile-long trek to the cemetery. The Filipino POWs across the road were going through the same motions in preparing their dead. They were losing two to three times as many men as we were, and it took them all day to transport and bury their dead.

Discipline grew harsher by the day. Deaths from severe beatings were common. Captain Yoshio Tsuneyoshi, the camp commander, decreed that fraternization between American and Filipino soldiers was punishable by death.

By this time, the guards expected us to count up to 1,000 in Japanese. In our work details, we were moved from one area to another in groups of fifty to one-hundred. When we re-assembled at the new area, we were lined up and expected to count off in Japanese. Mistakes could be fatal.

Early one morning, Ben and I came upon the body of a young Anglo soldier in his early twenties. He was lying in a pool of blood with his face smashed in from the vicious blows of a blunt instrument. He had been kicked and dragged in the dirt. He had been seen the day before standing at attention and was being drilled in the Japanese numbers in front of a Japanese soldier. He had made a mistake.

The practice of religion, particularly Christianity, was strictly forbidden by the Japanese commander. To be caught kneeling in prayer was tantamount to suicide. Religious devotions were done after dark and in complete seclusion.

Benedicto C de Baca was a very close friend from Peña Blanca. He was a Catholic and a genuine Christian. He was the only soldier I knew who would kneel down in prayer either in private or among his buddies before retiring at night. Benedicto was to become the organizer of a group of Catholics who would meet after dark and in secret to pray the rosary. It was in one of these prayer meetings that he demonstrated his capacity to share his religious beliefs.

One late evening in May, as I was walking to a meeting with Ben and other friends, another young soldier tapped me on the shoulder from behind.

"Hey, Montoya."

"What's up, David?"

"I want to find a place to pray. I don't have a religion. I was a Protestant when I was kid. When I grew up I quit going to church, but I need to learn to pray again."

Benedicto immediately came to mind. I was certain that he would welcome David with open arms.

I pointed to a certain barracks and whispered, "David, go in there and look in the darkest corner for a group huddled together, on their knees, praying the rosary."

"I remember bits of the Lord's Prayer."

"The group will recite, 'Our Father who art in heaven...hallowed be thy name,' every so often. Join them."

"There are no atheists in the fox holes."

On the second week of May 1942, the Japanese command moved all the senior U.S. officers to Tarlac, north of Clark Field. A lot of colonels were left behind, including Colonel Sage from our regiment. Before he left for Tarlac, General King named Sage commander of the American group at Camp O'Donnell.

With Colonel Sage as the senior officer in the camp, more officers of the 200th were placed in charge of work details. Lieutenant Jack Boyer from Battery H was placed in charge of a Sick Barracks. His job was to supervise the assignment of seriously ill POWs from working barracks to a ward. There was also a St. Peter's Barracks for the terminally ill.

Sergeant Luis G. LeRoux from my battery survived a month's stay at St. Peter's ward. He was stricken with dysentery some time in May. I remember visiting with him at that time. He was an exceptional individual. He was too weak to walk so he dragged himself from one end of the ward to the other. He was always bumming cigarettes. He never gave up. Eventually, he recovered enough to be reassigned to the Sick Barracks.

Second Lieutenant Jack R. Kennaman, also from Battery H, was placed in charge of the burial detail. He was tall, lean, soft-spoken, and level-headed. As an NCO working in the battery commander's office back in the states, I had known of Lieutenant Kennaman before his promotion to a commissioned officer. I liked to work with him.

One rainy day in late May, we set out on our burial detail. Our group was a convoy of fifty litters with fifty GI bodies. Ben and I, along with two other litter bearers, were leading the column with Lieutenant Kennaman walking beside us. Escorting the detail were two Japanese soldiers, each with an infantry rifle with fixed bayonet. The two soldiers were wearing raincoats. I was wearing a cavalry hat, GI-issue green under shorts, and my Army shoes. The rest of the men on the detail were similarly dressed. This was the practical way to work in the rain in the Philippines during the rainy season.

As we walked in the wet and slushy mud on the road, some of the litter bearers were losing their balance as they slipped on the mud. The slow-moving column of litters was making the guards nervous. The Japanese soldier in front of us confronted Lieutenant Kennaman.

"Kura, itchi bon, dahme, tho!" he shouted and motioned to us that we were moving too slowly, and kept lashing out with his bayonet at our stomachs to prove his point.

Lieutenant Kennaman tried his best to assure the guard that we would accelerate our pace. He even remembered the Japanese word *wakaru,* which means, "I understand."

Shortly thereafter we reached the cemetery. We proceeded to grave number one as directed by the Japanese as the heavy rain continued. The graves were four feet deep, eight feet wide, and twelve feet long. By this time, the hole was a third full of water. The tempo was a steady "rush, rush." *Kura, Amerika*

The guards were prodding and shoving us with their rifle butts. We had to lay the corpse down on the muddy surface with some degree of respect. Ben and I would have to crawl down into the grave to lay the corpse on the bottom of the grave. The bodies were laid down side-by-side and head-to-head. There were ten to twelve bodies to a grave. The majority of the bodies were dressed only in their under shorts.

We would improvise diapers from rags back at the camp for those who were completely naked. In spite of the primitive conditions in the camp, every one of us tried to respect the act of burying the body of one of our comrades.

Some of the bodies we had just interred began to float in the bottom of the grave. We had to weigh down and sink some of the bodies as the gravedigger's poured dirt over the bodies.

The torrential rain continued.

By late morning, my detail was ordered by the Japanese to re-group and prepare to march back to our camp. We would be escorted by three or four Japanese soldiers. We would have to stand at attention at the command of a Japanese officer to count off in Japanese. Early in our POW internment, this formality was fraught with danger.

Fortunately, that day the last count-off was flawless and we headed back to camp. My shoes were full of water. The rain was providing me with a much-needed shower.

As the detail started to move away from the burial grounds, someone nudged me.

"Hey, Montoya. Look at those bare arms sticking out of the ground."

I looked in the direction he was pointing. The sight was horrendous. The bodies we had just interred were beginning to surface. The bodies would be exposed to wild dogs at night.

Lieutenant Kennaman pleaded with the guards to allow his men to stay longer to rebury the corpses. The guards responded with a sequence of curse words and insults. Summoning our officer to the front of the formation, the enemy berated and kicked him.

"Amerika Dahme, Nay, Nay, Dahme Tho!"

That meant that Americans were worthless, and nothing would be done about the exposed bodies.

Our detail was re-grouped and we were marched back to Camp O'Donnell at an accelerated pace as the rain continued.

That night I could not sleep well. The tropical rain continued to pound on the fragile nipa palm roof in my barracks. My skimpy tee shirt and shorts were damp and cold from the moisture in the air. To stay warm, I would scoot over next to my brother Ben on the bamboo bed as I lay awake.

When we arrived at the cemetery the following day, we discovered that during the night wild animals had found the bodies left partially uncovered the day before. Lieutenant Kennaman immediately commanded the detail to re-bury the corpses. To have to touch and handle the remains of these desecrated heroes was more than I could bear. I cursed those "damned Japs" in one breath, and in the next I prayed for the final eternal rest of our men's souls in heaven.

At daybreak the following morning, the tropical rain stopped abruptly. At about the same time, I was awakened by a strong urge to urinate. I checked the pile of pebbles by my pillow. It was the eighteenth pebble. I had been up eighteen times overnight. I sat up quietly on the bamboo slate in order not to bother my buddies. The tropical air was heavy with humidity. The clothing I had slept in was damp, making me slightly chilled. I stood up as quietly as I could. I looked around for Ben. He was two bodies down from me. He was in a deep sleep and hardly breathing. It startled me. I nudged him with my toe. He opened his eyes.

"What's the matter, Brother?"

"Go back to sleep, everything's OK," I said. I was just making sure he was alive.

Every day we would wake up to the smell of death. The smell of clean bodies was tolerable, but ten out of twenty-five men in our barracks were dysentery patients. Even at this early hour, the black blowflies were lighting on their mouths, their noses, and their eyes. Some of the corpses still had their eyes open, as if pleading for help.

Ben and I were fortunate in that we were brothers, and we had a lot in common. Sometimes, at the end of the day, we would isolate ourselves in the dark recesses of a barracks and reminisce about our good times back home. We would pray together. The Twenty-third Psalm was especially comforting.

We all suffered from the lack of food and medicine, but those of us who filled our minds with positive thoughts survived.

Many other factors impacted our lives at the camp. We did not receive mail from home, nor did we write home. We had no magazines or books to read. Sports-minded soldiers were totally isolated from the news of their favorite ball teams back home. Setting our hopes on tomorrow or the day after seemed to be enough to carry us through the day.

My first goal was Christmas Day 1942. I expected to be back with the U.S. Army troops by then. Some miracle would happen, and I would either escape or be recaptured by the U.S. forces. This illusion carried me through the Christmases of 1942, 1943, and 1944.

News of the progress of the war and other matters was scarce and unreliable. Word of the fall of Corregidor on Manila Bay the first week in May was demoralizing. Most of the captured Americans from Corregidor were brought to O'Donnell.

These men were still fighting the Japanese army on "The Rock" in April during the "thirty seconds over Tokyo" bombing raid by General Jimmy Doolittle and his valiant B-25 bomber pilots. This is the news we were all waiting to hear. This is the news that would build up morale and perhaps save lives in the long run.

The end of the month brought a number of rumors. The most persistent one was about the transfer of the able-bodied prisoners to another location. I liked that scuttlebutt. In an environment of hunger, sickness, and death, it was nice to hear a hopeful rumor. I was ready for a change. The guards were getting more sadistic and inhumane by the day. Public beatings, maimings, and executions were the reality seven days a week. Lieutenant Kennamen was still in charge of burial details.

Smuggling was punishable by death, but some civilians were willing to risk their lives by smuggling food, medicine, and other essentials into the camp. Many Filipino civilians lost their lives by doing this for the Americans.

There was one instance in which an American was caught in the act of receiving contraband food and medicine from a Filipino woman. This happened in the wee hours of a dark and rainy night. The Filipino woman was shot several times in the chest and head. She was left to die in a pool of blood and mud.

Two sentries grabbed the American. They called for the nearest tower to direct their searchlight beam on the area. Sam Romero and I happened to be inside a barracks not more than twenty-five yards away.

We were awakened by the commotion at two o'clock in the morning. We feared that the guards would start looking for witnesses. They did not.

"Kura, Amerika, Dahme Tho!"

"Attention!"

The GI was forced to stand at attention. He was weak from hunger and his clothes were hanging, wringing wet, from his shoulders and his waist. Without warning, the Japanese soldier thrust a bayonet into the GI's rib cage.

"Help! Help someone! Oh, God."

But there was no one around to respond.

His tortured and bayoneted young body was dragged to a platform in front of the guardhouse the next day. We were ordered by the chief guard to walk by the corpse as we exited the front gate on our way to the cemetery. I noticed that the young American had been bayoneted repeatedly in the chest and neck. His left ear had been severed. His muddy Navy cap lay on his chest. He was about six feet tall, and in his early twenties. His clothing was saturated with mud and his own blood from his countless bayonet wounds. On his head was a four-month growth of blonde hair matted with mud and blood. He probably weighed no more than 125 pounds. The average four-month weight loss at the camp was between sixty and one-hundred pounds.

The next day, June 1, began a week of hope. The rumor regarding the moving out of all able-bodied prisoners was true! Since Ben and I and the rest of the burial detail had been physically active all this time, I felt confident we would be moved out. That was a good feeling. We were losing fifty to one-hundred, fifty Americans a day to disease.

By June 2, 1942, it was official. Able-bodied POWs would be moved to Camp Cabanatuan located northeast of Camp O'Donnell. Those of us fortunate enough to leave Camp O'Donnell alive considered ourselves to be very lucky.

Only a few small units of Army medical personnel and civilians were left behind to care for the terminally ill and to police up the area. Bodies would be found in culverts, under barracks, and in other secluded places.

About 2,200 Americans and 22,000 Filipino prisoners of war died at Camp O'Donnell from starvation, disease, and the inhumane treatment they received at the hands of our Japanese captors.

I recall vividly the day we left for Camp Cabanatuan. We were in groups of fifty and one-hundred men with two to four Japanese armed guards in charge. These guards were forever prodding and pushing their rifle butts against the ribs and behinds of stragglers. I was able to carry the totality of my belongings under my left arm. I was wearing an Army cavalry hat and a dirty pair of khakis and Army shoes in fairly good condition. My top was a makeshift Army shirt. It was dirty and tattered from carrying bodies on my shoulder. Ben, Joe Medina, Lolo Montoya, Sam Romero, Fred Concha, Lieutenant Kennaman, and I walked together.

Four hours into our walk the first day, I suddenly developed a sharp pain that radiated down my leg. It was in the nature of a crick or charley horse. I immediately had an intense fear of falling on the ground. The consequences could be deadly.

As we walked four abreast, Ben grabbed me by the right arm. "Horace, what the hell happened?"

"Ben, I've got a severe pain in my right hip, and I cannot put any weight on my right leg."

"Don't worry, Horace. Hold your elbows firm. Joe will steady you from the left and I'll grab your right elbow...keep walking as best as you can."

Meanwhile, the rest of the men in my group closed ranks around me to divert the attention away from my sudden incapacity. The tall Marine in front of me placed a three-foot piece of twine into my hand. The piece of rope had a loop at one end.

"Run that loop onto your right foot. Take the other end in your right hand. Lift your foot manually every time you step forward."

I was quick to grasp the concept. It worked. I was able to stay with the rest of the column. I simply pulled the cord every time I stepped forward with my right foot. It worked every single time. Someone was looking kindly at me from above. I knew that if I had fallen, the guards would have beaten me to death.

Surely goodness and mercy shall follow me all the days of my life...

I kept walking in spite of the pain. It began to ease off after three or four hours. To my good fortune, the skies were cloudy with only a possible rain shower. The long unpaved road ahead was uneven with potholes and ruts, making it difficult for me to maintain an even gait. The ground was dry, with clouds of dust rising up to clog our eyes and noses. I could taste the dust in my mouth. The fine dust would cling to the perspiration on our faces and necks. And there was not enough water. Few of the men were carrying canteens. My mouth was so dry I couldn't even spit.

By mid-afternoon, my leg had recovered to the extent that I was able to keep up with rest of men in my column. I had my buddies to thank for their help. I also was indebted to the Marine who happened to come to my aid when my leg gave out. All I knew about him was that he had been captured on Corregidor when that island fell to the Japanese army.

The first group of American POWs to leave Camp O'Donnell that first day numbered 600 men. We walked from sunup to sundown. The guards ordered the men off the road into an area about one city block square. We were ordered to sit on the ground as close together as possible. Guards were posted around us.

We sat in the late-afternoon tropical sun until about six o'clock. The guards picked ten men as a water detail. A guard would escort them to a nearby civilian well. One had to feel sorry for the men in the detail because of the assortment of water containers. They ranged from the regulation canteen, to glass bottles with a string around the neck, to empty pork and bean cans.

Later in the evening, we were each fed a rice ball about the size of a baseball. Nothing else was provided. We supplemented this with some of the weeds around us. We slept under the stars that night wondering what the next day would bring.

CHAPTER 10

✧ ✧ ✧

CAMP CABANATUAN

We arrived in Cabanatuan with approximately 475 men. On the march, we were followed by a group of Japanese army trucks in charge of gathering the seriously ill and the bodies of the dead. Some of the corpses were bloody from bayonet wounds while others were badly bruised. Some of these men had been punished for not being able to maintain the required walking speed in the ranks. Some of these souls were dead because they had had a malaria attack or had left the ranks to relieve themselves during a dysentery attack.

The trucks carrying the sick and the dead were bringing the stench of sickness and death from Camp O'Donnell. I thought we had left all that behind.

Camp Cabanatuan was comparatively clean and spacious. There were rows and rows of bamboo-constructed barracks with thatched roofs. A high barbed-wire fence encircled the camp. Some of the men in my detail were beginning to pass out from exposure to the hot sun. Dysentery and malaria was beginning to take their toll. One of the ill was my friend, Gustavo Lucero, from my hometown.

Three o'clock rolled around, and we were still in formation in front of the barracks waiting to be assigned to our living quarters. We were exhausted and hungry. We had been standing for four hours. We had had a ball of rice for supper the night before. Our water containers were dry.

"Kioski, Amerika!"

All of us immediately stood at attention. We also straightened out the columns of men with the proper distance between each row.

"Bango!"

We counted off and, fortunately, the number of men supposedly in the group was correct. Everyone seemed to have remembered his number in Japanese. We were marched to our assigned barracks. Ben and I were in the same building by chance. I was glad about that. There were many ways we could help each other. We could share our food and drinking water. With the specter of illness and death everywhere, we were available to help each other at any moment.

The first day at Camp Cabanatuan ended as we settled down in our own barracks. We were able to rest on the bamboo beds that evening. We were fed a bowl of steamed rice that night at eleven o'clock. I fell asleep wondering what the next day would bring for me.

There were three prisoner of war camps in the Cabanatuan area at one time. They were identified as Cabanatuan Camps #1, #2, and #3. They were opened sometime in May 1942. The camps were located approximately 12 miles from the city of Cabanatuan, about seventy miles north of Manila.

In 1942 and 1943, when I was there, Camp #1 was the main POW camp in the area. The American troops captured on Bataan and the 7,000 Americans from Corregidor were in this camp. It was made up almost exclusively of Americans. When we left Camp O'Donnell, we left our Filipino comrades behind. Most of them were later to be pardoned and sent home by order of the Japanese High Command.

It seemed that every week the population in the camp would increase by thousands. A lot of the late arrivals were Americans who refused to surrender to the Japanese Army on April 9. They had escaped into the hills, later to be tracked down by the Japanese infantry. Some of these units were medics. As such, some had life-saving drugs in their possession: quinine for malaria or sulphathiazole for dysentery.

To smuggle any kind of medicines into Cabanatuan was synonymous with committing *hara-kari*. This ritual of disembowelment was the honorable way out for a defeated Japanese officer in many instances during the War in the Pacific.

I estimate that the camp covered an area of 400 to 500 acres, one-third of which was dedicated to the day-to-day life of the approximately 5,000 men. These included barracks, the outside kitchens, the hospital area, as well as the Japanese guard house and their private quarters. The tract of land was bounded on one side by the highway leading to the city of Cabanatuan. The camp proper was traversed by a four-to-five-foot-deep community ditch that carried a very good stream of water. A lot of water went into cooking rice for thousands of GIs.

Come September that year the camp commander, Lieutenant Colonel Shineji Mori, had organized prisoners into details that were assigned to a specific activity – transporting water to the kitchens, collecting firewood, burying the dead. For the last four to six months of 1942, Americans were still dying at the rate of sixty-five to eighty a day. The "new" wore off this place in a hurry.

The men became walking zombies from one day to the next. The average American prisoner had lost from forty to eighty pounds during the first eight months of captivity. I went from 150 to 130 by October. Our battery captain, Dow Bond, went from 200 to 130 after a bout with dysentery. Bob Mitchell, a corporal in our battery, went down from 220 pounds to 140.

It was fascinating to listen to some of the men describing their dreams about food. Those from my regiment and from the southern part of New Mexico and of Mexican descent craved and dreamed about enchiladas, beans, and the like. Benny Ortiz from Gallup was haunted by dreams of beef steak with all the trimmings including "smashed" potatoes. To this day, every time I have mashed potatoes with my dinner I am reminded of Benny. He was a very close friend of mine.

My heart-breaker was dreaming about a breakfast of hot pancakes with prodigious amounts of butter, two fried eggs, bacon, sausage, shoestring potatoes, and coffee. I used to scream upon waking up from this dream, which was so demoralizing for me that I lay awake for hours getting over it. My only therapy was prayer and hope.

By the end of 1942, deaths per day were averaging 180 to 200. This figure was not as bad as it was in Camp O'Donnell. Perhaps one reason was the quality of care in the hospital was somewhat better here. With the help of the 115 Army Medical Corps physicians and corpsmen, the hospital area was in better hands.

Doctors Julian Long and Dick Riley from our regiment never got enough rest or sleep. They were not immune to attacks of dysentery, malaria, or other communicable diseases. They gave medicine that could have helped them to men who needed it more. But there were a few doctors who would steal food from the patients, hoard smuggled-in quinine and sulfathiazole, and dispense it illegally for a price.

Doctor William Bluber was a dentist. I was frequently a victim of toothaches and had to see him at least twice a week. Since there were no facilities for filling cavities, the only option was to extract the affected tooth. The doctor said that my toothaches were the result of the lack of calcium in my diet. And I recalled the inferior quality of teeth in the Filipino population. The lion's share of the young Filipinos were sporting gold teeth. They belonged to the more affluent families. Gold seemed to be plentiful on the islands.

Sometime towards the end of 1942, perhaps in late December, I had just picked up my portion of rice and greens to enjoy at the end of a working day. Belarmino Lopez, a blood brother, joined us. He had been very sick with dysentery, but he seemed eager to eat. This was a good sign. But soon, he was doubled up in excruciating pain. He had dropped his food on the ground to press his fists against his stomach. He died in a matter of minutes.

We gathered around Belarmino and prayed in our hearts for his departed soul. I covered his eyes and mouth with his hat to protect them from the flies. I felt a lump in my throat as I looked at him for the last time before the burial detail took him. Many more like Belarmino would die that same day in Cabanatuan under similar circumstances.

A host of other diseases became widespread in Cabanatuan in 1942 and 1943. Beriberi was crippling thousands of Americans. It was caused by severe lack of vitamin B1 (thiamine), and its symptoms were pain, an inability to move, and swelling. I had it for almost four months, and the pain kept me awake at nights. It was a common sight to see scores of prisoners at two or three o'clock in the morning soaking their feet and hands to ease the pain from acute beriberi.

Despite our inability to walk, the guards came by the barracks every morning recruiting workers for the farm. The guards would punch, kick, and shove the men around to make them go. And to add insult to injury, we had to work in our bare feet. The bristle and the dry grass residue would make our bare feet bleed by the end of the day.

Pellagra, meaning rough skin in Italian, was caused by total lack of vitamin B-3 (niacin). The victims would develop diarrhea and severe cases of dermatitis. The skin would crack and bleed, eventually turning into multiple scabs. The condition was most painful when it appeared around the mouth and eyelids. Any scratch or cut in any part of the body seemed to take weeks to heal. Pellagra would also cause the gums to bleed. With my perpetual problem with tooth decay, bleeding gums was the last thing I needed. I had to rinse my mouth and freshen my lips and cheeks every morning. There always seemed to be a trace of blood on my teeth the rest of the day.

Malaria is an infectious disease caused by an organism that is transmitted by the bites of infected mosquitoes. The disease is characterized by violent attacks of chills, fever, and excessive sweating. Cerebral malaria affected the mind of the victim. Men would scream and curse. They would swing their arms at an imaginary figure as though they were fighting. They would become incontinent. Since there was no medicine, we would have to tie their hands and feet to keep them from hurting themselves.

Late one evening as I was walking back to my barracks, Benny Ortiz called to me.

"Hey Horace, wait a sec. You know, your friend, Filadelfio Cordova? He is having severe malaria fit in number eleven."

I rushed over to the barracks to find Fil sitting on someone's chest on the ground. Fil was cursing out loud as he punched and kicked. He had cerebral malaria and had lost his wits momentarily. He was sweaty and red in the face as I approached him.

The man he was punching out was dead.

I told Fil to stop it as I grabbed his arms and held them gently. He understood as I looked at him. I helped him up and walked him into his barracks. Fil died that night and was buried the following day. His younger brother, Jose, as well as his half-brother, Telesfor Gonzales, died in a prison camp in the Philippines the same year. They all belonged to Battery H from Taos.

Although disease and malnutrition were responsible for the vast number of deaths of the men of Bataan, for the first year I had been able "to beat the devil around the bush." I survived bouts of diarrhea, malaria, dengue fever, and beriberi during my first year at Cabanaruan.

Beriberi was affecting the progress of the Japanese vegetable farm in Cabanatuan. Earlier in the first year all able-bodied men were beaten and forced to break ground for a 500-acre farm a few yards from our barracks. We were pressed into working in our bare feet on the farm. Beriberi was rendering us incapable of doing farm labor.

Without the proper nutrition, the only remedy for beriberi was soaking the feet and hands in cold water. It was simply a mild relief from pain, but we kept it up through the night. We had to be ready for the farm detail come six o'clock the next morning. It was so painful to walk to the working area that men would vomit their breakfast of rice and soup on their way to the farm. To make matters worse, the camp commander forbade the use of shoes when walking in the vegetable beds.

Staying alive was a monumental task.

CHAPTER 11

✵ ✵ ✵

THE 500 LEAVE FOR JAPAN

The group scheduled to leave Cabanatuan for Japan was composed of members of the U.S. Navy, Army, and Marine Corps.

The day of departure was a cloudy day in July 1943. We were ordered to line up in several columns alongside the barbed-wire fence. To our right was the Japanese guardhouse. This activity was planned by the commander to give the guards an opportunity to mistreat us one more time.

Every man was searched thoroughly for possessions of pencils, mirrors, or anything that could be used in an escape. I had a pencil stub between the toes on my right foot. I had hopes of keeping a diary in Spanish and in shorthand.

"Kioski!"

The Japanese NCO was standing in front of the formation at attention. He was grasping a sword in his hand.

The group of 500 Americans stood at attention with "Eyes Front."

"Bango Ya!"

We counted off in Japanese. Following these formalities the group of 500 was ready to leave Cabanatuan for Manila. Every man was issued a ball of steamed rice for his lunch on the trip. It was six o'clock in the morning.

We arrived in Manila twelve hours later. I ate my ball of rice at the pier as we awaited orders to move on. In the meantime, we were allowed to sit on the floor of the dockyards. This was, perhaps, a bonus for having counted off to an even 500. The guards made certain that there were no escapees. It was the transfer of POWs *en masse* from one camp to another when many of the attempted breaks from prison camps occurred.

As I sat, half squatting, on the dirty and slimy floor of the dockyards, I was actually enjoying the experience. The weather in the Manila harbor was cloudy and cool. We all were tired and hungry, but the chances of something more to eat were not favorable. Every American had eating utensils fastened to his waist. Every utensil was unique. Some of the men were carrying the original U.S. Army issue. Other men were not that fortunate. Their eating utensils consisted of tin cans, tin lids, and even hollow twelve-inch branches of bamboo trees. Before long, all the aforementioned eating utensils were either lost or had been confiscated by the enemy.

The pier was a beehive of activity. Hundreds of Filipino stevedores were rushing to and fro. Some were carrying objects on their shoulders. Others were pushing carts as they loaded and unloaded Japanese freighters at the docks. We pitied the laborers; we knew what tortures they were having to endure.

The Filipino native was a genuine *amigo* of the American soldier. We were well aware of this when we were fighting the Japanese on the islands. They showed their true colors as emissaries of good will during and after the fall of Bataan. Tens, perhaps even hundreds, of Filipinos of both sexes were shot and bayoneted by Japanese soldiers as the they tried to smuggle food or water to the Americans on the Death March. Many Filipino women were butchered by Japanese guards as they tried to smuggle food or medicines into camps O'Donnell and Cabanatuan.

As we watched the Filipino stevedores fetch and carry small freight, I noticed two squads of Japanese soldiers heading in our direction. We all anticipated some type of move. I saw the soldiers position themselves around our group as we continued to sit on the ground. The Japanese CO goose-stepped his way to the front of the formation, grinding to a stop as he faced us.

"*Kioski!*"

"*Bango!*"

We counted off to an even 500.

We were marched 200 yards down the pier to a staircase that dropped off into a loading area. The path led to an old Japanese freighter on the east end of Manila Bay. We stepped onto the deck of the antiquated vessel. It smelled of copper or coal or some other type of ore. The navigation instruments on the deck were Spanish Armada vintage.

The loading up of the 500-man detail aboard ship was now in the hands of the "new" Japanese soldiers. They always proved to be meaner. Darkness was beginning to descend as we started to load up.

"Hy-yako, Amerika, Hy-yako!"

They were on high alert because of their fear of an attempted escape. The guards were guiding us like cattle in the direction of an enormous hatch ahead of us. We eventually came to a ten-foot-square hole on the metal deck. Looking down the hold, I saw a rickety twenty-foot metal ladder dropping down into a dark and fetid bottom of a lower deck. It smelled of cow dung. The air was hot and humid. Everybody feared going down and never coming out.

This Japanese freighter, the *Clyde Maru,* was one of the infamous "Hell Ships."

Ben, Joe Medina, and I were among the first of the group to descend into the hold. Our trio stayed together in order to help one another. This was a new experience for me, traveling as a prisoner of war on board a Japanese ship. The waters of the Pacific Ocean were not safe from American Navy submarines. I did not see any markings on the top deck that would alert submarine crews that Americans were aboard.

I was at a point near the landing area of the staircase as the loading continued. I could hear the Americans say," Ouch!" or "Yellow slant-eyed bastards!" as they were being shoved and kicked deeper into the cavernous hold by the guards. Everyone had to stand up while the guards continued to pack us in.

By about nine o'clock that evening we were all loaded up. The guards, with their clubs and rifle butts in hand, left us below. They went up the ladder to the top deck. As the last guard reached the top, I looked up at the entrance-way. And for a brief moment, I could see the stars.

The last guard out slammed the hatch shut. The air was filled with curses for the Japanese.

"Goddamn Japs!"

"Yellow-bellied bastards!"

"Slant-eyed Nips!"

By 10 o'clock, the freighter was on its way. We were packed so tight that we could not sit or stand. Men were squatting with their knees up to their faces; some were passing out on their feet. The heat and the humidity were horrible. There was no water anywhere. Among Joe, Ben, and me, we had only one full canteen. We had to risk our lives to protect it, for thirsty and deranged men would kill for a drink. The men were using the forks and spoons from their mess kits as weapons.

Ben and I, and some of our rational friends, worked our way to a corner that had a better supply of air.

The fact is that they had packed 500 men into an area suitable for a hundred or fewer. There was no place to fall. Men were relieving themselves on the spot where they were standing or squatting down. Conditions were primitive. We were at the enemy's mercy – or lack of it.

At about midnight, the Japanese guards flung open the hatches above us. In the semi-darkness I could see containers being lowered at the end of some heavy cord. Steamed rice. It was like manna from heaven.

"Chow!" someone yelled, and the mad rush was on. The crazed men stomped on everyone in their path as they elbowed their way to the buckets.

Out of the numerous buckets of rice lowered down, Ben and I were able to retrieve two mess kits full for ourselves. I was finishing my portion of rice as I stood against the wall in my spot by the hatch. Joe Medina passed around the canteen for a fresh swig of water to wash down our rice.

The next day, we arrived at Santa Cruz, where we spent the day watching a host of Oriental coolies load manganese ore onto the ship. Two people, one behind the other, would be carrying a bamboo basket between their shoulders with, perhaps, a hundred pounds of ore. The loading lasted from six o'clock that morning until eight o'clock that evening.

Back at sea after a stop on Formosa, I could feel the steady "thump, thump" of the gigantic motors under me as they plowed their way north. Destination Japan. I was hopeful that life in a POW camp in Japan would be better than in Cabanatuan.

I was wrong.

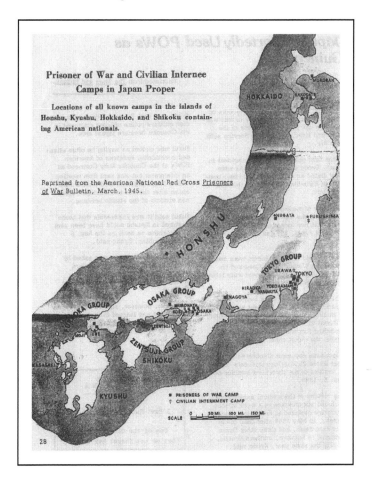

CHAPTER 12

✦ ✦ ✦

JAPAN: LAND OF THE RISING SUN

In early August, after sailing for days and days aboard a ship we christened the *Mate Mate Maru,* or the "Wait Wait Ship," we arrived at the seaport of Moji on the northern tip of Kyushu, the southern-most of the five principal islands of Japan. This was deep in enemy territory. There was no way to escape.

By Christmas Eve I'll be back in the hands of the Americans.

It was a sight to see the American prisoners of war as we stepped onto the pier. Our faces were gaunt, our skin was pale, our stomachs were flat. We were all exhausted, and we were hungry.

Ben, Joe Medina, and I watched from the pier for some of our buddies from the 200th. We were always thrilled to know that others of our men had made it this far.

Ben and I were among the first to set foot on dry land. There must have been a brigade of Japanese army guards waiting for us.

"Hy-yako, Amerika, Hy-yako!"

"Bango!"

The guards were swinging rifle butts and kicking the Americans in the shins and in the groins to speed us into *bango* formation.

Once the formation was organized, we were marched about a quarter-mile down the street to a railroad station. All of us were shabbily dressed. Many of the men were wearing Army khaki cut-offs. Others were wearing torn trousers. But every single one still had a makeshift mess kit hanging from his belt. My worn-out leather shoes were waterlogged from standing on the wet and filthy floor of the Japanese freighter for weeks on end. Although I was weak and hungry, I enjoyed the fresh air. It was a welcome change from the hold of the Hell Ship.

We were ordered to halt and come into a four-column military formation alongside a narrow-gauge train.

"*Bango!*"

Still 500.

We were loaded into the train one by one. I felt like a human being once again as I walked down the aisle between the seats of this modern passenger train. The interior was impeccably clean. There was a Japanese army guard standing at the head of the aisle inside the car.

We traveled south from Moji for about two hours. I estimated the distance to be sixty to seventy miles. The weather was moderate. We traveled through an urban area. Living conditions appeared to be somewhat crowded. I did not see any city parks or parking areas. There were countless Japanese army stations, and the pedestrians on the streets were mostly army personnel.

We arrived at Omuta on the western shore, about thirty-five miles across the bay from Nagasaki, in late afternoon. Omuta had a population of between 500 and 1000. We learned later that the men of the village worked in the coal mines a couple of miles inland.

The weather was moderate. The temperature was like that of early-fall weather back home in Taos, quite unlike the hot tropical weather we left behind in the Philippines.

We were met at the railroad station by a squad of guards, a squad of local militia personnel, and civilians. These army guards didn't look any different from those in the Philippines. In their right hands they carried an infantry rifle with a long, sharp, and shiny bayonet at the tip of the rifle bore. The bayonet was the most effective item in their possession to keep us in line.

As we marched down the street in columns of four, squads of Japanese soldiers flanked us on both sides. The soldiers were in full combat uniform. They were wearing army regulation leather shoes, some with metal cleats on the back of the heel. This accounted for the menacing "thud-thud" on the pavement as they strutted down the street.

The column of 500 American POWs on the streets of Omuta stretched for about 300 yards. The scattered buildings on either side appeared to be clean and freshly painted white. Overall it looked nice and clean. There were no lawns in front.

The spectators lining both sides of the street were mostly Japanese women and old Japanese men, some with long, white goatees. There was a smattering of Japanese children. They were all screaming expletives and insults. Furthermore, they had rocks, clubs, sharpened bamboo sticks, and small pieces of iron rods. These Japanese would swing their clubs and bamboo sticks against the face and torso of a defenseless American. Some of the Americans had blood flowing down the sides of their faces or a bleeding puncture wound on the side of the chest.

Some spectators cursed in English.

"Americans no good!"

"Americans must die!"

We left the civilians at the station and continued on in silence.

We walked in formation down a graveled street away from the beach. There were no buildings along the way. The Japanese guards were more restrained in their discipline, and there were no beatings.

I remember walking close to Ben. It made me feel secure.

We arrived at Fukuoka Camp #17 tired and hungry. We stood at attention at the front gate.

"Bango!

"Ichi, nee, san, si, go, roku, sichi, hachi, cu, ju..."

I listened closely, as the count went up. We had finally learned to count off in Japanese. This *bango* was flawless.

"Yon-yocu-roku-ju-yon," I screamed as my turn came up. That was 464, my official identification number as a prisoner of war in Camp 17 for the rest of my internment. Ben's number was 140, and Joe Medina's was 319. These numbers were stenciled on uniforms, on shirts, on caps and on entrances to barracks. The numbers were used on rosters instead of names.

Fukuoka Camp #17 was about seventeen miles northwest of Kumamoto and south of Fukuoka. The camp was about 200 yards wide by 800 yards long. The terrain was comprised of slag from the near-by coal mine. Mitsui Coal Mining Company had constructed laborers quarters. The Japanese Army took over the operations during the war.

A twelve-foot high, wooden fence enclosed the compound. Six feet off the ground, the Japanese had securely fastened two live, heavy-gauge electrical wires to discourage would-be escapees. There was an incident, later on, in which a Japanese soldier, on guard duty inside the camp, walked dangerously close to the wire. The bayonet at the tip of his gun made contact with the live wire. He was electrocuted.

We were ordered to *cho-tare* (goose-step) into the compound in columns of four. It was not difficult to us any more. We had practiced in Camps O'Donnell and Cabanatuan.

The grounds inside were kept clean. There were a few fir trees on the spacious parade grounds in the center of the compound. There were, perhaps, twenty to twenty-five barracks encircling the compound. There were ten rooms to a barracks. The rooms averaged 100 square feet. They had tarpaper roofs and windows with panes. This was a far cry from the bamboo barracks we had in camps O'Donnell and Cabanatuan. The floors were covered with four-by-six foot straw mats. At the end of each barracks was a stool raised from the ground to serve as a commode and urinal. The waste matter was collected in a wooden barrel to be removed twice a week.

The detail of POWs assigned to the removal of human waste in the barrels was nicknamed the "honey dippers." Two men were assigned to each barrel. We would run a ten-foot pole through the handle of the barrel and fling the ends of the poles over our shoulders and carry the barrel for 300 to 400 yards to the nearest vegetable garden. We were ordered to empty the human waste in small furrows alongside the rows of vegetables. This was the most dreaded activity in the camp. It was filthy and unsanitary.

The barracks were light enough during daylight hours. For night hours, each room had one 15-watt light bulb. There were no heating facilities, for the climate was mild. There were no beds. We slept in our working clothes on the straw mats on the floor. These mats were easily removable when necessary. The sand floor was dry and soft, ideal for concealing small objects.

Because of our weakened conditions, our bodies were very sensitive to dampness and penetrating cold. The average American POW was underweight by fifty to eighty pounds. Our hypersensitivity to around forty degrees Fahrenheit made it extremely difficult to sleep. We had to huddle in the middle of the room like a litter of piglets to stay warm.

On the second day at the camp, every American in the barracks was ordered to a mass formation in the spacious parade grounds in the center of the camp. After the customary *bango* ritual, we were informed that we were in a Japanese mining camp, and that we would be paid in Japanese currency for our labors.

We were at attention for three hours as the camp commander berated us. We were worthless and we were inferior soldiers. He raised his voice to a high pitch when he announced that we were going to be slaves of Japan for ten years, and that the United States would eventually be invaded by the Japanese Imperial Army.

The officer was no more than five-feet, four-inches tall, but he had a three-foot samurai sword hanging from his left hip. The Japanese officers were obsessed with the sword.

A young mining engineer translated the speech into English.

A few days after our arrival, we were assigned to the various barracks for good. Ben and I wound up in a nine-by-ten-foot cubicle with Joe Medina and Benny Ortiz, the "Gallup Kid." We had to share it with five other men. I liked Benny because he was friendly and chatty. He was the type that would cheer you up when you were down and out, but forceful when he had to be. Joe was agreeable and practical.

In those first few days, the Japanese command issued clothing. We each received a two-piece brown woolen outfit, which was probably left over from the First World War, and black tennis shoes with a split toe and a metal fastener in the back. We were provided with a four-by-six-by-one-inch wooden box for our steamed rice lunch when working outside the camp. We called them *bento* boxes. *Bento* is the Japanese word for lunch.

Another item on the issue list that day was toilet paper. We thought that was so considerate of the enemy. This luxury came in coarse, six-by-ten light tan sheets and was better adapted for use as typing paper.

When I received my ration of toilet paper, one thing came to my mind: my diary. Now I could start recording instances of beatings, tortures, and other atrocities committed by the Japanese against our men. It was extremely important to record names, dates, and the nature of the criminal act. I had been hiding a small pencil in my shoes all this time for this very purpose. The text would be recorded in Spanish in Gregg shorthand. I would hide the diary in the dry sand under my sleeping mat. Possession of a mirror or a pencil was grounds for execution. The enemy believed, correctly, that these simple pieces of hardware could be used to send messages or signals to someone outside the camp. My four roommates – Joe Medina, Luis Lopez, Benny Ortiz, and Ben – were sworn to secrecy.

That day at the parade grounds ended with work assignments. Some of the men were ordered to work as blasters and shovelers. Benny, Joe Medina, Ben, and I were inducted into the *saitan* (coal blasting) squad. It was the most strenuous work in the coal mine.

Other squads were assigned to build wood frames to secure the ceilings. These were the *iyomaks* squads. Loose slabs of rock in the tunnels are dangerous and unpredictable if they are not jacked up with pillars of lumber. These supports would help prevent small cave-ins in the various tunnels in the mine.

The coal mine in Omuta had been condemned prior to the war as too dangerous to work. It was owned by the Mitsui Mining Company and operated by the Japanese army during the war. The supervisors inside the mine were members of the Japanese Military Militia, which was made up of civilians. They were experienced coal miners. The hard labor was done by the prisoners of war.

Electricity was the source of power for the conveyers and lighting inside the mine. A very young, and effeminate, Japanese electrical engineer maintained the electrical power. Benny Ortiz dubbed him "La Putita," Spanish for "the little whore."

The camp, although run by a Japanese commander, was supervised by U.S. Army and Navy officers: A. C. Tisdell, Thomas Hewlett, and John R. Mamerow.

CHAPTER 13

✲ ✲ ✲

FUKUOKA CAMP 17

Camp 17, later known as Fukuoka Camp 17, was a white prisoner of war camp. We had Americans, British, and Australians, and men from the Dutch Islands south of the Philippines. We Americans were not allowed to fraternize with non-Americans, but we were always eager to look up the Australians. The average Aussie was six feet tall. To a man, they were friendly and had a wonderful sense of humor.

They wore their army regulation big hats whenever possible. And they were brave.

The British, on the other hand, were not as sociable. Although they were not rude, they were inclined to stick to themselves. They did a lot of singing as they drank their tea together.

The work awaiting us in the mines was a new type of torture. We were working fifteen-hour shifts, seven days a week, in suffocating tunnels under the ground. Furthermore, at the end of the day we were pressured, at the point of sword or bayonet, to walk a mile to our barracks. We were beaten and our bodies were emaciated.

Christmas Eve 1943 arrived and I was still alive.

As 1944 passed, the Battling Bastards of Bataan were working longer hours in the mine. We all looked like walking skeletons. There was little humor in our lives. Tempers were short. I was involved in a brief fistfight one day. I confronted another POW, accusing him of stealing my lunch as I worked down in the mine.

The stealing of rice was occurring frequently as men were being worked harder without enough to eat. The wooden *bento* boxes were packed with steamed rice by the kitchen personnel on every shift. It was the only sustenance during an eight- to ten-hour shift in the mine. It was worth fighting for.

Since the coal mine had been condemned during peacetime, every day we worked underground our lives were in grave danger. Cave-ins were commonplace. When they occurred, tons of rock and dirt fell from the ceiling directly on men working underneath. Men were crushed to death as they shoveled coal. In most fatal cave-ins, the supervisor was "supervising" from a safe area away from the danger.

The bodies of the ill-fated Americans buried underneath the tons of dirt were never recovered by the enemy. They simply sealed off the tunnel. I made it a point on those days to record the incident in my diary.

The idea of working in a coal mine in Japan was totally different from our dreams when we signed up for this detail work back in Cabanatuan. We thought that any change from working under "Air Raid" at the farm would be a step up.

Our supervisors were short and husky and carried clubs and used them. Men would be walking out of the mine at the end of the shift with bleeding lacerations on their scalps and faces or with split lips. Doctor Tom Hewlett, our senior American surgeon at the so-called hospital in the camp, would have to patch up these unfortunate victims.

His equipment and emergency-room resources were primitive. There were no bandages, no splints, and no sedatives or tranquilizers. He performed appendectomies, including one on Ben, with essentially nothing more than an ordinary U.S. Army mess kit knife.

Occasionally, the Japanese medical officer would authorize the use of *sake* as a painkiller. It was also used as a sedative for teeth extractions, but we had at least two Army dentists who had to performe dental extractions without even sake.

By mid-1944, hundreds of Allied prisoners in the Omuta coal mines were being exposed to incalculably dangerous working conditions. Every day and night more men sustained fractures on some part of the body. Some of these victims of accidents who were still able to walk were assigned to light duty. The more serious fractures were referred to Doctor Hewlett.

We were malnourished, exhausted, and desperate. Men would extract a painful tooth with their bare hands. They were setting off detonators in their hands in the mine. Prisoners, including a soldier from Taos, would offer their evening portion of rice to anyone who would break his left arm for him.

My diary was getting longer.

All this time, Doctor Hewlett's ward was being filled with all types of mine injuries that created a twenty-four-hour workday for him. Some were injured by rockslides as they shoveled coal into the conveyer belt. Some were survivors of cave-ins. Men were also injured by runaway ore cars as they carried eight-foot logs on their shoulders along a narrow and dark tunnel. (Except for the miserly lighting from our miner's caps, we were in total darkness.)

Larry Sandoval (Sandy) from our regiment had both his legs amputated above the knees after they were crushed in a cave-in. His buddies carried him around the camp in their arms like a baby. He became the official checker of the men's numbers as they entered the dining room to eat. He was a real trooper.

At midnight on New Year's Eve 1944, Ben I and walked with our night detail to the mine. It was dark and cold. It was a very touching moment. The Twenty-third Psalm came to mind.

I was cold, hungry, and tired. We had been on this street every day or night for the last eighteen months, and I could identify every physical characteristic by now, including potholes and even the number of steps I took. I was particularly contemptuous of the guard as he walked with gun and bayonet in hand. He was no more than an arm's length from me. I was never comfortable any time I was close to any of them.

This was the same guard who slammed his rifle butt to my head and kicked me in the crotch and ribs as I lay on the ground. He caught me in formation with a lit cigarette in my hand. Benny and Luis Lopez had to pick me up from the ground and practically carry me back to the camp. My hatred for that guard was so profound that I dreamed of seizing his bayonet and stabbing him to death.

We arrived at the mine entrance shortly after midnight. I clung to my *bento* box.

"Bango!"

The count was twenty-five. We were marched down to the mine's dressing room where we would remove everything but our shoes and change into our work clothes: a G-string. We carried an eight-by-ten-by-two-inch metal battery on our belts. This battery was connected by a wire to the light on our mining caps.

The last stop into the mine was the "holy room." This ritual was mandatory for everyone going down. The Japanese guard, with gun and bayonet in hand, would escort us in single file into this dark room. At the guard's command we would stand at attention and face a solid wall to the right. Situated on top, a few inches from the ceiling, was a small, dull, red light in a glass cage. It was, simply, a plain red light to us. But this apparatus was implicitly related to their god.

The ceremony was brief and to the point. The detail was ordered to stand at attention. It was a sight to see us standing erect in our G-strings. At the commands, *"Dat-su-bo"* and *"Sacu-bo"* we would remove our caps, bow, and replace our caps. After that three- to four-minute ritual, we were escorted into the mine. We had to carry picks, shovels, and eighty-pound jack-hammers on our shoulders all the way to the working area. In some cases, the distance was 800 to 900 yards. By this time we were already tired and hungry. Some would eat their lunch at that time. They would have to go twelve to fifteen hours before their next meal.

On this first graveyard shift of January 1945, I was walking close behind "Blinky," our supervisor. With a pick and a shovel in each hand, my *saitan* squad and I were trailing him down a dark and dusty tunnel. Upon arrival at the work tunnel, Blinky would designate two of us to drill eight-inch-deep-holes into the wall of coal. The jackhammer was powered with compressed air so that as Luis Lopez, my constant companion in the mine, and I rested the hammer on our shoulders, it repetitively forced the drill bit into the wall of coal. Blinky then packed the holes with dynamite. He set off the charges as we waited outside the tunnel. The blast would fill the tunnel with loose coal, which we had to shovel onto a conveyor belt. Perez, Ortiz, Lopez, and I would shovel coal for the next eight to ten hours until the tunnel was cleared. We would work hour after hour without a break.

Meantime, Blinky would sit in a dark corner and sleep. At times, I could get a few seconds of shuteye by leaning forward on my shovel and closing my eyes.

Our *bona fide* interludes of rest occurred only on occasional breakdowns of the conveyer belt. The Japanese repairman would come down from topside to do the repairs. A majority of the mechanical failures were the workings of our sabotage.

This midnight shift seemed notably longer. Luis and I had been shoveling coal into the conveyer belt for four hours by now. The handle on my shovel was slick from sweat. It had been a hot and muggy night in the mine. Suddenly, I felt Blinky right behind me. He woke up, luckily, and sensed the dropping of dirt and pebbles from the ceiling of the tunnel.

"*Kochi Koy!*"

We immediately retreated to the back of the working area. The ceiling was threatening to cave in.

Blinky had to prop up the ceiling and he sent me down the tunnel to fetch some lumber. I was in the process of selecting the right sized *naroogis* when out of the dark I saw

Blinky running towards me with a club in his hand.

"*Nanka, Nanka,*" he kept screaming as he began to beat me with his club. He was beating me because he felt that I was taking too long to return with the *naroogis*.

After the first blow to the head, my light fell to the ground. I couldn't see where he was coming from. I fell to the ground, and he kept pounding on me. I could feel the wood splitting my lips as I tasted my own blood. I flinched repeatedly as I felt the trauma to my scalp and my spine. I was sure he had broken my back. He walked away. I lay beaten on the ground. I groped around with my hand for my cap and light. When I found the light, I shook it and it lit.

I struggled to my feet and painfully walked back to the tunnel where Ortiz and Lopez were waiting for me. All they could do for me was soothe my wounds with kind words and compassion, but they said I looked like hell.

Blinky barked out of the darkness, "*Hyyako, taxan shigoto!*" That meant get back to work.

After that shift, I had to be helped to walk the half-mile to camp. My buddies would offer their shoulders so I could lean on them. I experienced sharp shooting pains in the small of my back. I knew my spine had been injured permanently.

I recorded the incident in my diary that evening. I retrieved the diary from the sand under the bamboo pad where I slept, and had Luis Lopez "bird dog" for me to protect me from any unsuspecting guard. I wrote down the date and place of the beating, the name of the Jap, his official title, and the description of the beating.

Two nights later, as I walked alone down a dark tunnel I met Gap Silva, a Gallup resident who was also in the 200th.

"Have you heard the latest rumor?"

"No, I haven't."

"You know the young Marine who's been in the brig for the last two to three months? He is going to be executed tomorrow."

The next day I was up bright and early to hide behind a barracks wall with a good view of the execution site and the parade grounds. I was risking my life by doing this. I was supposed to be in my barracks.

A young American was escorted to the middle of the parade grounds by a guard on both sides. Each was carrying an infantry rifle with a fixed bayonet in his right hand. The young Marine was tall and lanky. His hands were in handcuffs; his ankles were shackled.

From my vantage point behind a short wall, not more that fifty yards away, I stood straight and silent. I was sweating and trembling. The Marine was ordered, at the point of a bayonet, to kneel down on the ground. The young man appeared to be facing death bravely. I noticed that he was saying something as he looked up at the sky. He was praying in a hoarse and trembling voice.

The officer of the execution shrieked out, *"Banzai!"* and sliced the air with his gleaming sword. The guards on the left and the right sides of the Marine plunged their bayonets into his torso. The Marine let out a muffled wail before his head fell forward, limp and lifeless.

I sneaked back to my barracks and wept as I recited the Twenty-third Psalm. I had to describe every minute detail in my diary that day before going back to work that night.

In the spring of 1945, we learned of the death of President Franklin D. Roosevelt from our guards. They poked our ribs with their rifle butts, laughed in our faces, and said, *"Rosovelto patay."* "Roosevelt dead."

Time passed slowly at Camp 17, but there were promising signs that the Japanese were losing the war. I was encouraged every morning by the vast numbers of American bombers flying at 35,000 feet towards Tokyo. I never saw a single Japanese fighter plane intercepting them. The B-29s were dropping 500-pound clusters of incendiary bombs every fifty to one-hundred feet. The explosions would generate a temperature of 1,800 degrees Fahrenheit. Japanese civilians by the thousands ran for their lives or were burned alive.

At Camp 17, the Japanese Imperial Army violated the rules of the Geneva Convention by not displaying the Red Cross atop the main building. Japan was not a signatory of the Geneva Convention.

So it was within the realm of possibility that one of our own Air Force planes might drop explosives or incendiary bombs on our un-marked camp. Even so, the thunderous roar from these planes was music to our ears. We were strictly forbidden by the enemy to watch the bombers overhead; instead, we were sup-posed to stay inside a building or in the air raid shelter built in the middle of the camp area. Many a day we'd spend hours in the shelter waiting for the sizeable number of US planes to fly over the camp.

Many of us were severely beaten for being caught watching the bombers. I remember ly-ing on the ground squirming with pain after a ruthless thrashing for looking up at the bomb-ers, thinking that these guards would never succeed in extinguishing my determination to survive.

I was going to make it...and I was going to drag my brother, Ben, with me.

The flights of American bombers overhead was the omen that the eventual defeat of the Japanese Imperial Army was near. I couldn't have been happier. I do not recall any fatali-ties, thanks to the countless American POWs who risked their lives to make the evacuation possible.

I was assigned to a new barracks. Life went on. We went back to working sixteen to eighteen hours a day. We would sleep six hours and go back to the mine. Our rations of rice became leaner and leaner by the day. If we were lucky that day, kitchen personnel would supplement the rice with a pickle or a small turnip, but these, too, were becoming scarce.

In late July, our Battery H motor sergeant, Jim Lujan, died in the hospital. His body had wasted down to skin and bones with pulmonary tuberculosis. Ben and I were particularly grieved; we had known Jim since the beginning of the war.

Fukuoka Camp 17 was situated midway up the west coast of the island of Kyushu in the town of Omuta. Nagasaki is only thirty-five miles across the bay. Hiroshima and Tokyo are on Honshu, the island north of Kyushu. By the end of July, our B-29s had bombed a path from Kyushu to Tokyo. In three months of night raids, all the major industrial cities were in ruins. On one day in mid-July, there were more than 2,000 United States planes in flight over Japan.

For three days in early August, U.S. bombers were totally absent from the skies. There was, however, a high-flying U.S. observation plane in the air at all times. What was going on? Was an allied landing imminent? If so, we expected to be executed as soon as Allied forces set foot on Japanese soil.

On August 9, 1945, late in the afternoon, my crew of 150 prisoners were exiting the main mine entrance. We instinctively looked up for relief of the soul and fresh air. This day, thousands of feet up in the atmosphere, there was a cloud of silvery dust hovering menacingly above us – the aftermath of "Fat Man," the first atomic bomb. The skies cleared about twenty-four hours later.

The camp commander gave us the next day off. The prisoners working at the mine were called back to camp. I remember being on the three-to-eleven shift. We were notified at the last moment that we were off that day. The first thing we did was eat our rice lunch.

We were told it was Emperor Hirohito's birthday. The next day was another *yasumay* (rest) day. The "birthday celebration" would continue.

CHAPTER 14

✫ ✫ ✫

B-29s PAVE THE WAY

Not counting the lack of food and rest and the long days laboring in the mine, Ben and I had more than our share of bad luck. First and foremost, Ben lived through an appendectomy in the camp hospital.

One day as we walked to the camp in squad formation from the mine, there was a young man walking in the ranks with us. He was from San Antonio, Texas. He was friendly and gregarious. He was of average height, muscular, and stocky. His last name was Perez. He had a tendency to boast excessively about his football playing days at Alamo High and his prowess with the girls.

Since we had worked fourteen hours straight, we were tired, hungry, and skeptical of Perez's heroics, and so no one was listening.

"Shut up, Perez! We don't want to listen to you! We're to damn tired and hungry", said Benny Ortiz.

Perez shut-up.

My day was not over. As we goose-stepped into the camp, we were stopped by an officer in front of the guardhouse. After whispering something to the guard in charge, he called out my number.

"Yon-yocu-roku-ju-yon!"

My heart sank all the way to my feet.

They have found my diary.

I was pulled out of rank by a surly guard and pushed and shoved to the guardhouse. I was asked my number. The officer seemed to be more concerned with what he kept repeatedly shoving in my face: my personal name tag. It was a one-by-two-inch piece of thin lumber with my number "464", on both sides. The sin I committed that day was that I had hung the tag inside my room door instead of outside when I went to work that morning.

As a punishment, I was compelled to kneel on the ground in front of the guardhouse. I was strong-armed into maintaining an erect back and neck at all times. The soldiers in the guard-house would periodically come out and kick me in the ribs and my groin. I maintained that position until nine o'clock that evening. I went straight to bed.

The countless flights of B-29s over Camp 17 did wonders for the morale of the prisoners of war – American, English, Dutch, and Australian. Our only worry was that the Japanese com-mander had not affixed a sizeable red cross on top of the camp's main building.

Some time in June 1945, there was a mas-sive cave-in the coal mine. Ben was among the most seriously injured of the group of six prison-ers. The foreman and two POWs were crushed to death. My brother suffered contusions of the chest, a concussion, and two compound frac-tures in his right leg; one above and one below the knee.

A six-by-ten-foot slab of rock fell from the ceiling of the tunnel. The three men who died were crushed between the slab and the mine floor. Ben was lucky enough to have been knocked down to the floor against a small steel dump cart sitting in the middle of the tunnel. The sturdy cart was sitting solidly on the two railroad tracks. Luckily, the steel side of the vehicle was strong enough to hold up the massive slab of rock. After the dust settled in the tunnel, rescue crews inched their way to the cave-in area. I was told that my brother was unconscious when they got him out.

A few weeks after the cave-in, I was walking back to camp from the mine. I was in a fifty-man detail. We had just worked fifteen hours straight blasting coal. We were half-starved. We were dead tired. We walked in cadence with the uniformed soldier at our side.

Perhaps 400 yards from camp, someone in the front of the formation jumped up and screamed, "Fire! Our camp is on fire!"

Our camp had been hit by incendiary bombs dropped from American B-29s earlier that afternoon.

The men in my detail rushed into the gates of the camp. The air was full of burning cinders and smoke. Some men were carrying buckets of water to the fire. Others were retrieving equipment from the hot spots. Japanese guards were having a field day with their clubs and rifle butts.

The camp hospital seemed to be the center of the conflagration and Ben was stuck there with a fractured leg. I had to find him.

I picked up a bucket and filled it with water at the faucet. I drenched myself with water.

Most of the patients were being evacuated, safely, into nearby barracks. But I couldn't find Ben. Visibility was poor as I ventured deeper and deeper into the smoke-filled area. I had to put my left hand over my mouth. My eyes were burning like hell from the cinders in the air. I would bend over regularly to splash water over my face from the bucket I carried in my right hand.

All this time I was praying for my brother's safety. I was no longer tired, nor was I apprehensive. I could taste adrenalin. Only one thought was uppermost in my mind: I had to find my brother alive.

I kept calling Ben's name every few seconds. I asked anybody if they had seen my brother. Most would ignore me, while others would simply shake their heads. My heart was pounding. I was on my own. The air was full of smoke and ash, which made it difficult to breathe.

I hadn't ventured more then ten or twelve paces into the smoke-filled hospital before I could see two figures walking towards me. One of the men was having considerable trouble walking on his own, having to steady himself by leaning on the shoulder of his buddy.

"Ben! Is that you? Are you OK?"

As I rushed forward to embrace him, he grabbed my arm firmly to steady himself. "I've made it again, Horace! I'm short of breath and my eyes are burning like hell! Get me out of here – QUICK!"

I put my left arm around his waist, wrapped his right arm around my shoulder, and his medic friend and I got him to a safe area. The medic and I had to force our way through a mob of fire fighters. Every available prisoner of war in the camp was "recruited" at the tip of a bayonet to join the water brigade. There were, apparently, no fire station facilities in the area, for we had no assistance from the outside.

I had no more than set Ben down in a safe area when I heard someone behind me yell, "Your barracks is on fire!"

I turned around and sure enough there was the one-story hut where I lived, going up in flames. Black smoke was oozing out of the windows. I was distraught.

"My diary! It's going up in smoke. It's going to be destroyed!", I uttered.

My only alternative now was to remember and memorize excerpts of my diary as best I could. I knew that I would be interrogated and debriefed by United States Army personnel once we were repatriated.

CHAPTER 15

✫ ✫ ✫

SAYONARA TO CAMP 17

The end of the war was never announced to us officially. The Japanese commander deserted in the days that followed. The gossip was that he was stalked and followed by some Marine POWs and slain with his own samurai sword.

The atomic fall-out at the camp from the Nagasaki bomb on August 9 was more devastating than one can tell. There was the silvery mist over Omuta. Then there was the report by many that the ground beneath Nagasaki rolled like an earthquake. One report from the civilians was that the blast had killed all the fish in the bay.

It was rumored that in the event of an Allied landing on Kyushu, every Allied prisoner of war would be speared, clubbed, or shot to death by Japanese civilians. This militia would be composed of old men, women and, perhaps, able-bodied teenagers. This gruesome threat was also conveyed to us day in and day out by the Japanese guards before they fled.

To avoid chaos in the camp, the senior American officers assumed command. One of the first priorities was to protect the men in the camp from Japanese civilians outside the camp. To do this, we had confiscated small arms and ammunition from the fleeing guards left behind. The camp was now being policed twenty-four hours a day by American prisoners who were armed with 25 caliber Japanese infantry rifles. At noon on August 15, 1945, the Emperor announced over Japanese national radio that the "Japanese Empire had been conquered and forced to surrender." In the history of Japan, this was the first time that commoners had ever heard the voice of their Emperor.

Life changed dramatically for the men in the camp. We were filling up on rice from the abandoned Japanese warehouse. The American cooks even found flour and the essentials for bread. We were getting sick from overeating. Having been hungry for so long, eating often became an obsession. We would even get up at night, just to eat.

The skies over the island of Kyushu were deserted except for a solitary U.S. reconnaissance plane. No other aircraft had been recently sighted from Camp 17. However, identifying the area as a prisoner of war camp was necessary for purposes of self-preservation.

Two or three men who had worked in the kitchen broke into the Japanese warehouse, requisitioned several bags of lime, took it to the middle of the parade ground, and in ten-foot letters wrote, "P 0 W."

Two or three days later, a B-29 flew over the camp at an unusually low level. We saw a small object fall right in front of us. We ran to investigate what it was.

We found a metal wrench tied to a piece of heavy cardboard. On it was inscribed a message to the effect that the camp would be supplied with food, medicine, and clothing by way of parachutes, in three days.

We were all very excited and unable to sleep at night. Liberation and real American chow!

That evening, the senior American officer chaired a meeting for all the men in the camp.

"Men, as you all know by now, our B-29s will begin supplying our needs by way of airdrops. Listen carefully, men! During the airdrop, take cover inside a building! A loaded, unopened parachute can kill you!"

On the appointed day, we heard and saw a monstrous plane sweep over the camp at about 1,000 feet. The plane was flying in a northerly direction. Moments later we saw the plane make a U-turn and head back towards the camp. I saw the plane drop down its landing wheels for drag and open its bomb-bay doors. I ran for cover.

Following the historic drop, the pilot retracted the wheels, closed the bomb-bay doors, and gunned the engines. The plane became a speck in the sky as it disappeared over the East China Sea.

Down came the multicolored chutes, each one with a 55-gallon barrel hanging precariously in the air. They hit the ground with a loud *thud,* spilling goodies all over – food, clothing, and medicines.

There was a loud shout from the men as the B-29 gunned its engines on its way back to the Marianas Islands, more than 1,000 miles away. The bombardier had to be commended on his aim. Better than ninety percent of the chutes landed inside the camp. The ones landing outside the fence were quickly retrieved by details of American POWs.

Once the dust settled, every man came out from his hiding place. The barrels were chock-full of cans of corned beef, sardines, salmon, tuna, pork and beans, powdered milk, evaporated milk, fruit, jellies, ground coffee, syrup, bundles and bundles and bundles of Hershey bars and other popular American candy, soda crackers, sweet cookies, boxes of corn flakes, a variety of condiments, salt, and granulated sugar.

There were cartons of Luckies, Camels, Wings, and Chesterfields. And U.S. Army khaki shirts and trousers, GI web belts, army high-cut shoes, socks, GI light-green underwear, soap, and shampoo.

Our camp hospital was not forgotten. Doctor Hewlett and his hospital staff were provided with hospital bedding and a multiplicity of medical and surgical supplies.

The airdrop brought about a dramatic change at Camp 17. We were sporting new clothing over clean bodies. Our pants fit loosely from our forty-month weight loss, but we didn't care. That's what the belts were for.

We started to become impatient. Many of us went into the countryside in search of American troops. Some even commandeered trains to Tokyo and Yokohama in search of U.S. Army troops. We were intoxicated with hope.

I stayed close to the camp. Ben was not capable of long walks without help. I could not leave the camp without him. I had to help him get back home. The approximately fifteen other patients in the camp hospital were convalescing well.

On September 17, the senior U.S. Army officer in the camp told us that the next day we would be boarding a Japanese train at Omuta for Nagasaki. Omuta was within walking distance of the camp.

We wept with joy. "God Bless America!"

Many of the men had posted U.S. flags made from parachutes outside the barracks. I was filled with emotion and patriotism as I stood at attention and saluted one of the homemade flags. Then I rushed to the hospital to share the good news with my brother, Ben. He was sitting in his bed with his right leg in a cast.

We embraced and sobbed together, ever so thankful that we had survived. After a brief prayer of thanksgiving, I helped him prepare for the trip the following day.

The next day was overcast at Camp 17. There were about 430 Americans, including the men in the hospital. We were the survivors of the original 500 that left Cabanatuan in August 1943.

The evacuation started at about seven o'clock. Several yellow buses were used to carry the hospital patients, including Ben. He waved as his bus passed by. The next time I saw him was in Manila a month later. By that time he was in a U.S. Army uniform. His right leg was still in a cast.

Meanwhile back at Camp 17, I was getting ready to walk to freedom.

I was assigned to a group of fifty Americans as we began our walk. Some of the men were joking. Others were singing. Others were bitter at the "Japs" in general. Tojo was the main target.

I took a last look at the camp as I walked away. I felt a momentary sense of sadness, not for the two years that I had spent there, but for the two-year diary I had lost in the fire.

We arrived at the train station, boarded, and found places to sit. I looked out the window from my seat in the coach and spotted one of my Japanese civilian foremen in the crowd outside. He was known as "Twitchy" and "Black Shirt." Twitchy was gruff on the outside but kind inside when I worked under him in the mine. He would bring me salt and ground red chile for my rice. He was a masterful coal miner and always protected us from mine cave-ins.

"Twitchy" walked over to my window as I waited for the train to pull out. He was very upset. His hands were shaking. A Japanese propaganda source was circulating the lie that American occupation forces would resort to torturing women and children. "Twitchy" was especially concerned about his six-month-old baby. I assured him that our occupying troops would not hurt his family and that, unprovoked, GIs were really nice guys.

It was an enjoyable and scenic trip. We left Omuta and traveled north for about sixty-five miles. We then headed south. Our destination was Nagasaki, thirty-five miles around the bay. In the distance, I could see the waters of the South China Sea.

Nagasaki was in total ruin. There were no human beings around. The ground was covered with three to four inches of gray ashes. The air had a ghostly appearance.

We arrived at the depot of the American authorities. There were temporary buildings, Army tents, first-aid stations, and a Red Cross office. We were served coffee and doughnuts. We were then ushered into Army khaki uniforms.

When I saw the insignia of a staff sergeant, my new rank, on my left sleeve, I was deeply touched.

CHAPTER 16

✲ ✲ ✲

HOMEWARD BOUND

Our assimilation back into the U.S. Army was fast and with little fanfare. We were issued khaki uniforms to go with the high-cut combat boots. In trying on my new boots, I could sense a painful skin ulcer in my lower right leg. I did not report it for fear of being assigned to the disabled group.

Every former prisoner of war was advanced a small portion of his Army pay. The American

Red Cross volunteered to contact our loved ones back home for free. The gifts and services from that organization to the repatriated Americans were seemingly infinite. They gave us stationery, toilet articles, postage stamps, and a choice of books to read. They even volunteered to write letters to our loved ones.

In a short de-briefing session, I told the officers about the diary. I assured the interviewer that names, places, and circumstances of Japanese brutality were still fresh in my mind. I was told to be readily available for future interviews by representatives of the U.S. government.

I left Nagasaki on the British warship *Speaker*. It appeared to be three football fields long, four stories high, and was painted white. Once aboard, I was escorted to the deck below the hospital area.

I was assigned to a small, private hospital room. I was told to change into pajamas and I was informed that I would be classified as a bed patient in a Navy hospital. There was no one else with me. I traveled the next few days in luxury.

We arrived in Okinawa on September 20. I was glad to change into my regular uniform.

I noticed that my khaki trousers were a bit snug. I'd gained twelve pounds but was still grossly underweight.

I had been separated from the rest of my co-workers from the coal mine. They were scattered all over the South China Sea aboard different ships. Their destination was the same: home.

On Okinawa I was assigned to a bunk in an Army tent. There were five other soldiers in the tent with me. They were all friendly and accommodating and seasoned combat veterans of the war in the Pacific, not ex-prisoners of war.

I cried when I saw "Old Glory" rising to the top of the pole one morning at five o'clock – the first time in four years. I had ham and eggs for breakfast. I saw my first Hollywood movie one evening after supper.

The landscape in Okinawa was lifeless and dull. The inhabitants, some of whom worked in the Army compound, were not very sociable. Their attitude towards the Americans was understandable; they were war weary. Ninety-five thousand Okinawans died in the battle for the island. Seventy thousand Japanese soldiers were killed, committed *hara-kari*, or were captured. The number of Japanese POWs was low.

After a week on the island, I was summoned to the commander's tent. I was told to report to the B-24 bomber hanger at two o'clock the following morning to be flown to Manila. I was cautioned to travel light.

I was up the following morning at one and reported to the hanger promptly at 1:30. I identified myself to the crew of the airplane. They all seemed to be in their early twenties, yet they acted like seasoned veteran pilots.

During the early-hour mixer, we feasted on coffee and chocolate doughnuts. Having been deprived of chocolate doughnuts for more than four years, I ate about eighteen. I knew I would suffer miserably.

We took off for Manila aboard a B-24 Liberator at seven. It was a clear day. The view from 30,000 feet up in the air was breathtaking. About a half-hour after we leveled off, I saw the pilot and the co-pilot leave the cockpit. They were waving their arms and gesturing for everyone to join them.

Below and behind the controls, there was a large, empty floor with a sheet spread out on it. Someone tossed in a pair of dice. We all reached for our money and sat down. A member of the crew placed a gallon of Old Crow bourbon in the middle of the playing area. The bottle was passed around the circle. Those in the mood politely took a swig and kept the game going as they loosened their grip on their money.

All this time, the B-24 was flying on a steady course towards Manila, courtesy of the automatic pilot.

After about five or six hours in the air, we were approaching Manila, and the flight crew resumed their positions in the cockpit. Everyone was happy about this.

"Prepare for landing!"

We all rushed back to our seats on the inside wall and secured ourselves with the web belts attached to the metal seats. I looked out the aircraft window at the thick jungle vegetation that looked like a green carpet over the islands. The view from the air was indescribable.

We landed at Nichols Field, just outside Manila, at about noon. The minute I set foot on the tarmac, my left lower leg became painful. The skin ulcer on the outside of my left ankle had become seriously infected. I had to sit and remove my left boot to relieve the pressure.

Once the Military Police discovered that I was a returning American ex-POW from Japan, they put themselves at my disposal. They volunteered to transport me anywhere I needed to go. There was nothing they would not have done for me. I had not been sitting long at the airport when an MP jeep drove up to where I was sitting. Two MPs jumped off and walked up to me.

"What's the problem?"

"I have a painful left leg. I am not able to walk comfortably on it."

The younger MP took a closer look at my infected ulcer. He shook his head and ordered his companion to help me get on the jeep. I was transported to the nearest Army hospital. On October 2, 1945, I was admitted to the U.S. Army's 312th General Hospital in Manila.

During the next two or three weeks, I was evaluated for intestinal parasites, skin ulcers, a spinal injury, and a host of avitaminosis-related health problems. I had multiple molar extractions. My deficiency in B vitamins was a major concern of the medical staff. In spite of the ban on alcohol in hospitals, I was issued, on a regular basis, two cans of beer a day to supplement my B-vitamin intake.

In the meantime, I was questioned about my diary. Sessions with the investigative officers took place at the most inopportune times, but I was always cooperative. The investigators were interested in specific incriminating evidence of any Japanese brutality against American POWs.

One evening after "lights-out," the night nurse came up to my bed and whispered, "Sergeant Montoya, you're going home tomorrow. You will fly aboard an Army hospital plane. Be ready in your pajamas and robe by three o'clock tomorrow morning."

The next day, October 29, 1945, I was transported in an Army ambulance to an Army airport for my flight to San Francisco.

As we headed to the airport just outside Manila, I had to bite my lip to keep from breaking down.

I boarded a four-engine C-54 Army Air Corps airplane. It was silver colored and very attractive. I was assigned to a top bunk, one of the many bunks attached to the side of the wall. I was ordered by the Army nurse to get in and lie down as she helped me with the covers. There were two nurses running the show. Both wore white and one had a red cross on her cap and uniform.

Without much delay, the exit door was slammed shut and we were off. One hour into the flight and 30,000 feet above the Pacific Ocean, the young and attractive Red Cross nurse came to check on me in my bunk. Of course everything was fine, and she went about her other duties. A few hours later we stopped over on Guam, about 1,500 miles west of Manila. Our next stop was at the island of Kwajalein. Late that evening we arrived in Honolulu.

We had traveled approximately 5,000 miles that day. We spent that night at the U.S. Army hospital at Hickam Field, and all slept well.

Early the next day, we were bound for San Francisco. I looked out to my right through the porthole at the hundreds of miles of ocean. It was an awesome sensation.

I thought of my experiences at O'Donnell, Cabanatuan, and Camp 17, and of my buddies whose remains were left in makeshift cemeteries and the mineshafts. What would I say to their loved ones back in Taos?

"Get ready, Sergeant. We're beginning to descend. We'll be in San Francisco soon", the nurse said.

I gathered my few belongings from around me and packed them in my ditty bag. I secured my billfold in my pajama pocket. I braced myself to walk again on good old American soil. I could sense the moment was going to be tearful and emotional.

EPILOGUE

It was late afternoon on November I, 1945, when the B-24 landed at Hamilton Field in San Francisco.

Once I set foot on U.S. soil, I could not hold back my emotions. I knelt down momentarily and wept. The individuals around me were kind and supportive as they helped me back on my feet. I walked unattended to the waiting army vehicle.

That evening, I was admitted to Letterman General Hospital in San Francisco as a transferee from the Army hospital in Manila.

The grounds surrounding the hospital building were beautiful. The main building, which was well maintained, had a distinctive character. This, I believe, was an extension of the noble mission of the doctors and nurses who worked inside.

During the admission process, a cadre of Red Cross volunteers surrounded me. They looked very impressive in their official uniforms. I have never been treated so well in my life. I was provided with free toilet articles, stationery, cigarettes, and most important, a long-distance call to my mother and family in Taos. This call was the best thing that the Red Cross volunteers could have done for me.

I was told on the phone that my oldest sister, Lydia, had died in childbirth. I was proud to hear of the wartime exploits of my three remaining brothers, who had stayed behind at home when Ben and I left for the Philippines in September 1941.

My sister, Claudine, told me that Eli had served with the medics in the U.S. Army in Germany. Jose was Seaman First Class in the Navy aboard the USS Aircraft Carrier *Guadalcanal* stationed in the Atlantic. Rudy, the youngest, was a U.S. Navy seaman attached to the U.S. Merchant Marines.

My four brothers and I returned home safely.

I was gratified by the way in which people in the street and restaurants expressed their appreciation for our service to our country. Often some unknown customer would pick-up the tab in a restaurant or nightclub simply because we were U.S. servicemen.

After a two-week stay at Letterman General, I was transferred to William Beaumont Army Hospital in El Paso for further treatment.

I loved El Paso. It was not so much for its aesthetic beauty, but because of the memories of the good times I had spent with my buddies on leave and on weekends during basic training. One of the only soldiers on the base with a car was Evans Garcia from Santa Fe. In spite of our kidding, he was very proud of his Spanish given name: Evangelista. I remember going to town on a Saturday with no more than three dollars in my pocket. Evans, Joe, and I would pool our money and enjoy ourselves.

Now, I was a patient in Ward 55 at William Beaumont.

The medical staff was doing wonders for my health. The pterygium growth was surgically removed from my right eye. The doctors ridded me of the intestinal parasites I had acquired through the soles of my feet as I worked in the farm in Cabanatuan and stabilized my jaundice. The dental staff had to extract most of the molars in my upper jaw.

I spent Christmas at home in Taos on a convalescence furlough. I was still in the Army, so I had to wear my Army uniform everywhere I went. My health was good enough to enjoy civilian activities while I was home.

My strolls down the streets of Taos were always bittersweet. Most of the men from Taos who did not come home died in Camp O'Donnell. On occasion, families would want to know the fate of their loved one. If I was actually involved in the burial of their loved one, I assured them of the love and respect we Americans had demonstrated at his burial.

After two weeks of rest and relaxation I headed back to El Paso. I planned on a night's layover in Santa Fe. Many friends and buddies from Taos, including Ben, were patients at Bruns Army Hospital there.

That night in Santa Fe, coming out of the movies with my friends, I met Maria Loyola Torres, a young, attractive, and well-dressed girl from Ranchos de Taos. Her friends and family called her Dolly. She was a dental supply clerk at the Army hospital.

I walked her home to her apartment. She liked me in spite of my swagger. Her memory haunted me for the next two years.

By late spring 1946, I was back home on an extended furlough. My salary as a staff sergeant came regularly. Other than occasional nightmares and brief periods of depression, my health was improving. I occupied myself with chores around our small farm.

One Sunday morning in May, two Army officers appeared at my front door. They knew about my diary in Fukuoka Camp 17 and wanted to talk to me about names, places, and incidents of Japanese Army brutality against Allied soldiers.

They said that I was a likely witness to testify at the War Crimes Tribunal in Manila later that year. All expenses were to be paid by the U.S. government.

That summer, I became seriously concerned about the prospects of testifying in such a prestigious international court. On a regular basis, I would sit down to refresh my memory about episodes of cruelty and inhumanity that I had recorded in my diary. Those memories would remain with me forever.

They never called me.

In October, I received an order from the Army to report to Fort Sam Houston in San Antonio on November 26 to be separated from the Army.

I had returned to the University of New Mexico under the GI Bill for the Spring 1947 semester as a business administration major.

One year later, on February 9, 1948, Dolly and I were married at St. Francisco de Assisi Church in Ranchos de Taos. My best friend, Paul Trujillo, was my best man.

In April 1948, I had to drop out of UNM when I obtained a position with the Bureau of Veterans Affairs in Albuquerque. I knew that my work at the VA Hospital would allow me to spend my days helping fellow veterans, many of whom were my prisoner of war buddies. I retired in April of 1977.

Dolly and I raised five children and we live happily in Albuquerque. Ben, now deceased, retired after approximately thirty years with an agency of the U.S. government.

CABANATUAN PRISON CAMP DEATH LIST.   *11*

This is a list of the deaths occurring in the Cabanatuan Prisoner of War Camps from 3 June 1942 through 12 March 1944. The records were buried to keep them from falling into Japanese hands. Some blanks appear for the original documents were illegible due to age and damage that occurred during burial. The names of many prisoners executed in these camps and buried by the Japanese do not appear on any death lists. Executions were carried out in one of two primary ways, ie. by firing squad or by beheading with a samurai sword.

There were three Prisoner of War Camps in the Cabanatuan area. These camps were identified as Cabanatuan #1, #2 and #3. These Camps were opened in mid May 1942. The Cabanatuan #1 camp was located approximately 12 miles from the city of Cabanatuan. Camp #3 was located approximately 8 miles from the city of Cabanatuan. The 7,000 Prisoners of War interned in camp #1 were troops captured on Corregidor Island on May 6, 1942. In September 1942 camp #1 was closed and the remainder of the prisoners were transferred to Cabanatuan Camp #3. Camp #1 was converted to rehabilitation training camp for Filipino Prisoners of War. Camp #3 remained in use until it was liberated by a United States Ranger Battalion in January 1945.

NAME	SERIAL NUMBER		DATE OF DEATH
Clark, Clifton L. Pvt. Co. K.	6284091		5---42
Long, Jessie F Pfc. 31 Inf.	6384595	Co. H.	6---42
McKnight, J.H. Sgt.	6792212		6-3-42
Hatherill, Neal E. Pvt. 31 Inf.	16013510	Co. M.	6-3-42
Farley, John A. Cpt. HPD	W-901415		6-3-42
Gilliam, Calvin J. Pvt.	13017053		6-4-42
O'Bryan, Edward M. Pvt.	6542666		6-4-42
Rector, Paul Pvt. 803 Engr.			6-4-42
Haynes, Edward E. 93 Bomb	6297746		6-5-42
Hayes, J.D.Pfc.	18036361		6-5-42
Packer, L.H.	39677386		6-5-42
Lepping, Vernon G. Pfc.	6914215		6-5-42
Rogers, Harry A. Pfc. 200 CAC	20843486		6-5-42
Koppen, Howard A. S/Sgt. 20 Pur.	6913795		6-5-42
Rose, Ben Jr. Pfc.	7086343		6-5-42
Wallace, Joseph A. Sgt.			6-5-42
Watson, Alvin F. 1/Sgt. 515 CAC	20842742		6-6-42
Clayton, Robert E. Pfc.			6-6-42
Pounds, Chester O. Pvt. 200 CAC	38011805		6-6-42
Gulso, Robert V. Pvt.			6-6-42
Clevenger, James R. Pfc 194 Tank	20700225		6-6-42
Roley, John Pvt.	15066199		6-6-42
Rodriguez, Albert Pvt. 200 CAC	38012536		6-6-42
Rigney, Elbert Lee Pfc. 4 Marine	277242	.	6-6-42
Snittjer, Vernon C. Pvt. 19 Bomb	6860942		6-6-42
Unknown #1			6-7-42
Jones, Elwood E. Pfc. 34 Pur.	17015638		6-7-42
Metts, Raymond L. Pfc.	14011914		6-7-42
Unknown #5			6-7-42
Autry, John B. Pvt. 31 Inf.	6577024	Co. F.	6-7-42
Rhoades, Harold B. Sgt. 7 CWS	19056429		6-7-42
Oliver, William V. Cpl.	69508708		6-7-42
Yager, Louis W. Pfc. 194 Tank	20720286		6-7-42
Beach, Melvin H. Pfc.	13024475		6-7-42
Conner, Donald F. Pfc.	19032278		6-7-42
Hardy, Richard J. Cpl. 200 CAC	38012400		6-7-42
Fenwick, John R. Cpl. DEML	7025114		6-8-42

```
Unknown #2                                                    6-8-42
Sass, Martin E. Sgt. 515 CAC          36008019               6-8-42
Ossir, Carl Pvt.                       7033198               6-8-42
Howlett, Joseph C. Pvt. 12 MP                                6-8-42
Buckman, George H. Pvt.               19030056               6-8-42
Unknown #3                                                    6-8-42
Higgins, James J. 31 Inf.             18048883  Co. H.       6-8-42
Kemp, Ray L.                           6275826               6-8-42
Shepard, Ben F.                       19024158               6-8-42
Champagne, Francis E.                 19054319               6-8-42
Lee, Wallace C. 194 Tank              20700243               6-8-42
Cotton, Neal Pvt. 24 Pur.              6584422               6-8-42
Burden, James R. Pvt. 192 Tank        35017643               6-8-42
Christensen, Victor L. Pfc.            686397                6-8-42
Unknown #4                                                    6-8-42
Loveland, Donald B. Cpl 3 Pur.         6538575               6-8-42
Pearce, Ruben Pvt. 31 Inf.            19071444  Svc. Co.     6-8-42
Beck, Boyd H. Pvt. 31 Inf.            17014222  Co. B.       6-9-42
Robey, Walter L. Pvt. 192 Tank        35000901               6-9-42
Smith, James G S/Sgt. 200 CAC         38057355               6-9-42
Viitanen, Arnold E. Pvt. 200 CAC      38011997               6-9-42
Dolski, Peter P. Pvt.                 17025244               6-9-42
Maczka, Louis A. S/Sgt.                6905649               6-9-42
Montoya,                               1217
Brown, Albert F.
Swett, Leslie F. Pvt.                 11013307               6-9-42
Sheets, Samuel L.                     38068611               6-9-42
Bennett, Herbert A. Pvt.              18010400               6-9-42
Johnson, Erford M. Pvt.               12024698               6-9-42
Cruz, Jose C. Pfc. 515 CAC            38012441               6-9-42
Nance, Paul C. Sgt. 31 Inf.           17000700  Co. H.       6-9-42
Griffith, Newell Cpl.                                        6-9-42
McKee, Harvey L. Pvt. 31 Inf.         18036369  Co. I.       6-9-42
Martin, Joseph R. Pvt. 27 Mat.                               6-9-42
Brod, Alvin C. Pvt. 194 Tank          39501688               6-9-42
Murray, Robert E. Pvt. 409 Sig.       33053729               6-9-42
Martinez Ted G. Cpl. 200 CAC          20843126               6-9-42
Unknown #6                                                    6-9-42
Carr, Charles I. Jr. Pfc. 192 Tank    36017202               6-9-42
Brantley, H.E. S/Sgt.                  6290997               6-10-42
Caldikas, John F. Pfc. 515 CAC         3603466               6-10-42
Hansford, Charles Pvt.                 6998535               6-10-42
Opgrand, John L. Pfc.                  6569611               6-10-42
Shriver, Robert Pvt.                   6949466               6-10-42
Train, Robert David Sgt. 17 Pur.       6913165               6-10-42
Richard, Arnauld Pvt.                 17015570               6-10-42
Fleming, Claude Pvt. 200 CAC          38011966               6-10-42
Mansfield, Quinton Pfc. 228 SC        11017106               6-10-42
Wood, George L. Cpt.                 0-168103                6-10-42
Franklin, Clarence E. S/Sgt. 3 Pur.  R-1047599               6-10-42
Borunda, David G. Pfc. 200 CAC        38011813               6-10-42
Jaffries, E. H. Cpl.                   6937773               6-10-42
Good, Harrold Sgt.                     6254892               6-10-42
Scott, T/Sgt.                                                6-10-42
Basinger, Paul R. Pvt.                18029997               6-10-42
Gallano, J.R. Pvt. USMC                                      6-10-42
Rose, Joseph D. S/Sgt.                 6948286               6-10-42
Schmitz, William F. Cpl. AC.          17003225               6-10-42
Hamilton, Earl B. Pvt. 31 Inf.         6291184  Co. C.       6-10-42
Snyder, Densel T. Pfc.                19019216               6-10-42
```

```
Hoffman, Robert Sgt.                      6948855              6-10-42
Goff, Harvey L. Cpl                      19016290              6-11-42
Quesenberry, William Sgt.                 6891343              6-11-42
Seymour, E.A. Pvt.                        7000507              6-11-42
Day, Milcom R. Pvt. 19 AB                 6571575              6-11-42
NcCoy, J.C. Pvt.                          6960525              6-11-42
Maranda, Lawrence F. Pvt. 194 Tank       37026111              6-11-42
Norton, John W. S/Sgt. 515 CAC           20842963              6-11-42
Barkley. Charles R. Capt. Inf.           0-336945              6-11-42
Trujillo, Ralph J. Pfc. 200 CAC          20843179              6-11-42
Sheltler, Reuben R. Pvt. 27 Mat.          6976741              6-11-42
Babbain, Joseph J. Sgt. 17 Pur.          11014157              6-11-42
Stanevitch, Bronis J. Pfc. 31 Inf.       19010899   Co. L.     6-11-42
Wood, Everett R. 1st. Lt. Inf.           0-317491              6-11-42
Robbins, Leonard F. Pfc.  31 Inf.         6149169   Co. H.     6-11-42
Robbins, Allen D. Pvt.                                         6-11-42
McAllister, Lawrence J. Pvt.             19019536              6-11-42
Williams, Edgar V. Pvt. 31 Inf.          19056300   A-T Co.    6-11-42
Ramírez, Salvador H. Pfc. 200 CAC        20843305              6-11-42
Hamilton, Joyl H. Pvt.                   38030568              6-12-42
Craig, Howard E. Sgt.                     6556132              6-12-42
Hoffarth, Dayton C. Pvt.                 37048825              6-12-42
Mares, Charles C. Sgt. 200 CAC           20844124              6-12-42
Braddock, Beauford C.                     7001278              6-12-42
Murray, John H. Pfc.                      6953671              6-12-42
Vela, Fidal Pvt. 515 CAC                 58030028              6-12-42
Miller, Gordon Pvt.                      13030437              6-12-42
Hughes, Lloyd A. Pvt.                    20964195              6-12-42
LeMarr, Ronald T. Pvt. 19 Bomb           19051390              6-12-42
Carpenter, K.L. Cpl.                     17001775              6-12-42
Dorman, David T. Pvt.                     6274793              6-12-42
Goemmer, Milton J. Pvt. Tank              7040122              6-12-42
Gray, C.F. Pvt.                                               6-12-42
Fisk, Frank Jr. Cpl.                      6882058              6-12-42
McNamara, James V. Pvt.                   6917428              6-12-42
Leitzel, W.F. Pfc.                       36102657              6-12-42
Smith. X. Lawrence Pvt.                                       6-12-42
St.Germain, Orel Sgt. 31 Inf.             6862853   Co. H.     6-12-42
Barnett, Billy Cpl. 31 Inf.              18036325   Co. D.     6-12-42
Thompson, Richard R. Pfc.                 1018631              6-12-42
Cooper, E.W. Pvt.                        19020117              6-12-42
Downey, Phil R. 2Lt. 16 Bomb             0-421888              6-12-42
Jennings, Willard D. Sgt. 192 Tank       20600380              6-11-42
Colburn Quintan D. Pfc. 200 CAC          38012630              6-12-42
Buffington, George M. T/Sgt.              6250162              6-13-42
Dodge, Justin F. Pvt. QMC                 6934683              6-13-42
Boles, Eugene E. Pvt.                    19002567              6-13-42
Hule, Thomas J. Pvt.                      6937004              6-13-42
Neubauer, Adrian Pvt.                    36213944              6-13-42
Jarmulowicz, M.E. Pvt. 24 Pur.           11020688              6-13-42
Davidson, Bernice L. Pvt. 2nd. Obs.      19028892              6-13-42
Elsasser, Harold E. Pvt. 31 Inf.         19020676   Co. L.     6-13-42
McGahan, John J. S/Sgt.                  19019433              6-13-42
Koocharook, J.T. Pfc.                     6542406              6-13-42
Knight, William L. Cpl. 200 CAC          20842714              6-13-42
Kintz, Robert E. Pvt.                     6592640              6-13-42
Klocker, George M. Pvt. 200 CAC           3801347              6-13-42
Sauer, Clarence C. Pvt.                   6913345              6-13-42
Cohn,                                                         6-13-42
Buterbaugh, Harold H. Pvt.               13024339              6-13-42
```

```
Hartman, William  Pvt.                    19048328                         6-13-42
Barreras, Elisea H. Cpl. 200 CAC          20842694                         6-13-42
Wingfield, Harry Pvt.                      19003636                         6-13-42
Chamberlain, stephen 1 Lt. 26 Cav.        0-411896                         6-14-42
McMurray, Welborn G. Lt/Col.              0-198944                         6-14-42
Steel, Hubert Pvt. 194 Tank               20523464                         6-14-42
Unknown #7                                                                 6-14-42
Maginnis, David G. Pvt. 27 Mat.           11017100                         6-14-42
Gagnon, Arthur J. Pfc. 31 Inf.             6148663     Co. M.              6-14-42
Morris, Gem E. Cpl.                        6580732                         6-14-42
Erickson, Vernon A. Pvt.                   6913591                         6-14-42
Ford, Leroy G. Pvt.                        6911714                         6-14-42
Huntington, William Pvt.                  19000334                         6-14-42
Smith, Brite Pvt.                          6290861                         6-14-42
Ryan, Daniel F. Pvt.                      19006227                         6-14-42
Kutz, Clayton N. Pvt.                     33055476                         6-14-42
Clem, Grover R. Pvt.                      19028175                         6-14-42
Barbrak, Joe Pvt.                          6655625                         6-14-42
McBurney, Douglas J. Pfc                  19018944                         6-14-42
Hancock, Joseph G. Cpl. 17 Pur.           16000656                         6-14-42
Suttle, George H. Pvt. 31 Inf.            19038616     Co. L.              6-14-42
Montgomery, Fred M. Pfc.                   7002788                         6-14-42
Thomas, John Jr. Pvt. 31 Inf.             6542406      Co. D.              6-14-42
Johnson, H.V. Pvt.                        17000647                         6-14-42
Murphy, Frank Pvt.                                                         6-14-42
Miller, Harold J. Pfc. 28 Mat.            6915686                          6-14-42
King, Eddie M. Pvt. 194 Tank              20945456                         6-14-42
Maxson, Dwight E. Pfc. 194 Tank           37025752                         6-14-42
Pederson, Roger C. Pvt.                   19017601                         6-15-42
Britton, Neal Richard S/Sgt. 17 Pur.16020317                              6-15-42
Darr, Franklin E. T/Sgt. 24 Pur.          6851422                          6-15-42
Harvey, Alban Pvt.                        13004908                         6-15-42
Handley, John E. Pvt.                     6981630                          6-15-42
Barber, Thomas Cpl.                       18048121                         6-15-42
Adams, Nevel E. Pvt.                       6652702                         6-15-42
Cramer, R.M. Pvt.                         39302842                         6-15-42
Sallee, Joseph G. Pvt.                    1718528                          6-15-42
Archuleta, Marque Pfc. 200 CAC            38012237                         6-15-42
Buhle, Melvin Pfc.                        16000349                         6-15-42
Merkel, Alvin J. Cpl. USMC                                                 6-15-42
Smith, Leo B. S/Sgt.                      6803438                          6-15-42
Nunn, Grover W. S/Sgt. 31 Inf.            6273432      SVC. Co.            6-15-42
Brazzel, Rufus Pfc. 17 Ord.               38022995                         6-15-42
Snyder, Russell B. Jr. Pvt.               6948573                          6-15-42
Anderson, G.A. Pvt.                       38007503                         6-15-42
Woody, G.W. Pfc.                          39233552                         6-15-42
Spring, Robert G. Pvt.                    19052539                         6-15-42
Kuhn, Elmer C. Pvt. 680 Ord.              19052252                         6-15-42
Ehrbar, Lloyd E. Pfc. 192 Tank            35001041                         6-15-42
Yeats, Allen M. Sgt. 21 Pur.              19016505                         6-15-42
Debler, Donald D. Sgt. QMC                6575630                          6-15-42
Grieco, Michael Pvt. 31 Inf.              11010226     Hq. Co.             6-15-42
Oppenhiem, James R. 1 Lt. CE              0-328592                         6-16-42
Laska, Carl Cpl.                          6936914                          6-16-42
Hulyk, Robert Pvrt.                       13009082                         6-16-42
Huffman, Verle G. Pfc. 31 Inf.            6276112      Co. C.              6-16-42
Weis, Wilbur S. Pvt. 31 Inf.              12032802     * C.I.              6-16-42
Mayo, Fred Cpl. 31 Inf.                   6566810      Co. A.              6-16-42
Chalifox, Joseph Pvt. 27 Mat.             11017166                         6-16-42
Crotzer, Fred Pvt. 19 Bomb                13030365                         6-16-42
```

```
Dowling, Leslie Pvt. 31 Inf.          19017743   SVC. Co.    6-16-42
Zimmer, Lloyd P. Pvt.                 16017462               6-16-42
Pugh, Howard V. Jr. Sgt. 19 Truck     6931692                6-16-42
Phillips, Burell Cpl. 31 Inf.         6386259    Co. L.      6-16-42
Cohen Abraham Pvt. QMC                6519808                6-16-42
Funk, Virgil F. Cpl. 515 CAC          36008422               6-16-42
Wendland, Robert A. Pvt.              19014670               6-16-42
Webber, Roger Pvt.                    11016727               6-17-42
Ables, Hubert A. Cpl.                 19002901               6-17-42
Brown, Tom D. Pvt. 31 Inf.            6266226    Co. I.      6-17-42
Lujan, Joe L. Pvt. 200 CAC            20844115               6-17-42
Montgomnery, Cecil L. Pvt. USMC       280980                 6-17-42
Wattenhofer, Herman Pfc. QMC          6892004                6-17-42
Boles, Leo Pvt. 31 Inf                15067899   Co. D.      6-17-42
Larson, Howard Sgt. 149 Tank          20700200               6-17-42
Vandervuller, Glenn 1/Sgt. QMC        6767150                6-17-42
Jackson, J.R. Pvt. 31 Inf.            19017253   *           6-17-42
Allen, Henderson W. L/Col. QMC        0-117755               6-17-42
Millam, Harold C. Sgt. 454 Ord.       14049123               6-17-42
Sims, Jack Pfc.                       7002774                6-17-42
Crompton, Charles V. Pfc. 192 Tank    20645300               6-18-42
Milleren, Fred 2/Lt. 31 Inf.          0-890234   Co. D.      6-18-42
Cantrell, Cpl.                        20832792               6-18-42
Cavett, James D. Sgt. 3 Pur.          18014625               6-18-42
Salcedo, Henry 200 CAC                38012234               6-18-42
Holland, Jack J. Pvt. 24 Pur.         6914368                6-18-42
Whitford, Leo Cpl. 5 Inter.           6976728                6-18-42
Clark, C.L. Pvt. 31 Inf.              35125302   A-T Co.     6-18-42
Brantley, Clarence Cpl. 200 CAC       38053822               6-18-42
Starks, Merlon Howard Pfc. 2 Obs.     19052223               6-18-42
Glasscock, Charles J. S/Sgt. 24 Pur.  6571800                6-18-42
McCracken, Henry C. S/Sgt. 24 Pur.    657946                 6-18-42
Ziglinski, Joseph P. Pvt. QMC         19014983               6-18-42
Eckert, Allen W. Pvt. 31 Inf.         20900704   *           6-18-42
Gallegos, Antonio Pfc. 200 CAC        20842505               6-18-42
Rodrigues, Geraro Pfc. 200 CAC        38030900               6-18-42
Espalin, Damacia Pvt. 200 CAC         38011852               6-18-42
Jarvis, William C. Sgt. Inf.          19015753   *           6-19-42
Fusilier, Lodger Cpl. AC              6839043                6-19-42
Neal, Clarence W. Cpl. 17 Pur.        16011621               6-19-42
Hetze, Gustaf Pvt. 31 Inf.            19016754   Co. M.      6-19-42
Curtis, George M. Cpl. AC             6959056                6-19-42
Smith, George D. Pvt.                 7027691                6-19-42
Wickman, Charles W. Jr. Pfc. 31 Inf.  6151768    Co. M.      6-19-42
Ralston, F.D. Pvt. QMC                19060845               6-19-42
Zimmerman, R.C. Pvt.                  19013614               6-19-42
Kirby, J.L. Pfc. 693 Ord.             19003167               6-19-42
Sener, C.L. Pvt.                      19017250               6-19-42
Deymek, Emanuel J. Cpt. QMC           0-164789               6-19-42
Pastor, Joseph S/Sgt. 5 Inter         13009805               6-19-42
Chase, Julius T. Pfc. 693 Ord.        19002571               6-19-42
Zona, Albert Pfc. 27 Mat.             19011574               6-19-42
Romero, Santiago Pvt. 200 CAC         20843159               6-19-42
Greenwood, Vernon R. Cpt. F.A.        0-283559               6-19-42
Dunn, James Pfc. 24 Pur.              12007458               6-20-42
Collins, Marshall L. Cpl. 27 Mat.     6978841                6-20-42
Gist, Charles F. Pvt. 7 Mat.          19044207               6-20-42
Whitman, J.J. Pfc. 228 Sig.           6949649                6-20-42
Pennington, M. Pvt. 27 Bomb           20546168               6-20-42
Corbett, John J. Pfc.                 13024445               6-20-42
```

236

```
Upton, Max S. M/Sgt. Inf.              6573884   *           6-20-42
Downes, Robert T. T/Sgt. 2 Obs.        6788121               6-20-42
Everly, Marvin E. Pvt. 31 Inf.         19017936  Co. E.      6-20-42
Rodhauer, Carol Pvt.                                         6-20-42
Torcson, Howard Cpl. 34 Pur.                                 6-20-42
Paschke, Gerald Pvt. 2 Obs.            19017543              6-20-42
Reynolds, Ralph E. Pvt. QMC            6731598               6-20-42
Belcheff, Teddy Pvt. 16 Bomb           35027980              6-20-42
Hall, Harry J. Pvt. 808 MP.            6564583               6-20-42
Andrews, Thomas E. Pvt.                17013698              6-20-42
Goodfellow, James Pvt. 31 Inf.         6898895   Co. M.      6-20-42
Pocus, Andrew S/Sgt. 34 Pur            6920052               6-20-42
Chavez, Ray S. Pvt. 515 CAC            38012113              6-20-42
Beaudeon, Charles R. Pvt. 200 CAC      36106585              6-20-42
Garcia, Ramon Pvt. 200 CAC             20842506              6-20-42
Wright, Durward H. Sgt. 515 CAC        38012680              6-21-42
Packer, Earl C. Cpt. 31 Inf.           0-272176  Hq. Co.     6-21-42
Diaz, Joseph G. Pvt. 515 CAC           20843313              6-21-42
Russell, James A. Pvt. 31 Inf.         19006155  Co. B.      6-21-42
Steen, Arnold Pfc. 192 Tank            20645277              6-21-42
Blazevich, John Pvt. 200 CAC           38011916              6-21-42
Franklin, W.S. S/Sgt. 27 Bomb          6955608               6-21-42
Hutchens, Joseph L. Pvt.               19012213              6-21-42
Landry, Clifford J. T/Sgt. 93 Bomb     6829994               6-21-42
Wirtz, Elmer C. Jr. Cpt. 86 FA         0-348911              6-21-42
McClure, David H. Pvt. 31st. Co. E.    19052467-Bro. Dale Svc. Co 6-21-42
Schmidt, John Sgt. 194 Tank            35004787              6-21-42
Perry, Jack F. Cpl 7 Mat.              18029918              6-21-42
Rice, Joseph S/SGt. 24 Pur.            6127503               6-21-42
Nix, Jesse C. Pfc. 17 Bomb             7002650               6-21-42
Klonka, Edwin J. Sgt. 5 Bomb           6832558               6-22-42
Stair, William E. Pvt. 28 Mat.         13006762              6-22-42
Burnham, George E. Civilian                                  6-22-42
Hodges, James J. Pvt. AC               34034135              6-22-42
Odell, James G. Pvt. 515 CAC           38012026              6-22-42
Snyder, Francis G. Pvt. AC             16039173              6-22-42
Dunlap, M.F. Sgt. SC                   6853754               6-22-42
McDougal, David Pvt. 31 Inf.           19006278  Co. I.      6-22-42
McCaulley, Frank B. Pfc. 31 Inf.       6781904   Co. K.      6-22-42
Hoggatt, Chester E. Pfc. MP            17019466              6-22-42
Rall, Harold Pfc. 31 Inf.              7031137   Co. C.      6-22-42
Macklin, James E. L/Col.QMC            0-15783               6-22-42
Runyon, Stanton Pvt. 803 CE            6574386               6-22-42
Vigil, Max Pvt. 27 Matl.               18046248              6-22-42
Wysong, Jeff A. Cpl. 200 CAC           38011959              6-22-42
Leon, Boris A. S/Sgt. 3 Pur.           6583188               6-22-42
Michel, Ralph E. Cpl. 31 Inf.          14038409  Co. K.      6-22-42
Burnham, John L. Pfc. 7 Matl.          19018838              6-22-42
Hiner, Carl H. Pfc. 17 Ord.            19018546              6-22-42
Hufsmith, Richard E. Pvt. 20 Pur.      19020140              6-22-42
Sweeney, Thomas F. Pvt.                6946613               6-23-42
Warren, Robert B. S/Sgt. 17 Pur.       6913116               6-23-42
Laudeman, Richard R. Pfc. 2 Obs.       15058825              6-23-42
Stearly, Everett W. S/Sgt. 93 Bomb     6714072               6-23-42
Foltz, John F. Pvt. 27 Bomb            13948775              6-23-42
Mussen, Alman Pvt CWS                  19048616              6-23-42
Mahr, Walter J. S/Sgt. Tank            20600370              6-23-42
Hoskins, Philip W. Pvt AC              11010598              6-23-42
Russ, Jason B. S/Sgt. 27 Bomb          6259013               6-23-42
Swank, Richard E. Pvt. 31 Inf.         16013458  *           6-23-42
```

```
Bianco, F. Pvt. 515 CAC              37055696                      6-23-42
Powell, DeHaven Pvt. 31 Inf.         18050404  Co. C.              6-23-42
Foreman, L. Pvt. 7 Mat.              19000008                      6-23-42
Martsolf, Lawrence F. Pvt. 454 Ord.  33039453                      6-23-42
Malcolm, Robert B. Pvt. 17 Bomb      16039170                      6-23-42
Hicks, W.B. Pfc. 60 CAC              16017856                      6-23-42
Barnett, William Cpl. CWS            19021228                      6-23-42
Montgomery, Lorris L. Pfc.           19002543                      6-23-42
Wethnell, Thomas M. Pvt. 31 Inf.     18001278  Hq. Co.            6-23-42
Boucher, A. Pfc. QMC                 R209145                       6-24-42
Driver, Jack D. Pvt. 192 Tank        38029825                      6-24-42
Powelson, Robert L. Jr. Pvt. 27 Bm.  14027394                      6-24-42
Brown, Vincent C. Pvt. 808 MP        10308381                      6-24-42
Tunney, Eugene C. Pfc. AC            33000624                      6-24-42
Karcher, Howard Pvt. 17 Bomb         6916320                       6-24-42
Reynolds, Harman A. Pfc. 200 CAC     38012104                      6-24-42
Morris, Orivel K. Pvt. 31 Inf.       14042422  A-T Co.            6-24-42
Ratay, Paul A. Pvt. 192 Tank         35020472                      6-24-42
Fraser, Hugh K. 1/Lt. CE.            0-391218                      6-24-42
Horn, Robert A. Sgt. 27 Mat.         6581967                       6-24-42
Hagestad, Clementh M. Pfc.           9028793                       6-24-42
Maloy, Grooms K. Pfc. 454 Ord.       14036531                      6-24-42
Raper, Hulan L. Pvt. 454 Ord.        14050626                      6-24-42
Hultquist, J.C. Maj. CAC             0-306255                      6-24-42
Tremplay, Edward J. 2/Lt. AC         0-411740                      6-24-42
Edwards, Darrel C. Pvt. 515 CAC      38055439                      6-24-42
Hansen, Roy O. Pfc. AC               19019897                      6-24-42
Shafer, George W. Pvt. 7 Matl.       19051039                      6-24-42
Ramirez, Cenobino Pvt. 200 CAC       38029803                      6-25-42
Dillon, Travis C. Sgt. 34 Pur.       6960167                       6-25-42
Donald, Robert L. Pfc. 228 CAC       14049704                      6-25-42
Watson, Mac O. Cpl. AC               6296929                       6-25-42
Kent, William C. Pfc. 194 Tank       14005463                      6-25-42
Holton, George E. Pvt. 200 CAC       20842711                      6-25-42
Shaul, Edwin Pvt. AC                 16026650                      6-25-42
Alderete, Ramon S. Pvt. 200 CAC      38011944                      6-25-42
Stanton, Marion P. Pfc. 454 Ord.     14024994                      6-25-42
Duncan, James Pfc. 17 Pur.                                         6-25-42
Charles, E.S. Pvt. 192 Tank          35001419                      6-25-42
Pettigrew, Dan Pvt. 17 Bomb          14026312                      6-25-42
Johnson, Ray N. T/Sgt. 3 Pur.        6243455                       6-25-42
Jones, Robert N. Pfc. 228 Sig.       19012448                      6-25-42
Tillson, William B. Pvt. 28 Matl.    19012448                      6-25-42
Schwartz, Jackson Sgt. 19 Bpomb      6685508                       6-25-42
Mackey, Donald O. EM1c USN           411-87-11                     6-25-42
Parra, Simon R. Cpl  200 CAC         20943365                      6-25-42
Verville, Joseph R. Cpl. AC          11013322                      6-25-42
Kairunas, joseph J. Pvt. 200 CAC     36106537                      6-25-42
Blank, Ralph E. Pfc. 31 Inf.         19020963  Co. E.             6-25-42
Romero, C. Pvt. 200 CAC              38012597                      6-25-42
Jensen, Jack W. Pvt. 19 Bomb         19050502                      6-25-42
Baumgartner, H.V. Pvt. Ord           15061422                      6-25-42
Marx, Clyde F. Pfc. 31 Inf.          16003014  Co. I.             6-26-42
Zuber, J. Pvt. 4 Pur.                11010329         Executed    6-26-42
Graham, Robert J. Pvt. fm.  808      19044326  Co. F. Executed    6-26-42
Gastelam, J.R. Pvt. 60 CAC           19013521         Executed    6-26-42
Reed, Fred J. Pvt. 31 Inf.           6273307   A-T Co. Executed   6-26-42
Penvose, Irvin Pvt. 31 Inf.          6576036   Co. B. Executed    6-26-42
Sison, Kenneth L. Cpl. 60 CAC        7001692          Executed    6-26-42
Hunt, Thomas E. S/Sgt. 515 CAC       38012121                      6-26-42
```

Name	Serial	Unit	Date
Jones. Paul P. 2/Lt. 91 Bomb	0-427554		6-26-42
Pernestte, M. Pvt. CWS	13017715		6-26-42
Van Arsdale, John D. Pvt. 31 Inf.	6562289	Co. M.	6-26-42
Siegel, Jock Sgt. 745 Ord.	6681287		6-26-42
Revelia, Ward Sgt. 31 Inf.	R-1031556	Co. G.	6-26-42
Carroll, George E. T/Sgt. 19 Bomb	6835633		6-26-42
Wilkes, Edmund W. Maj. 31 Inf.	0-19509	Co. B.	6-26-42
Van Ronke, A. Pvt AC			6-26-42
Hardesty, Florence M S/Sgt. 12 MP	6826333		6-26-42
Jackson, Harry Pvt. QMC	19038244		6-26-42
Harvey, Henry H. Pvt. 31 Inf.	6142636	Hq. Co.	6-26-42
Welter, Christopher Pfc. 31 Inf.	6790384	Co. D.	6-26-42
Jones, Ollie C. S/Sgt. 91 Bomb	6250237		6-26-42
Ledbetter, Gene Pvt. QMC	6937045		6-26-42
Trunk, J.C. Pfc. 803 CE	32036181		6-27-42
Contreas, Frank Pvt. 200 CAC	38012631		6-27-42
Gotchy, Patrick Pfc. QMC	19052959		6-27-42
Joiner, Thomson Pvt. 31 Inf.	6561439	Co. M.	6-27-42
Baca, Ernest Pvt. 200 CAC	20840360		6-27-42
Pope, James Pfc. 515 CAC	38012009		6-27-42
Hardy, Wilkie Pvt. 454 Ord.	7083944		6-27-42
Tafoya, Jesus M. Pvt. 515 CAC	38012224		6-27-42
Baum, B.G. Cpl. USMC	265672		6-27-42
Cordova, Edward Pvt. 200 CAC	38011206		6-27-42
Obershelp, R.H. Pvt. 2 Obs.	17016560		6-27-42
Veile, Carles P. Sgt.	6691784		6-27-42
Heaton, Lloyd G. Sgt. 28 Mat.	6879818		6-27-42
Fear, Delber R. Pvt. AC	15060202		6-27-42
Collins, James B. M/Sgt. 19 AB	R-562841		6-27-42
Henke, Albert C. Pvt. 31 Inf.	17015790	Co. M.	6-27-42
Llewellyn, Arthur J. Pfc. 28 Mat.	6854430		6-27-42
Hughes, Joseph S. Pvt. 75 Ord.	6540886		6-27-42
Bick, Paul C. Sgt. 19 Bomb	6564906		6-28-42
Helm, W.G. Cpl. 24 Pur.	1601562		6-28-42
Davis, Robert H. Pfc. 48 Matl.	11013610		6-28-42
Smith, Charles K. WO AC	6102050		6-28-42
Bolton, Lewis B. Pvt. 21 Pur.	14029519		6-28-42
Bartlett, Arnold L. Pvt. 27 Bomb	11015710		6-28-42
Hanson, David C. Pfc. 27 Bomb	16006593		6-28-42
McCloskey, Robert B. Cpl 31 Inf.	6979966	Co. C.	6-28-42
Eberhard, Roland R. Pfc. AC	17070467		6-28-42
Jauriqui, Jose C. Pvt. 200 CAC	38012561		6-28-42
Kleppinger, Jack Pvt. AC	7086415		6-28-42
Thomas, Lawrence E. Pfc. SC	15010584		6-28-42
Wilson, Walter C. Cpl. AC	13025047		6-28-42
Adams, E.W. Cpl. SC	6717812		6-28-42
Taylor, Thomas E. Pvt. 31 Inf.	17002831	Co. D.	6-28-42
Rawson, Raymone V. Sgt. 454 Ord.	14040574		6-28-42
Hinson, Noel Sgt. 31 Inf.	6378211	Co. G.	6-28-42
Amos, Howard H. Capt. FA	0-391935		6-28-42
Stagner, Pat L. Pfc. AC	6268369		6-28-42
Whitehead, O. L. Cpl. 7 Matl.	19011656		6-28-42
Lynch Condia, Pvt. 31 Inf.	14047096	A-T Co.	6-28-42
Curry John M. WO AGD	6346918		6-28-42
Chmielewski, R.V. Pvt. QMC	39677368		6-28-42
Curd, Charles W. Pfc. 17 Pur.	11009103		6-28-42
Wrigley, H.F. Pvt. QMC	R-365177		6-28-42
Kintz, Frank J. Jr. Pfc. AC	6583375		6-28-42
Agrens, Harold E. 2/Lt. QMC	0-381592		6-28-42
Eby, William E. Pvt. 409 SC	19021222		6-28-42

```
Williams, James R. S/Sgt. 515 CAC   20843487            6-28-42
Worley, Herbert Jr. Pvt. 31 Inf.    19057074  Co. B.    6-28-42
Mumford, Wm. M. Pfc. 19 AB          11020601            6-28-42
Garrison, Russell S. Pvt. 194 Tank  39006535            6-28-42
Kramer, Kenneth L. Pvt. AC          19016258            6-29-42
Hudson, J.L. Pfc. AC                 6397156            6-29-42
Heggemeier, Paul A. S/Sgt. 5 Inter.  6856582            6-29-42
Cavender, R.B. Pvt. 31 Inf.         17030324  Co. F.    6-29-42
Craig, C.D. Cpl. 34 Pur.            18010369            6-29-42
Duncan, William Pvt. 20 AB          17003911            6-29-42
Tipton, Verle J. Sgt. 454 Ord.      14003752            6-29-42
Godden, Arnim E. Pvt. 7 Matl.        6937912            6-29-42
Lecky, Richard L. Pvt. 27 Bomb      15069245            6-29-42
Brown, John R. Pvt. 31 Inf.         19013261  Co. D.    6-29-42
Edwards, Wade Pvt. SC               39602557            6-29-42
Harnline, Theodore E. S/Sgt. 20 Pur 19018302            6-29-42
Bahr, D.G. Sgt. 3 Pur.               6920690            6-29-42
Ryan, Daniel Pfc. CWS               19006227            6-29-42
Capps, Grant B. Pfc. 17 Pur.         6914950            6-29-42
Kimmel, Buryl B. Pvt. Ord.          19002348            6-29-42
Webb, M.S. Cpl. Ord. Tanks          15047087            6-29-42
Bright, Jack R. Pvt. AC             18029826            6-29-42
Nelson, Norman L. Sgt. 33 QMC       19028268            6-29-42
Pheil, Raymond Pvt. 23 Pur.         13024675            6-29-42
Archuleta, M.R. Pvt. 200 CAC        38012334            6-30-42
Thompson, L.R. Pfc. 515 CAC         20800302            6-30-42
Johnson, George M. Pfc. 93 Bomb     19030304            6-30-42
Hughes, Donald Cpl. 409 SC          11018786            6-30-42
Clarno, John A. Pvt. 24 Pur.         6932549            6-30-42
Arnold, James T/Sgt. QMC                                6-30-42
Forsyth, Grant A. Cpl. 93 Bomb       6581308            6-30-42
O'Brien, James W. Pvt. 192 Tank     20500745            6-30-42
Lydic, Wilson F. USMC                301443            6-30-42
Sterman, Earl R. Sgt. 200 CAC       20843602            6-30-42
Hightower, Charlie C. Pvt. 200 CAC  38012311            6-30-42
Lorenz, Delbert T. Cpl. 525 CAC     36203206            6-30-42
Musson, Ralph I. 2/Lt. 27 Bomb      0-424777            6-30-42
Larlec, Douglas Pfc. 17 Pur.         100??82            6-30-42
Radcliff, Clarence Pvt. 515 CAC     30452514            6-30-42
Tkaczuk, Raymond Sgt. 2 OBS         11020714            6-30-42
Newland, Pvt. 20 AB                 25056423            6-30-42
Ewart, R.W. Pvt. QMC                 6025695            6-30-42
Ferguson, George Sgt. QMC            6845380            6-30-42
Gabrielson, C.E.                     6931943            6-30-42
Vallantine, James E. Pfc. 27 Bomb   14014521            6-30-42
Henry, Jacob Pvt. 194 Tank          38100425      .     7-1-42
Geiger, Hubert D. Pfc. 454 Ord.     14038791            7-1-42
Rouse, M.M. Pfc. 93 Bomb            19038019            7-1-42
Rice, Harvey 1/Lt. 194 Tank         0-374798            7-1-42
Leavitt, Earnest E. Pvt. 75 Ord.     6149290            7-1-42
Burgerhondt, John J. Pvt. HPD       19012731            7-1-42
Erickson, Arthur E. Pvt. AC         11024205            7-1-42
Reilly, Donald J. Pfc. 194 Tank     20900684            7-1-42
Prucher, George R. M/Sgt. Tank      20645238            7-1-42
Berger, D.R. Pvt. 192 Tank          20645250            7-1-42
Anderson, Clifford O. Pvt. 27 Bomb  37090568            7-1-42
Wright, William H. Pfc. 3 Bomb      19300442            7-1-42
Bassett, James P. Pvt. 21 Pur.      15018719            7-1-42
Camash, Joseph Pvt. QMC                                 7-1-42
Johnson, George M. Pvt. 2 OBS       11020714            7-1-42
```

```
Padilla, Josa F. Pvt. CWS          19054787                    7-1-42
Whitemore, George Pvt. AC          13030451                    7-1-42
Fisher, Edward 2/Lt. Inf.          0-890355                    7-1-42
Moore, Elbert Pvt. Ord             38032111                    7-1-42
Skramstead, Irwin C. S/Sgt. 3 Pur.  6820461                    7-1-42
Schenk, Leo L. Pfc. AC              6938037                    7-1-42
Foote, Roe V. Pvt. AC              19046398                    7-1-42
Bunyan, Frank Pfc. 31 Inf.         19054940   Co. C.           7-1-42
Keeling, Birchel Pfc. 194 Tank     20523481                    7-1-42
Simon, Russell D. Pvt. 192 Tank    20500244                    7-1-42
Johnston, Howard D. L/Col.         0-12475                     7-2-42
Bates, W.M. Pvt. 31 Inf.           17021087   Co. E.           7-2-42
Bergmann, John C. Pfc. 17 Pur.     16000623                    7-2-42
Schmidtz, Chas. W. Pfc. 19 Bomb    19028812                    7-2-42
Smith, Beverly P. Pfc. 19 AB        6998835                    7-2-42
Hoffman, Emiel O. Pvt. QMC         39677378                    7-2-42
Picone, Thomas Pvt. 31 Inf.        14060790   Co. H.           7-2-42
Connors, John A. Pvt. HPD          12011183                    7-2-42
Padilla, John J. Pvt. 200 CAC      29844195                    7-2-42
McIntosh, Alexander C. Pvt. 200 CAC 20844195                   7-2-42
Roe, Herschell W., 1/Lt. FA        0-309101                    7-2-42
Chilcoat, Harold R. Pvt. CWS       19004354                    7-2-42
Clark, Louis L. Pfc. 200 CAC       20843933                    7-2-42
Sanchez, Adelardov Cpl. 515 CAC    38012204                    7-2-42
Matthias, Walter F. Jr. Pfc.       16010586                    7-2-42
Trout, Robert W. Pfc. 5 Inter.      6667971                    7-2-42
Graham, Raymond Cpl. 192 Tank      35102133                    7-2-42
Lassmann, Charles 2/Lt. AC         0-427449                    7-2-42
Smith, Samuel S. Pfc. AC            6948606                    7-2-42
Finkboner, Wilber Pvt. AC           6938065                    7-2-42
McDonald, Clarence Pfc. AC          6953621                    7-2-42
Kindlesparker, Frk F. S/Sgt. 17 Ord 15061475                  7-2-42
Raymen, Henry E. Pvt. AC           33000612                    7-3-42
Tafoya, Gabriel Pvt. 200 CAC       38012217                    7-3-42
Snell, Harry C. Maj. Ord.          0-240593                    7-3-42
Welch, Paul E. Cpl. 31 Inf.         6549233   A-T Co.          7-3-42
Lewis, Charles Pvt. 19 Bomb        19038077                    7-3-42
Levy, Lester B. Pvt. 28 Matl.      15013329                    7-3-42
Walsdorf, Robert L. Pvt. AC         6911984                    7-3-42
Grayson, Clyde M. Pfc. 194 Tank    20900715                    7-3-42
Wills, Edward Pvt. 192 Tank        20523501                    7-3-42
Pagel, Donald E. 1/Lt. AC          0-404060                    7-3-42
Fechner, Paul A. Pvt. 803 CE       35154537                    7-3-42
Hughes, Kent Pfc. 192 Tank         20643285                    7-3-42
Martin, Vernon A. Pvt. 31 Inf.      6857070   Hq. Co.          7-3-42
Wilson, Willliam L. Pvt. 454 Ord.  35030548                    7-3-42
Allen, Robert Pvt. 803 CE          19017462                    7-3-42
Fox, Ray Cpl. 17 Pur.               6725441                    7-3-42
Cristensen, Stanley E. Sgt. 21 Pur. 6938206                    7-3-42
Boepple, Bernard C. S/Sgt. 3 Pur.   6953693                    7-3-42
Baptista, Edward J. Cpl. 91 Bomb   11024433                    7-3-42
Jones, Carl W. Pvt. 515 CAC        38055544                    7-3-42
Busbin, Earl J. Sgt. 429 SC        19054611                    7-3-42
Ball, J.E. S/Sgt. 192 Tank         20600432                    7-3-42
MacDonald, Frederick Pvt. 7 Matl.  19030389                    7-3-42
Crouder, F.H. Pvt. 200 CAC         46106491                    7-3-42
Woods, Melvin K. Pfc. AC            6949951                    7-3-42
Jacobs, Arlyn C. Pfc. 60 CAC       16008775                    7-3-42
Keener, John R. Pfc. 27 Bomb       13037263                    7-3-42
Miller, Irwin Pvt. AC              13006783                    7-3-42
```

Name	Rank/Unit	Serial	Unit	Date
Goforth, Donald H.	Pfc. 31 Inf.	14043887	Co. F.	7-4-42
Christensen, Albert R.	S/Sgt. & Mat.	19016494		7-4-42
Biedieger, David R.	S/Sgt. 34 Pur.	6272656		7-4-42
Alexander, Granville W.	Sgt. MD.	18021137		7-4-42
White, C.I.	Pvt. 60 CAC	17002897		7-4-42
Unks, Donovan L.	S/Sgt. AC	6253614		7-4-42
Jordon, Henry E.	Pfc. 2 Obs.	6668633		7-4-42
Meyers, Ford H.	Pvt. 93 Bomb	19012799		7-4-42
Stahlman, Paus S.	Cpl. 409 SC	7022743		7-4-42
Harris, Clyde	Sgt. 31 Inf.	17018700	Svc. Co.	7-4-42
Parker, John	Pfc. 803 CE	18015301		7-4-42
Mayhew, Allen E.	Cpt. 91 CAC	0-337521		7-4-42
Cheney, C.G.	Sgt. 3 Pur.	6296959		7-4-42
Spencer, Robert	Cp. SC	12023817		7-4-42
Emerson, Ralph W.	Cpl. 24 Pur.	12023817		7-4-42
Morris, Walter	Sgt. AC	6915664		7-4-42
Symington, John F.	Pvt. 31 Inf.	69738775	Co. M.	7-4-42
Skinner, Edward F.	Cpl. 31 Inf.	6145104	Co. M.	7-4-42
Boutwell, Rufus L.	S/Sgt. 91 Bomb	6971494		7-4-42
Hall, Harold A.	Pvt. 75 Ord.	19051592		7-4-42
Darr, James	Pvt. 7 CWS	18029921		7-4-42
Havlicheck, Grady J.	Pvt. MD	19017306		7-4-42
Fitzgerald, V.F.	M/Sgt. AC	R-83804		7-4-42
Mondati, James	Sgt. 19 AB	6937860		7-4-42
Smith Roy L.	S/Sgt. AC	6373805		7-4-42
Buell, Corbin N.	Pvt. 194 Tank	37006445		7-4-42
Thompson, Donald V.	Pfc. 19 Bomb	6958068		7-4-42
Ruckman, Oscar	Sgt. 200 CAC	20843578		7-4-42
McDermott, Barnard	Sgt. 31 Inf.	R-1522488	Co. A.	7-4-42
Demaray, Ralph E.	Cpl. 7 CWS	36152247	Co. D.Replacement	7-4-42
Brown, E.R.	1/Cl. USN	3758426		7-4-42
Starnes, Charles	Sgt. 31 Inf.	6295201	Co. M.	7-4-42
Looney, Robert K.	Pvt. MD	13032379		7-4-42
Williams, Edwin V.	Cpl QMC	19054971		7-4-42
Coulter, Adrian J.	Pfc. 194 Tank	37025747		7-4-42
DuBois, Robert E.	Pvt. 200 CAC	20842701		7-4-42
Brozovich, George	Pvt. 34 Pur.	15012908		7-4-42
Norris, Jimmy	Pvt. 200 CAC	38011256		7-4-42
Benner, Charles A.	M/Sgt. AC	6538365		7-5-42
Dondich, Alexander	Pfc. 7 CWS	19056925	*	7-5-42
Hirsh, Robert W.	Pfc. 194 Tank	6569362		7-5-42
Ottmer, William C.	Pfc. 429 SC	19028609		7-5-42
Thomas, Charles E.	Pvt. 7 CWS	19039160	Co. K.Replacement	7-5-42
Johanson, Gilbert A.	Pvt. 31 Inf.	17018731	Co. C.	7-5-42
Clark, John S.	Pvt. Pvt. 31 Inf.	7021072	Hq Det 1/Bn	7-5-42
White, Glen L.	Pvt. 194 Tank	37037364		7-5-42
Hernandez, E.E.	Pvt. 515 CAC	38029615		7-5-42
Hickman, Rodney H.	Cpl. QMC	6952360		7-5-42
Curtis, Arnold R.	Pfc. 808 MP	20938876		7-5-42
Howard, Clarence	Sgt. 3 Pur.	18026108		7-5-42
Byard, Robert A.	Pfc. 200 CAC	20843805		7-5-42
Serio, Frank J.	Pfc. AC	13024348		7-5-42
Mislay, Michael	Cpl. 27 Matl.			7-5-42
Miller,	Pfc AC			7-5-42
Sadler, Adolph	Pvt. 24 Pur.			7-5-42
Lavighe, R.F.	Pvt. 17 Bomb	11013653		7-5-42
Martinez, Pete		6276084		7-5-42
Ziembo, Henry J.	Pfc. 19 AB	6977383		7-5-42
Fotte, Earl F.	Pfc. QMC	6935214		7-5-42
Lofton, Woodrous P.	Pvt. 194 Tank	38020935		7-5-42

242

```
Soper, George G. 1/Lt. AGD          0-360966                        7-6-42
Wilson, Robert Paul Pvt. 48 Matl.   14029183                        7-6-42
Day, Alfred R. Pvt 27 Bomb          16019564                        7-6-42
Gummersall, Henry P. HPD            19011474                        7-6-42
Gosney, Victor L. Sgt. 194 Tank     20900679                        7-6-42
Garrnet, Perry W. Pvt. 21 Pur.      18029882                        7-6-42
Carter, William M. Pfc. AC          6947645                         7-6-42
Johnson, Elmer M. Pvt. 14 Bomb      6979212                         7-6-42
Schervan, Theodore Pvt. 27 Mat.     11010341                        7-6-42
Cheholts, Harry Pvt. 7 CMS          19017627   Co. G.Replacement    7-6-42
Taylor, Floyd D. Pfc. 31 Inf.       17002833   Co. G.              7-6-42
McFarland, David R. Sgt. 3 Pur.     6588742                         7-6-42
Ortiz, Frank Pvt. 200 CAC           38011249                        7-6-42
Lucas, Eugene Pfc. 745 Ord.         18004979                        7-6-42
Moulton, James C. Pvt. 200 CAC      20843151                        7-6-42
Kalish, Harvey M. Pvt. AG           11010496                        7-6-42
Jordon, Walter A. Sgt. 808 MP       18001771                        7-6-42
Absher, James W. Pfc. 429 SC        14049744                        7-6-42
Pawlikowski, Jesse Pfc. 2 Obs.      6564545                         7-6-42
Greene, William J. Pvt. 194 Tank    39006623                        7-6-42
Biggood, Gerald M. Pvt. 19 Bomb     20903355                        7-6-42
Sandoval, Arthur R. Cpl. 515 CAC    20844146                        7-6-42
Fierro, Miguel S Pvt. 200 CAC       38011857                        7-6-42
Fabry, Paul Pvt. 20 Ab              13006664                        7-6-42
Baca, Edward Pvt. 200 CAC           38035320                        7-6-42
Burnett, Ross W. Pvt. AC            19018893                        7-6-42
Black, Jack M. Pvt. 808 MP          6398248                         7-6-42
Daniels, Elgin W. Pvt. 4 CWS        17027608                        7-6-42
Parke, Allen A. Pvt. 59 CAC         17001762                        7-6-42
McKellup, Paul V. Cpl. 12 MP        6558500                         7-6-42
Midboe, Howard T. Pvt. 429 SC       19018046                        7-6-42
Rhodes, J. Pfc. 7 Mat.              17013521                        7-6-42
McAllister, Grover C. Pvt. 27 Bomb  14014452                        7-6-42
Ayers, Odell W. Pvt. 20 AB          13014818                        7-6-42
Regina, Samuel Anthony Pvt. 20 AB   33033866                        7-7-42
Taylor, Keith E. Pvt. 17 Ord.       15061415                        7-7-42
Tatro, Charles F. Pvt. 808 MP       11019003                        7-7-42
Robinson, George W. Sgt. 515 CAC    20843823                        7-7-42
Sherman, Kenneth Cpl. 31 Inf.       6554974    Co. B.              7-7-42
Dixon, Melvin E. Pfc. 24 Pur.       6936422                         7-7-42
Fitzgerald, J.C. 1/Lt. Inf.         0-386334                        7-7-42
Jones, Curtis C. cpl 515 CAC        20843941                        7-7-42
Quintana, Martin Pvt. 515 CAC       38012453                        7-7-42
Chapin, Melton F. Pvt. 440 Ord.     16012266                        7-7-42
Harrison, Harry Cpl. 31 Inf.        6955648    Co. F.              7-7-42
Williford, Ralph C. Pvt. 194 Tank   20932906                        7-7-42
Warren, Roderick E. Cpl. 515 CAC    20843792                        7-7-42
Bence, Robert B. Pfc. 34 Pur.       13030327                        7-7-42
Shanks, LaVerne R. Pvt. 680 Ord.    13027376                        7-7-42
Alkire, John W. Pfc. AC             19019178                        7-7-42
Archuleta, Amedo G. Pvt. 200 CAC    38012407                        7-7-42
Bertrand, Robert P. Pvt. 20 AB      11017188                        7-7-42
Cummins, Claire C. Pfc. 693 Ord.    19054602                        7-7-42
Medalock, F.D. Sgt. 93 Bomb         19054602                        7-7-42
Armijo, Carlos A. Cpl. 515 CAC      38012489                        7-7-42
Throp, Joseph M. Pvt. 194 Tank      20900755                        7-7-42
Conoway, Rolland L. Sgt. 34 Pur.    18003407                        7-7-42
Gilbert, Walton L. Pvt. 34 Pur.     20939265                        7-7-42
Bostedt, J.O. Cpl. 3 Pur.           17011358                        7-7-42
Kenneson, Russell F. Pvt. 48 Matl.  11015381                        7-7-42
```

```
Swaggart, Rex Cpl. 515 CAC          36106367                        7-7-42
Abbott, Gideon B. Pvt. 27 Mat.      11013328                        7-7-42
Liversberg, Leon J. Pvt. 19 Bomb    13031346                        7-7-42
Scanlon, Jennings, B. Sgt. 192 Tank 20523462                        7-8-42
Roberts, Benjamin M. Pvt. 48 Mat.   6956067                         7-8-42
Wotten, William T. S/Sgt. AC        6563850                         7-8-42
Pacheco, B. Pfc. 515 CAC            20842728                        7-8-42
Rominger, Norman W. Pfc. 19 Bomb    19030292                        7-8-42
Kahn, Julius Pvt. 803 CE            32081719                        7-8-42
Hatlevig, Kenneth R. Pfc. 192 Tank  20645260                        7-8-42
McCann, Gerald Pvt. 7 CWS           32092865   Co. E.Replacement    7-8-42
Kaplan, George Pfc. 680 Ord.        6139458                         7-8-42
Haws, Lamont J. Sgt. 680 Ord        19010506                        7-8-42
Schiess, R. Pvt.                                                    7-8-42
Stetler, Delos W. Pfc. 31 Inf.      19052073   Co. E.              7-8-42
Anderson, Alvin A. Pfc.             6558161                         7-8-42
Smith, William E. Pvt. 454 Ord.     14040115                        7-8-42
Lunasse, Edgar C. Pvt. 200 CAC      38011980                        7-8-42
Dixon, James O. Cpl AC              6266504                         7-8-42
Finch, Harvey L. Pfc. 194 Tank      20700228                        7-8-42
Burris, Nalcon Sgt. 7 Matl.         6914336                         7-6-42
King, Fred Pfc. 192 Tank            20645264                        7-8-42
Nicholson, Kenneth Cpl. AC          6584477                         7-8-42
Horton, George E. Pvt. SC           13009698                        7-8-42
Garcia, Fidel Pfc. 515 CAC          38012165                        7-8-42
Calliahan, Clinton B. Pvt. AC       36125958                        7-8-42
Mathewson, Dtanley G. Sgt. 228 SC   6130770                         7-8-42
Vaughan, Milton J. 2/Lt. QMC        0-890106                        7-8-42
Simons, John Sgt. 27 Bomb           6384965                         7-8-42
Bisset, Warren R. Pvt. 680 Ord.     19000559                        7-8-42
Douglas, Eugene T. Pfc. 680 Ord.    18051589                        7-8-42
Curranza, Angle Pfc. 7 Mat.         19038524                        7-8-42
Simmens, Robert H. Cpl. 20 AB       6938035                         7-8-42
Shouse, Blaine W. S/Sgt. 91 Bomb    6743064                         7-8-42
Mitchell, Robert N. Sgt. 194 Tank   20900653                        7-9-42
Mariette, Rex S. Cpl. 17 Pur.       16010595                        7-9-42
Corbett, Frederick G. Cpl. 745 Ord. 6978272                         7-9-42
Wasson, DeWayne E. Pfc. 192 Tank    20645245                        7-9-42
Langland, Wayman Sgt. 5 Inter.      6677192                         7-9-42
Harren, Claude W. Pvt. 194 Tank     20149134                        7-9-42
Spalek, Robert Cpl. 31 Inf.         6262629    A-T Co.             7-9-42
Boyle, Frederick Pfc. QMC                                          7-9-42
Jenson, Leathem Pvt. QMC                                           7-9-42
Nelson, Jessie J. Pvt. 31 Inf.      17014244   A-T Co.             7-9-42
O'Brien, P. S/Sgt. QMC              6129151                         7-9-42
Jencik, John T. Pfc. 31 Inf.        6239398    Co. C.              7-9-42
Hilard, Guy W. Pfc. 200 CAC         20843806                        7-9-42
Ferris, John Civilian                                              7-9-42
Freeman, William H. Pvt.            11008268                        7-10-42
Condon, Frank H. Pvt. 194 Tank      39156410                        7-10-42
Weber, Irving Cpl. AC               19051636                        7-10-42
King, Harry Pvt. 31 Inf.            13025004   *                   7-10-42
Akey, Vernon P. Pvt. 803 CE         18013746                        7-10-42
Clevenger, Pearlie L. S/Sgt. 192 Tank 20700207                     7-10-42
Looney, Chas. H. Pvt. 192 Tank      14016182                        7-10-42
Olsen, Gerald O. Cpl. 17 Ord.       15061403                        7-10-42
Mullis, Jas. H. Jr. Pvt. 27 bomb    14011888                        7-10-42
Games, W.F. Pvt. 406 SC             19002754                        7-10-42
Chavez, Barto Pvt. 200 CAC          38012333                        7-10-42
Sauer, Robert S. Cpt. 31 Inf.       0-237051   Co. E.              7-10-42
```

```
Norenberg, Earl Pvt. 31 Inf.          16008523   Co. E.        7-10-42
Hjulstad, Alvine Pvt. 194 Tank        37025797                 7-10-42
Claunch, Arthur Pvt. QMC               6960530                 7-10-42
Abel, Charles E. Cpl. 2 OBS            6936224                 7-10-42
Mitchell, W.S. Pvt.                    6281388                 7-10-42
Hicks, Lawrence E. Sgt. 31 Inf.        6629433   Co. B.        7-10-42
Boggs, William C. S/Sgt. AC           16011421                 7-10-42
Greenough, Harold Pvt. QMC            19038503                 7-10-42
Edmund, Mills N. Pvt. 27 Bomb         34118581                 7-10-42
Pysz, Walter S/Sgt.                   21614341                 7-11-42
Rye, Elmo M. Pfc. 2 Obs.              16017675                 7-11-42
McGraw, John J. Pfc. AC                6580821                 7-11-42
Grinchsel, Charles B. Sgt. 20 Pur.    11608286                 7-11-42
Gilmer, Claude Cpl. 194 Tank          20700232                 7-11-42
Jordan, Frank Pfc. 17 Bomb            11010494                 7-11-42
Yeager, Leland D. Pvt. 680 Ord.       39007447                 7-11-42
Moss, John D. Cpl. 515 CAC            20843560                 7-11-42
Thompson, Harvey W. Pvt. QMC          19038810                 7-11-42
Fabrizio, Maurice A. Sgt. 7 Mat.       6291052                 7-11-42
Robertson, Frank K. Pvt. QMC          19024152                 7-11-42
Murphy, John E. Pvt. 31 Inf.          16008558   Co. B.        7-11-42
Moore, Clifford J. Pfc. 16 bomb       11013684                 7-11-42
Kirkman, Howard Pfc. 680 Ord.         19017764                 7-11-42
Campbell, John F. Pfc. 192 Tank       20645229                 7-11-42
Quitmeyer, Arnold R. Sgt. MD           6936172                 7-11-42
Bookwalter, E.J. Pvt. QMC             15057274                 7-11-42
McCallum, Richard S/Sgt. CWS          14037577                 7-11-42
Campbell, Verne G. Pfc. 194 Tank      37025834                 7-11-42
Bernardo, J.J. Pvt. 194 Tank          39002457                 7-11-42
Rabbitt, Thomas J. Pvt. 3 Pur.        13025098                 7-11-42
Becker, Julius Pvt. 7 CWS             19056963                 7-11-42
Wesley, Macey W. Pvt. QMC             19046314                 7-11-42
Veillette, Byron L. S/Sgt. 194 Tank   20700193                 7-11-42
Chower, Max W.O.  31 Inf.                        Svc. Co.      7-12-42
Smith, Raymond C. Pfc. 228 SC         19028768                 7-12-42
Lawson, John F. Pvt. 194 Tank         39231031                 7-12-42
Horton, LeRoy C. Cpl. 7 CWS           19013626                 7-12-42
Terhune, Yandell C. S/Sgt. 192 Tank   20523435                 7-12-42
Stevens, Clifford G. Pvt. 194 Tank    20900750                 7-12-42
Zempel, Clarence J. Pvt. Ord          18046279                 7-12-42
Wright, Frank L. S/Sgt.               19017702                 7-12-42
Mangel, Milo B. S/Sgt. 3 Pur.          6574293                 7-12-42
Klein, Lawrence N. Pvt. QMC            7033586                 7-12-42
Glass, Harry b. 2/Lt. FA             0-980456                  7-12-42
Wilson, Henry E. Pvt. 31 Inf.         19017702   Hq. Co.       7-12-42
Wilson, James R. Pvt. 19 AB           17030547                 7-12-42
Adams, Roland C. Cpl. 17 Pur.         11022028                 7-12-42
Smith, Clarence Jr. Pvt.              17002787                 7-12-42
Lefebvre, Francis W. Cpl.             11010378   *             7-12-42
Horton, Hrold Sgt. 27 Bomb             7001090                 7-12-42
Schacki, Gene J. Pfc. 17 Ord.         15016374                 7-12-42
Ellingson, Ardel S. Pvt. 31 Inf.       6565896   Co. G.        7-12-42
Gordon, Lewis L. Sgt. 34 Pur.          6693519                 7-12-42
Sloan, Max R. Pfc. 27 Bomb             6268041                 7-12-42
Miller, Merrill F. S/Sgt. 803 CE       6065360                 7-12-42
DeCant, Chester S. Pfc. 192 Tank      20500758                 7-12-42
Dominckowski, A. Pvt. 60 CAC           6133458                 7-12-42
Phenix, L. E. Jr. Pvt. 803 CE         12006799                 7-12-42
Bailey, Gordon M. Pfc. 31 Inf.         6980706   Co. G.        7-12-42
Bolan, Walter A. Pvt. 19 AB            6563476                 7-12-42
```

245

```
Boye, Albert F. Pfc 429 SC          39302771                      7-12-42
Demarets, Gilbert Pvt. 91 Bomb       7002616                      7-12-42
Stover, Russell Pvt. 31 Inf.         6704206   Hq. Det. 3 Bn.     7-12-42
Cackburn George H. Cpt. Inf.         0-346723                     7-12-42
Edwards, Billy Cpl. 19 Bomb          6957207                      7-12-42
Lassor, Richard D. Pvt. 48 Matl.    10017696                      7-12-42
Bryant, Francis E. Pvt. 31 Inf.      6290089   Co. I.             7-12-42
Lyons, P. John Pvt. 24 Pur.          6910539                      7-12-42
Mills, John A. Jr. Sgt. 27 Bomb      7008834                      7-12-42
Barry, Howard C. Sgt. 194 Tank      39378190                      7-12-42
Reader, Penrod L. Sgt. 16 Bomb       6915752                      7-12-42
Nesbitt, Joseph L.                  13013444   *                  7-12-42
Degraftenreid, Joe B. 2/Lt. AC       0-411945                     7-12-42
Zavota, Antonio Pvt. AC             11011688                      7-12-42
Pomillo, Anthony, Cpl. 200 CAC      37053685                      7-12-42
Kelly, Andrew J. Pvt. 194 Tank      37026128                      7-12-42
Hiatt, Richard C. Pvt. 31 Inf.      17018657   Hq. Det. 1 Bn.     7-12-42
Hamilton, Charles Pfc. 3 Pur.        6548189                      7-12-42
Boyer, F. Pvt. 7 CWS                37053244                      7-12-42
Bostick, Robert Pvt. 91 Bomb        14014387                      7-12-42
Lerma, Juan S. Pvt. 200 CAC         38012190                      7-12-42
Morrow, J.P. Pfc. 31 Inf.            6254359   Hq. Co.            7-13-42
Anders, John W. Pfc. 28 Matl.        6892020                      7-13-42
Barnes, W.M. Cpl. 200 CAC           38012654                      7-13-42
Vanasse, Andrew W. Pvt. 31 Inf.     11007574   Hq. Det. 1 Bn.     7-13-42
Nackley, N.P. Pvt. 31 Inf.          17016180   Co. L.             7-13-42
McDonald, Arthur Cpl. QMC            6562172                      7-13-42
Murphy, James A. Pfc. 17 Bomb        7002108                      7-13-42
Irvine, Frederick Pvt. 14 Bomb      16012619                      7-13-42
Williams, Melvin S. Pfc. 24 Pur.     6284009                      7-13-42
Young, George Pvt. 31 Inf.          10306791   *                  7-13-42
Shamblin, Fred A. Sgt. 93 Bomb       6880537                      7-13-42
Wagner, Harry W. Sgt. 24 Pur.        6828892                      7-13-42
Hayward, J.E. Pvt.                  19052513                      7-13-42
Vargus, Eddie G. Sgt. 27 Bomb        6265027                      7-13-42
Beck, Garrison B. Sgt. 515 CAC                                   7-13-42
McDon Emmit A. Pvt. 194 Tank                                     7-13-42
Thompson, Francis E. Jr. Cpl. 7 Mat.19049417                      7-13-42
Church, Darrell Cpl. 31 Inf.         6890727   Hq. Det. 2 Bn.     7-13-42
Calkins, Lew L. Sgt. 200 CAC        20842673                      7-13-42
Koppenhaven, Geo. Pvt. QMC          13029096                      7-13-42
Johnson, Earl B. Pfc. 21 Pur.       19015094                      7-13-42
Lovering, Fred W. Pvt. 192 tank     20600467                      7-13-42
Meyer, Vermont L. Pfc. 200 CAC      38012127                      7-13-42
Blanton, Garland D. Sgt. 19 Bomb     6914076                      7-13-42
Jepson, Lloyd C. Pvt. 19 Bomb       19046035                      7-13-42
Smith, Henry L. Pvt. 515 CAC        36050828                      7-13-42
Turner, Irby C. Pvt. 31 Inf.        14060875   Co. F.             7-13-42
Matlack, Charles E. Ppt 803 CE       6936770                      7-13-42
Foshee, Dorsey W. Pvt. 194 T\ank    20900710                      7-13-42
Mitchell, Charles Sgt. 200 CAC      20843757                      7-13-42
Wood. Henry F. Cpl. 16 Bomb         32044013                      7-13-42
McKenzie, A.W. Pvt. 31 Inf.         11009530   Co. L.             7-13-42
Degreness, Henning O. Pvt. 31 Inf.   6859010   Hq. Co.            7-13-42
Stover, Donald A. Sgt. 27 Mat.       6735523                      7-14-42
Howland. Warren A. Pfc. 680 Ord.     6572609                      7-14-42
Reinhardt, Lawrence W. Pfc. QMC     19004029                      7-14-42
Sproat, Carl R. Pvt. 21 Pur.        15048196                      7-14-42
Wilson, C.M. Pvt. 31 Inf.            6852931   Co. K.             7-14-42
King, David B. S/Sgt. 5 Inter        6571267                      7-14-42
```

```
Eddy, Eugene L. Pvt. 7 Mat.          19051899                        7-14-42
Goscha, Ambrose A. Pfc. 23 Pur.       6291037                        7-14-42
Monroe, Wilbur Pvt. 48 Matl.         18014366                        7-14-42
Harding, Leslie Pfc. 19 Bomb          6571973                        7-14-42
Luce, Denny M. Pfc. 3 Pur.            6953597                        7-14-42
Richards, Noel M. Pvt. 31 Inf.       17031024   Co. M.              7-14-42
Roper, O. Sgt. 515 CAC               38012331                        7-14-42
Tarbet, W. V. 1/Lt. CE               0-338678                        7-14-42
Luther, Robert N. Cpl. 200 CAC       20843968                        7-14-42
Goll, Kermit L. Cpl. 515 CAC         38030936                        7-14-42
Smithies, Verdel S. Cpl. MD          19018966                        7-14-42
Hill, John B. PVt. 75 Ord.            6265786                        7-14-42
Endsley, Nolan Pvt. 17 Bomb           7002920                        7-14-42
Beaver, Earnest A. Pvt. 7 Matl.       6529144                        7-14-42
Thomas, Kenneth C. Cpl. 194 Tank     37025881                        7-14-42
Savoie, David C. Pfc. 200 CAC        38012626                        7-14-42
Morton, H.S. Lt/Jg. USNR                                            7-14-42
Ivey, Charles D. Pfc. QMC            38002277                        7-14-42
Halton, Charles J. Sgt. AC            6582548                        7-14-42
Kramer, Alton R. T/Sgt. 7 Matl.       6564887                        7-14-42
Willrodt, Joseph E. Pvt. 194 Tank    20900760                        7-14-42
Valyon, Richard Pfc. 16 Bomb         11017277                        7-14-42
Porter, Glemwood Pvt. 31 Inf.         6930920   A-T Co.             7-14-42
Gionfriddo, E.A. Pfc. 17 Pur.        11010319                        7-14-42
Medley, Claudel Pvt. 16 Bomb          6969597                        7-14-42
Heinrich, Jacob Cpt. Inf.            0-257751                        7-15-42
Brown, Herchel G. Pfc. AC            15061980                        7-15-42
Remington, J.W. 2/Lt. QMC            0-324389                        7-15-42
Donnelly, Francis E. Cpl. 515 CAC    38012521                        7-15-42
Raymond. Wm. L. Pfc. 17 Pur.          6913485                        7-15-42
Solis, Lasaro Pvt. 31 Inf.           18035290   Co. M.              7-15-42
Davis, Wells S. Sr. Pvt.              6152472                        7-15-42
Young, Ralph W. EMKRL USN           316-34-90                       7-15-42
Shope, Robert Sgt. 93 Bomb            6577853                        7-15-42
Manzone, Joe C. Pfc. 31 Inf.         12028024   Co. G.              7-15-42
Mangold, Melton M. Pfc. 7 Matl.      16016294                        7-15-42
Deacon, John C,. Cpl.                16005485                        7-15-42
Clark, Vincent D. Pvt. 20 Pur.       19014681                        7-15-42
Kearney, Ralph J. S/Sgt. 20 Pur.      6393831                        7-15-42
Trumble, Benjamin E. 2/Lt. Inf.      0-890407   Co. C.              7-15-42
Jankipweiz, Joseph S. Pvt.893 CE     32036236                        7-15-42
Bridgeman, Patrick F. Pvt. 31 Inf.   19020776   Co. L.              7-15-42
Doucette, Joseph C. Pvt. 28 Matl.    11020622                        7-15-42
Thomson, Norman D. Sgt. 29 Pur.       6579592                        7-15-42
Skinner, Clifton R. Pfc. 17 Bomb      6971421                        7-15-42
Scott, John 1st. 31 Inf.             0-364132   Co. F.              7-16-42
Everts, Marvin Pvt. 194 Tank         20943827                        7-16-42
Dominguez, Joe N. Pfc. 4 Matl.         290920                        7-16-42
Ellis, Edward R. Sgt. 17 Pur.        18037551                        7-16-42
Hughes, Norman F. Pvt. 745 Ord.       6578433                        7-16-42
Brink, Alfred E. M/Sgt. 200 CAC      20844122                        7-16-42
Leahy, A. 2/Lt. 31 Inf.              0-890301   Svc. Co.            7-16-42
Van Beuning, John G. Cpl. 200 CAC    36050857                        7-16-42
McIntosh, Joe 1/Lt. CE               0-394696                        7-16-42
Casseday, Robert B. T/Sgt. CE         6276656                        7-16-42
Keele, William D. Pfc. QMC           19014936                        7-16-42
Calvin, Bernard J. Pfc. 17 Pur.      11017556                        7-16-42
Cash, Robert W. Pvt. 27 Mat.         17025678                        7-16-42
Mashatt, Henry Pl Pvt. 20 AB         11020716                        7-16-42
Meyer, William H. S/Sgt. 515 CAC     20842688                        7-16-42
```

247

Young, Charles E. T/Sgt. SC	39159623		7-16-42
Gutterman, Jacob Pvt. 803 CE	12020716		7-16-42
Murphy, Bernard J. Cpl. 3 Pur.	17021310		7-16-42
Aaron, James Pvt. 31 Inf.	14047056	Co. K.	7-16-42
Young, James W. Pfc. 7 Matl.	19011233		7-16-42
Engle, Kenneth W. Pvt.	32033721		7-16-42
Lane, Ivan E. Pfc. 19 AB	19019505		7-16-42
Morgan, Thomas H. Sgt. 19 Bomb	6297727		7-16-42
Kolb. Edward L. Sgt. 192 Tank	20600415		7-16-42
Quintana, Pat A. Cpl. 515 CAC	20843128		7-16-42
Frey, Clinton E. Pvt. 93 Bomb	19050844		7-16-42
Clark, Paul F. Pvt. SC	19017201		7-16-42
Lee, Willis W. S/Sgt. 24 Pur.	6395983		7-16-42
Lopez Nicolas Pvt. 200 CAC	38031294		7-16-42
Salasar, Manuel Pvt. 515 CAC	38029763		7-16-42
Nestor, William Sgt. 803 CE	6814001		7-17-42
Ammon, William C. Pfc. 28 Matl.	7020726		7-17-42
Vincent, Homer Pvt. 228 SC	6297783		7-17-42
Douglas, W.L. Jr. Sgt. 19 Bomb	6551933		7-17-42
Law, James E. Pfc. 93 Bomb	6915985		7-17-42
Rimgler, Harry E. 1/Sgt. 31 Inf.	6631692	Co. B.	7-17-42
Wright, Leslie N. Pfc. 21 Pur.	19014002		7-17-42
Johnson, Norman J. Pvt. 91 Bomb	18044253		7-17-42
Columbero, Tony Pfc. 20 AB	6571780		7-17-42
Covey, Hershell L. S/Sgt. 24 Pur.	6656424		7-17-42
O'Brien, Wayne Cpl. 200 CAC	36203177		7-17-42
Slee, William Pfc. 27 Matl.	16029233		7-17-42
Diemer, R.R. Pvt. 803 CE	35017671		7-17-42
Johnson, Harry F. S/Sgt. 429 SC	6546359		7-17-42
McMahon, Arthur J. Civilian			7-17-42
Schavanek, Joe Pfc. 200 CAC	20843584		7-17-42
Copeland, Gido Pvt. 200 CAC	38011158		7-17-42
Lichty, Donald R. Pvt. 31 Inf.	19020684	Co. C.	7-18-42
Barnett, Arthur Pfc. 31 Inf.	6903568	Svc. Co.	7-18-42
Powers, Charles Pfc. 8 Matl.	19028288		7-18-42
Greenberg, Herman Pvt. 200 CAC	36106751		7-18-42
Frank, W.S. Pvt. 31 Inf.	12004304	Co. I.	7-18-42
Frame, Kenneth Sgt. 200 CAC	20842703		7-18-42
Fromyer, Phillip S. Pvt. 24 Pur.	13009866		7-18-42
Franco, Porfirioc Jr. Pvt. 200 CAC	18012544		7-18-42
Godinho, Walter S. Pvt. AC	11024502		7-18-42
Calanchi, Louis B. Pvt. 200 CAC			7-18-42
Max, Joseph S/Sgt. 19 Bomb	6948921		7-18-42
Harrison, Gordon R. Pvt. Ord.	14037641		7-18-42
Graves, Jasper E. Sgt. 3 Pur.	13001467		7-18-42
Wilson, Thomas D. Cpl. 31 Inf.	17018698	Co. G.	7-18-42
Fitzgerald, Joseph F. Pvt. CWS	32044030		7-18-42
Robertson, J.W. Pfc. 48 Matl.	6971454		7-18-42
Silva, Joseph H. Pfc. SC	12028854		7-18-42
Givins, James C. Pvt. 698 Ord.	18035213		7-18-42
Perea, Tom Pvt. 200 CAC	38011844		7-18-42
Hedlund, Richard E. Cpl. 31 Inf.	6856886	Co. L.	7-18-42
Chowder, Max WO 31 Inf.		Svc. Co.	7-18-42
Parker, William H. Pfc. 7 Matl.	6680585		7-18-42
Renick, Richard E. Pvt. AC	6580586		7-18-42
Warren, Ira Pvt. 194 Tank	35206933		7-19-42
Tyler, R.L. Sgt. 5 Bomb	6296953		7-19-42
Thomas, Norman R. Pfc. 48 Matl.	14026129		7-19-42
Alt, Titus L. Pfc. 31 Inf.	6894469	Svc. Co.	7-19-42
Bass, Franke E. Pvt. 17 Pur.	19000785		7-19-42

```
Crook, Wesley W. Pfc. 31 Inf.        19010289   Hq. Det. 3 Bn.    7-19-42
Goings, White S. Jr. Sgt. 93 Bomb    19050351                     7-19-42
Hurt, James A. Cpl. 17 Pur.          16039734                     7-19-42
Kellet, Walter Cpl. 17 Pur.          16020322                     7-19-42
Schultz, Henry E. Pvt. M.D.          20916287                     7-19-42
Smith, Elwood L. Pvt.                12023724                     7-19-42
Sumlin, John Q. Pfc. AC               6583275                     7-19-42
Sutton, Vernon Pvt. 31 Inf.          19052488   Co. D. Bro- Orv   7-19-42
Bennett, Franklin H. Cpl. 429 SC     19018035                     7-19-42
Eeds, Charles M. Cpl. 48 Matl.        6485852                     7-19-42
Emerick, James B. Pvt. 31 Inf.        6264252   Hq. Co.           7-19-42
Evans, Wayne M. Pfc. 59 CAC          19054551                     7-19-42
Green, Elden B. Pvt. 7 Matl.         19051897                     7-19-42
Holman, David E. S/Sgt. 54 Bomb       6460729                     7-19-42
Jenne, C.A. Jr. Sgt. 21 Pur.         19011209                     7-19-42
Johnson, Leo S/Sgt. 31 Inf.           6339238   Svc. Co.          7-19-42
Lex, Lillard Pfc. M.D.               18043887                     7-19-42
Mashburn, William C. Pvt. HPD        34054152                     7-19-42
Pierce, Arthur Pfc. 803 CE           11007114                     7-19-42
Tash, J.R. Pvt. 31 Inf.              17016200   Co. F.            7-19-42
Sexton, Doyle W. Pvt. 19 Bomb        19011223                     7-19-42
Regester, Lester L. Pvt. 680 Ord.    39602376                     7-19-42
Crotty, Thomas Lt.(SG) USN                                        7-19-42
Johnson, Burling GM2c USN            321-17-79                    7-19-42
McLeod, Eugene P. Sgt. 24 Pur.        7030329                     7-19-42
Leckron, Cecil B. Pvt. 7 CWS         35004707                     7-19-42
Kujawski, Raumonmd W. S/Sgt. DEML    19056801                     7-19-42
Fast, Arthur H. T/Sgt. AC             6554443                     7-19-42
Thoeny, Robert L. Cpl 21 Pur.        19018367                     7-19-42
Bryan, Morris S. Pfc. 93 Bomb         6592458                     7-19-42
Kimble, Roy E. Pfc. 21 Pur.           6587294                     7-19-42
Vogel, Herbert Pfc. 803 CE           32082065                     7-19-42
Sloan, Harry C. Cpl. 48 Matl.         6236507                     7-19-42
Christy, George Pvt. 194 Tank        20720091                     7-19-42
Gilliam, Jessie J. SK2c USN          287-40-32                    7-19-42
Kosticki, Pfc.                       13011128                     7-19-42
Stroud, Marvin Pvt. 31 Inf.          15081807   Co. H.            7-19-42
Caizer, J.T. Pvt. 31 Inf.            19014816   Co. A.            7-20-42
Colson, Edward L. Pvt. 60 CAC        17014147                     7-20-42
Borden, Jerald A. Cpl. 60 CAC         6982111                     7-20-42
Stafford, George Pvt. 2 Obs.          6888288                     7-20-42
Dodrill, Garrett F. Pfc. 27 Matl.     6754266                     7-20-42
Lewis, Harold S. Capt.               0-267080                     7-20-42
Skokowski, alexander Pfc.             6141601                     7-20-42
Barron, Ernest C. Pvt. 200 CAC       38012576                     7-20-42
Hyatt, Willie W. Pfc. 454 Ord.       14040636                     7-20-42
Walters, Harold C. T/Sgt. 20 Pur.     6249090                     7-20-42
Reed, Douglas J. Pvt. 31 Inf.        19056955   Co. G.            7-20-42
Jones, Beaumont Pfc. 454 Ord.        34141741                     7-20-42
Duchscher, Edward A. Pfc. 429 SC      6568865                     7-20-42
Macormic, Ora A. Pfc. 7 CWS          37053503                     7-20-42
Erwin, Jack 1/Lt. M.I.               0-337557                     7-20-42
Lawson, Raymond P. CM  USN                                        7-20-42
Talbott, Carol M. Capt. 31 Inf.      0-21313    Co. K.            7-20-42
Moses, John B. Cpl. 515 CAC          38030988                     7-20-42
Hoague, Thoedor Pvt. 17 Bomb         11015328                     7-20-42
Ash. Philip H. 2/Lt.                 0-417679                     7-20-42
James, John A. Cpl. 200 CAC          38012587                     7-20-42
Farland, Paul E. Pvt. QMC             6954417                     7-20-42
Brown, Bill W. S/Sgt. 515 CAC        20843135                     7-20-42
```

```
Sestak, M.J. Pvt. 24 Pur.            6982032                  7-20-42
Ward, Bill H. 1/Lt. 26 CAV           0-37022                  7-20-42
Landrus, William W. Cpl. 34 Pur.     19000724                 7-21-42
Line, George W. Pvt. 93 Bomb         19002188                 7-21-42
Espinosa, Damian Cpl. 200 CAC        20843321                 7-21-42
Sherman, Herbert Pvt. 515 CAC        38012004                 7-21-42
Campbell, Craig F. Pvt.              19006320                 7-21-42
Baile, Samuel H. Pfc. 680 Ord.       36150420                 7-21-42
Hammond, Robert H. Pvt. 19 AB        18044271                 7-21-42
Donaldson, David Pvt. QMC            19038342                 7-21-42
Dyer, Harold D. Pvt. 31 Inf.         18049206     Co. F.      7-21-42
Hall, John D. Pvt 31 Inf.            14043892     Co. F.      7-21-42
Quimby, Fred E. Pvt. 27 Matl.        11015230                 7-21-42
Miller, LaMont Pvt. 93 Bomb          19002244                 7-21-42
Trotter, George W. T/Sgt. 31 Inf.    6740643      Hq. Co.     7-21-42
Valek, Antone C. Jr. AMM1c USN       223-38-59                7-21-42
Hendon, Theodore W. Pfc. 194 Tank    20956906                 7-21-42
Horn, Wilbur R. Pvt. AC              12010731                 7-21-42
Ernst, Raymond M. Pvt.  DEML         19002795                 7-21-42
Grimmer, F.H. Capt. CAC              0-325929                 7-21-42
Brown, Carl A. M/Sgt. QMC            6821785                  7-21-42
Perreira, Dan Pvt. 31 Inf.           11030575     Co. E.      7-21-42
James, Herbert F. Pvt. 7 Matl.       19050246                 7-22-42
Smith, Kenneth R. Sgt. AC                                     7-22-42
Hubbard, Sidney J. Pfc. 93 Bomb      19040414                 7-22-42
Crow, Alvin D. Sgt. 31 Inf.          6377548      Co. E.      7-22-42
Koppenheffer, Dan C. Pfc. 31 Inf.    6943500      Co. D.      7-22-42
Burnett, Walter E. 1/Lt. 803 CE      0-413686                 7-22-42
Miller, Clayton Pvt. 194 Tank                                 7-22-42
Crane, Wibur L. Pfc. AC                                       7-22-42
Nugen, Donald R. Pfc. 31 Inf.        6559937      Hq. Co.     7-22-42
Scott, Leo G. Pfc. AC                6980649                  7-22-42
Badgerow, Keigh M. Pvt. 19 Bomb      19023863                 7-22-42
Brennison, William T/Sgt. 27 Matl.   R-1024670                7-22-42
LeVelle, Edward G. Sgt. 200 CAC      20843717                 7-22-42
Varn, Milton H. Pvt. 16 Bomb         14027316                 7-22-42
Wheeler, William W. Pfc. 803 CE      7033012                  7-22-42
Chapman, Raymond Pvt. 515 CAC        38031189                 7-22-42
Howe, Warren F. Sgt. 91 Bomb         11010517                 7-22-42
Luckey, Ronald T. Sgt. 20 Pur.       6915891                  7-22-42
Hall, Russell L. Pvt. QMC            39156982                 7-22-42
Denny, Wallace S/Sgt. QMC            20523427                 7-22-42
Pierce, Raymond Pvt. 31 Inf.         6296107      Co. I.      7-22-42
Pierce, John Pvt. 31 Inf.            19017692     Co. K.      7-22-42
Keniston, H.S. Jr. Pvt. 17 Bomb      11010484                 7-22-42
Kresal, Eugene Pfc. 31 Inf.          16008522     Co. D.      7-22-42
Yankelevitz, Harold Pfc. 91 Bomb     30230389                 7-22-42
Fisher, Byron W. Pvt. 21 Pur.        15066251                 7-22-42
Wilson, John R. T/Sgt. 34 Pur.       6208886                  7-22-42
Miller, Douglas W. Pfc. 200 CAC      20843500                 7-23-24
Houghton, Robert D. Pvt. 200 CAC     38012038                 7-23-42
Carpenter, Paul S. Pfc. 454 Ord.     14040620                 7-23-42
Tremble, Milan G. Pvt. 60 CAC        19010878                 7-23-42
Guillen, Othan Q. Pvt. 200 CAC       38031223                 7-23-42
Westcott, David R. Pvt. AC           11011498                 7-23-42
Hasket, Thomas G. Pfc. 31 Inf.       6573788      Co. M.      7-23-42
VanKleek, William L. Pfc. 7 Matl.    19020972                 7-23-42
Vorrhies, R.C. Sgt. 803 CE           6570398                  7-23-42
Carroll, Thomas R. Pfc. 31 Inf.      6912188      Med. Det.   7-23-42
Cecco, Alexandera S/Sgt.             R-3582088                7-23-42
```

```
Austin, John Cpl 515 CAC            20843566                      7-23-42
Spears, Mitchel D. Pvt. 192 Tank   35101390                      7-23-42
Dery, Roger C. Pfc. 192 Tank       20640523                      7-23-42
Corcoran, Parick F. Pvt. 31 Inf.   19017391   A-T Co.            7-23-42
Kunik, Martin L. Pvt. 31 Inf.       6889913   Co. H.             7-23-42
Nichols, Oliver R. Pfc. 93 Bomb    19002941                      7-23-42
Vaughn, Ralph G. Sgt. 680 Ord.     19005620                      7-23-42
Sodd, Stephen Pfc. 2 Obs.          17025232                      7-23-42
Carranza, Jess Pfc.                 6769353                      7-23-42
Hassen, George Sgt. 31 Inf.         6553515   Co. G.             7-23-42
Gostwa, Joseph G. 1/Sgt. 31 Inf.    6841476   Co. K.             7-23-42
Powless, Warren W. Pvt. 31 Inf.    16008591   A-T Co.            7-23-42
Wernher, Walter A. S/Sgt. F.D.      6948955                      7-23-42
Johnson, Richard H. Cpl. 803 CE    15014446                      7-23-42
Frye, Walter Pfc. 31 Inf.          18015275   Co. E.             7-24-42
Porter, William F. Pvt. 803 CE     14030912                      7-24-42
Landis, George M. Pvt.             13030359                      7-24-42
Melton, Charlton R. Cpl. AC         6394149                      7-24-42
Kiewel, Douglas F. Pfc. 3 Pur.     17011028                      7-24-42
Ticken, Hubbard J. Pfc. 200 CAC    38030526                      7-24-42
Sherman, Glen N. Pvt. 31 Inf.       6729226   Hq. Det. 1 Bn.    7-24-42
Jackson, Alman Pfc. AC             11016594                      7-24-42
Whitmore, Llewelyn B. Pfc. 27 Matl. 6933647                     7-24-42
Yarmalovicz, Tony Cpl. 803 CE       6139235                      7-24-42
Lahnar. Clarence E. Cpl 31 Inf.    17007467   Co. M.             7-24-42
Dewey, Leland K. Maj. CAC          0-216507                      7-24-42
Watson, Clarence A. Pfc. QMC       18063146                      7-24-42
Lundgren, Victor C. Pfc. 4 USMC      275604                      7-24-42
Holcomb, James E. Pvt. 48 Matl.     6969499                      7-24-42
King, Harold E. S/Sgt. 21 Pur.      6860584                      7-24-42
Feltner, Robert A. Pfc. 27 Matl.    6894913                      7-24-42
Maidhoff, Daniel A. Pvt. SC        12027965                      7-24-42
Hernandez, Lorenza Pfc. 200 CAC    20843330                      7-24-42
Eldridge, P.G. Pfc. 192 Tank       14012433                      7-24-42
Rayburn, J.L. Pfc. 24 Pur.          6801756                      7-24-42
Sterken, Jerald Pfc. 192 Tank      20645307                      7-24-42
Smith, Raymond E. Pfc. 16 Bomb     11017303                      7-24-42
Abbott, Howard Pvt. 31 Inf.        17002434   Co. H.             7-24-42
Masters, Ray E. Pvt. 803 CE        36115744                      7-25-42
LaRue, Richard Pfc. 24 Pur.        11010622                      7-25-42
Taylor, Leonard W. Pvt. 31 Inf.    18036363   Co. H.             7-25-42
Potts, Boyd C. Pvt. 7 CWS          19052724                      7-25-42
Dawson, Kenneth Pvt. 17 Ord.       15016280                      7-25-42
Viano, Glen A. Pfc. 93 Bomb         6915643                      7-25-42
Buckley, John Pfc. 14 Bomb          7071003                      7-25-42
Wilson, Knight H. Pvt. 2 Pur.      15064981                      7-25-42
Roland, Lee I. Pvt. 17 Pur.        11020452                      7-25-42
Hlivjak, Frank Jr. Cpl. 31 Inf.    19051708   Co. B.             7-25-42
Powell, Edison L. Pvt. AC          12011162                      7-25-42
Conner, Robert M. Cpl. USMC          272424                      7-25-42
Urbig, Charles A. Cpl. 5 Inter.    11011356                      7-25-42
Ziolowski, Stefan Sgt. 17 Pur.      6912855                      7-25-42
Smart, LaVerne L. Pvt. 31 Inf.     16041672   Co. B.             7-25-42
Hartman, Howard J. Pvt. 93 Bomb     6899825                      7-25-42
Walden, Graham D. Cpl. AC          11020272                      7-25-42
Eesley, Lyle Pfc. 192 Tank         35001528                      7-25-42
Porter, John E. Pvt 27 Matl.        6274789                      7-25-42
Jackson, Paul W. Pvt. QMC           6558121                      7-25-42
McColl, Parker Pfc. 200 CAC        20843970                      7-25-42
*Vaughan, Milton J. 2/Lt. QMC      0-890106                      7-8-42
   *Vaughn's Wife Elizabeth POW a at Bacolod, Negros
```

251

```
Muse, John Willis 2/Lt. AC          0-413483              7-25-42
MacGowan, R.A. Capt. Ord.           0-359912              7-25-42
Rosberg, Nils H. S/Sgt. AC          6564120               7-25-42
Wilson, Max Pvt. 21 Pur.            19051655              7-25-42
Finnigan, James Pvt. 803 CE         32044411              7-25-42
Wampler, Donald L. Sgt.             7025239               7-25-42
Tubbs, Jesse E. S/Sgt. 192 Tank     20645223              7-25-42
Yockey, Arthur N. Pvt. 31 Inf.      39160664   Co. H.     7-25-42
Hamman, Gerald W. Pvt. 31 Inf.                 * C.I.     7-25-42
Watson, F.L. Pvt. QMC               13029093              7-26-42
Sinkule, Howard A. Pvt. 19 AB       7022852               7-26-42
Merritt, Carl E. Pvt. 7 CWS         33043392              7-26-42
Slaton, H.K. Sgt. 7 Matl.           6273726               7-26-42
Stephenson, Walter L.Pvt. SC AW     15065643              7-26-42
Carpenter, Alva J. Pvt. Ord.        19017736              7-26-42
Redcay, Raymond Pfc. 31 Inf.        17019517   Co. E.     7-26-42
Smalley, Vernon C. Pfc. MP          17015181              7-26-42
Finley, Leslie Cpl  31 Inf.         19056399   Svc. Co.   7-26-42
Rogers, John S. Cpl. 31 Inf.        6352921    Co. H.     7-26-42
Grant, Vaughn P. Pvt. 4CFS          11030584              7-26-42
Murray, Richard R. Pvt. 409 SC      39602374              7-26-42
Deutch, Robert Pvt. SC AW           1202790               7-26-42
Senz, Louis M. Pfc. 19 Bomb         19012329              7-26-42
Taylor, William M. Pfc. 200 CAC     20843984              7-26-42
Miner, Perry E. Pvt. 7 Matl.        19018950              7-26-42
Whipple, Daviv S. Pvt. 27 Matl.     19028335              7-26-42
March, Herbert F. Pvt. 24 Pur.      6560240               7-26-42
Harris, Glenn A. Pfc. AC            19000251              7-26-42
Whitener, Richard M. Pfc. 91 Bomb   14056099              7-26-42
Bodnar, Stanley L. Pfc.             11008255              7-26-42
Vigil, Tito Pvt. 515 CAC            38011241              7-26-42
McConnell, Hanry J. Pvt. 2 OBS      11011423              7-26-42
Lescaut, Joseph E. Pvt. 16 Bomb     11024358              7-26-42
Trujillo, Manuel Pvt. 200 CAC       20842177              7-26-42
Atencio, Santa Cruz Pfc. 200 CAC    20843693              7-27-42
Camflerman, Martin W. Jr. Cpl. 192T 20660396              7-27-42
Ross, Edwin E. Pfc. 17 Bomb         6971446               7-27-42
Phillips, John H. Sgt. 31 Inf.      6576013    Hq. Co.    7-27-42
Donnelly, John L. Pvt. 7 Matl.      19030538              7-27-42
Hurst, Robert Pvt. 429 Sig.         14057738              7-27-42
Beck, Boyd Pvt. 31 Inf.             17014222   Co. B.     7-27-42
Simmons, Ralph C. 2/Lt. 31 Inf.     0-890392   Co. C.     7-27-42
Rannells, Kenneth D. Pvt. 698 Ord.  19056321              7-27-42
Colson, Warren M. S/Sgt. 34 Pur.    6258716               7-27-42
Hathaway, Wayne E. M/Sgt. M.D.      6253235               7-27-42
Nourse, Joanas E. Pvt. 48 Matl.     11015370              7-27-42
Morris, Marvin D. Cpl 4 Marines     279934                7-27-42
Torres, George S. Pvt. 200 CACA     38013322              7-27-42
Martin, Clarence E. Pvt. 745 Ord.   17013176              7-27-42
Barlosky, Leo J. Cpl 7 CWS          6897                  7-27-42
Seibert Earl E. Pvt. 803 CE         33054972              7-27-42
Titcomb, Louis A. Cpl. 19 Bomb      11024227              7-27-42
Beighton, Carl M. Pfc. 31 Inf.      19019438   Co. B.     7-27-42
Hasson, George Sgt.    31 Inf.      6553515               7-28-42
Poole, Everett T. Pvt. 19 Bomb      19014882              7-28-42
Owens, Joseph A. S/Sgt. 27 Matl.    6232988               7-28=42
Armstrong, A.I. Sgt. 200 CAC        38012276              7-28-42
Gusmano, John T. Pfc. 808 MP        6979625               7-28-42
Jubenal, Robert E. Sgt. AC.         6565146               7-28-42
Weisfeld, Julius S/Sgt. 3 Pur.      6978772               7-28-42
```

```
Turner, Clifford N. Pvt.              19048330                              7-28-42
Murchie, Howard F. 93 Bomb            19050504                              7-28-42
Baudo, Joseph Pfc. Ord.               33054820                              7-28-42
Ryan, Warren F. Pvt. 2 OBS            19013457                              7-28-42
Weatherwax, George F. Pvt. 7 CWS      32044055                              7-28=42
McDonald, Harold D. Cpl. 194 Tank     20900734                              7-28-42
Ulmer, LaVerne E. Cpl. 24 Pur.        6930760                               7-28-42
Bishop, George F. Sgt. 59 CAC         6567320                               7-28-42
Scarborough, Alvin R. S/Sgt. 454 Ord  7009322                              7-28-42
Colter, Robert L. Pfc. 91 bomb        14014485                              7-28-42
Ropp, John W. Pvt. 2 OBS              19056758                              7-28-42
Thurman, Milburn Pfc. 7 CWS           19002475                              7-28-42
Hinson, Cecil T. Pvt. 2 CWS           14037802  Co. D.Replacement7-28-42
Jones, Willie O. Pvt. 48 Matl.        14014948                              7-28-42
Jones, Melvin E. Sgt. 200 CAC         20843570                              7-29-42
Silverman, Samuel Pvt. 31 Inf.        20904198  Hq. Co.                     7-29-42
Strickland, Clifford H. Pvt. 803 CE   6954316                               7-29-42
Yeates, Ballard K. Pfc. 21 Pur.       19010957                             7-29-42
Lucero, Jose L. Pvt. 200 CAC          38012371                              7-29-42
Larick, Charles A. Pvt. 31 Inf.       19038779  Co. K.                      7-29-42
Jones, Edward J. Pfc. 31 Inf.         12002840  Co. K.                      7-29-42
Novinski, John Pfc. 7 CWS             3302126                               7-30-42
Hicks, James L. Sgt. 31 Inf.          6576324   Hq. Co.                     7-30-42
Fields, Sam Pvt. Tanks                38020407                              7-30-42
O'Connell, Alfred Loren Cpl AC        6578859                               7-30-42
Scott, Winfield W. L/Col. F.A.        0-15916                               7-30-42
Flener, Charles M. Cpl. FEAF          6547967                               7-30-42
Asher, Kenneth B. Pvt. 680 Ord.       19054763                              7-30-42
Bidwell, George F. Pfc. CWS           19052016                              7-30-42
Sauter, John R. Pfc. 803 CE           7074186                               7-30-42
Stewart, James B. Sgt. QMC            19002646                              7-30-42
Cole, Lloyd O. Pfc. 194 Tank          20900697                              7-30-42
Tidwell, Durell A. Cpl. 200 CAC       20843605                              7-30-42
VanGelder, Edmund F. Sgt. 192 Tank    20645290                              7-30-42
Thompson, Lee Pfc. 31 Inf.            6313229   Hq. Det. 1 Bn.              7-31-42
Barnhill, James G. Cpl. QMC           6796517                               7-31-42
Sparks, Gerald W. Pvt. 803 CE         6957647                               7-31-42
Hodgins, Charles L. 1/Lt. 31 Inf.     0-230742  Co. A.                      7-31-42
Bronge, Robert F. Sgt. 192 Tank       20600362                              7-31-42
Curry, I.N. Pvt. AC                   18029488                              7-31-42
Jemenko, Frank T. Pvt. Ord.           15058945                              7-31-42
Seligman, Leonard D. Pvt. 19 AB       16028578                              7-31-42
Lemew, Joseph H. Pvt. 93 Bomb         6296088                               7-31-42
Clayton, James C. Pfc. 803 CE         6957650                               7-31-42
McCall, Alfred R. T/Sgt. CE           R-316621                              7-31-42
Stott, William J. S/Sgt. 16 Bomb      6367994                               7-31-42
Siegele, Arthur Pvt. 680 Ord.         19054764                              7-31-42
Carter, John T. S/Sgt. AC             6582538                               7-31-42
Horton, Ralph M. Cpl. CWS             19052323                              7-31-42
Olsen, Ingvald  Civiliam                                                    7-31-42
Easter, Lucien L. Pfc. 48 Matl.       14017206                              7-31-42
Roberts, Lester L. Sgt. 200 CAC       20842376                              7-31-42
Williams, Homer C. Pfc. AC            7000141                               8-1-42
Phelps, William L. Sgt. 515 CAC       20842731                              8-1-42
Bloxham, Christopher L. Pvt. 31 Inf.  19010589  Svc. Co.                    8-1-42
Haggen, Frederick N. 1/Lt. USMC                                            8-1-42
Hicks, Owen Pvt. 31 Inf.              19060851  A-T Co.                     8-1-42
Gurule, Juan F. Pvt. 515 CAC          38011203                              8-1-42
Wampil, Joseph W. Pvt. 27 Bomb        6070962                               8-1-42
Bramlett, George R. Pfc. 16 Bomb      14006598                              8-1-42
```

```
Baggett, William T. Pfc. QMC          19038327              8-1-42
Province, John Jr. Pvt. 31 Inf.       15081841  Co. H.      8-1-42
Marchese, Nick J. Pvt. 192 Tank       36016332              8-1-42
Via, Clyde R. Pvt. 31 Inf.            18023233  Co. M.      8-1-42
Shafsky, Francis A. Sgt. 31 Inf.       6865103  Co. F.      8-1-42
Owens, Herbert P. Cpl. AC              6564662              8-1-42
Haase, Richard P. Pfc. 808 MP         19011331              8-1-42
Blauer, Robert L. Sgt. 515 CAC        36008671              8-1-42
Glomb, William Pfc. 31 Inf.            6983518  Co. B.      8-1-42
Drake, Wayne E. Pfc. 31 Inf.          18050429  Hq. Co.     8-1-42
Brady, Lester L. S/Sgt. 48 Matl.       6911397              8-1-42
Dawson, Edward A. Pvt. 31 Inf.         6364362  Co. I.      8-2-42
Daudman, Lloyd Sgt. 48 Matl.           7002721              8-2-42
Huffines, Curtis L. Pvt. 16 Bomb      14029331              8-2-42
Dariani, Joseph E. Cpl  24 Pur.        6147040              8-2-42
Mickle, Fred E. Pvt. SC               14057615              8-2-42
Gallegos, Jose B. Pvt. 200 CAC        38012136              8-2-42
Luif, Edward A. Pvt. QMC              34053999              8-2-42
Aker, Owen P. Jr. Pvt. 19 AB          13018491              8-2-42
White, John R. Pfc. 7 Matl.           19051847              8-2-42
Nelson, Leon W. Pvt. 31 Inf.          19006257  Co. H.      8-2-42
Elsworth, David H. Pvt. 31 Inf.        6572780  Hq. Co.     8-2-42
Pate, Jameh H. 2/Lt. AC               0-422149              8-2-42
Wilson, Robert A. pvt. 200 CAC        20842751              8-2-42
Kolacek, Walter Cpl. 515 CAC          38029542              8-2-42
Clegg, N.R. Pfc. 28 Matl.                                   8-2-42
Myers, Henry P. Sgt. 18 Bomb          19044032              8-2-42
Beard, Clarence E.  59 CAC            19045981              8-2-42
Pierce, Charles R. Pfc. 16 Bomb       11015300              8-3-42
Johnson, Richard E. 2/Lt. SC          R-1029117             8-3-42
Abelson, LaVeern 2/Lt. AC             0-386903              8-3-42
Gacie, John J. 2/Lt. 52 Inf.          0-890177              8-3-42
Rymes, Hugh Cpl. 16 bomb               7002689              8-3-42
Mecks, Mason C. Pvt. 19 AB            14019835              8-3-42
Romero, Frutoso Pvt. M.D. 31 Inf.     18035282  Med. Det.   8-3-42
Bushaw, John F.A. 1/Lt. 192 Tank      0-403497              8-3-42
Bryant, T.B. S/Sgt. 200 CAC           20843550              8-3-42
Martin, J.M. Pfc. 75 Ord.              1867123              8-3-42
Malcolm, Dewey E. Pfc. 19 Bomb         6934725              8-3-42
Baxley, Hudson Pvt. Ord.              14040614              8-3-42
Grow, Charles D. M/Sgt. AC             6684386              8-3-42
Kohut, Joe M. Pvt. 60 CAC             17016331              8-4-42
Wise, J. H. SM1c USN                  38-113-28             8-4-42
Barker, Lawrence L. S/Sgt. 48 Matl.    6392672              8-4-42
Courey, George Pvt. 28 Matl.          17029069              8-4-42
Martin, Henry M. Cpl. 31 Inf.         32019144  Co. B.      8-4-42
Patterson, Cecil R. Pfc. Ord.         18051663              8-4-42
Herberle, Leonard Civilian                                  8-4-42
Prieskorn, Elmer J. Pfc. 20 Pur.       6953611              8-4-42
Mitchell, John F. Pfc. 93 Bomb        18059210              8-4-42
Jolley, Clinton A. Pfc. 31 Inf.       19015687  Co. A.      8-5-42
Overstreet, Robert E. Pvt. 194 Tank   20900738              8-5-42
Utterback, Homer E. S/Sgt. 5 Inter.    6831403              8-5-42
Carlson, Martin C. Sgt. 7 Matl.        6580423              8-5-42
Stefek, Paul N. Sgt. 31 Inf.          R-939212  Svc. Co.    8-5-42
Hart, Melvin L. Sgt. 17 Pur.           6913297              8-5-42
Taylor, Irving F. 2/Lt. QMC           0-371345              8-5-42
Turner, Ross C. S/Sgt. 20 Pur.         6265578              8-5-42
Mikologezyk, John M. Cpl. 31 Inf.      6907019  Hq. Dt. 3 Bn.  8-6-42
Hasty, Lynn T. Pvt. 31 Inf.            6258026  Hq. Co.     8-6-42
```

Russo, Angelo I. Pfc. 31 Inf.	13002831	Co. M.	8-6-42
Armstrong, Jack Pvt 31 Inf.	17016227	Co. A.	8-6-42
Hamilton, Leonard Cpl 31 Inf.	13000792	Hq. Co.	8-6-42
Bowlin, James C. Pvt. 31 Inf.	6935475	Co. M.	8-6-42
Chance, Robert T. Pvt. AC	11010376		8-6-42
D'Auria, Albert Pvt. 31 Inf.	3303148	A-T Co.	8-6-42
Killinger, Phillip E. Pfc. 192 Tank	35002567		8-6-42
Utinsky, John P. Civilian			8-6-42
Hoskins, Earl C. Pfc. 200 CAC	20842513		8-6-42
Lawson, John H. Pvt. 93 Bomb	13035022		8-6-42
Edwards, Leo H. Sgt. 27 Matl.	6938050		8-6-42
Flecken, Paul I. Sgt. SC AW	6943033		8-6-42
Muse, Lindsey F. S/Sgt. 19 Bomb	6258683		8-6-42
Ingram, Loren R. Pvt. 24 Pur.	19014683		8-6-42
Bishop, Shiell R. Pvt. 48 Matl.	14027440		8-7-42
Swain, Richard B. Pfc. 200 CAC	20842978		8-7-42
Bunn, Vigil S. Pfc. 4 MC	280445		8-7-42
Farren, Charles T. Pvt. 745 Ord.	6139691		8-7-42
Rich, Darrel E. Sgt. 60 CAC	19011440		8-7-42
Hynes, George J. Cpl 525 CAC	20843940		8-7-42
Inman, Harman R. Pvt. QMC	19045736		8-7-42
Hammon, Fred J. Sgt. CAC	20842939		8-7-42
Bodgen, Felix S/Sgt. CAC	6080044		8-7-42
Johnson, Frank J. Pvt. Ord.	19052538		8-7-42
Gregory, Loren J. Pvt. QMC	14038158		8-8-42
Sivel, Richard J. Pfc. 27 Bomb	16027916		8-8-42
Morrison, Dean J. Pvt. 808 MP	17001687		8-8-42
Pleshko, William 1/Lt. Ord.	0-412475		8-8-42
Juhl, William D. Cpl. 31 Inf.	6863828	Co. G.	8-8-42
Cochran, Clifton E. Pvt. 7 Matl.	18029865		8-8-42
Pickle, C.A. Pvt. 31 Inf.	20943024	*	8-8-42
Cambell, William T. Pvt. 31 Inf.	13034880	Co. C.	8-8-42
Nesbitt, George Jr. Pvrt. PDMT	17029742		8-8-42
Weiner, Henry A. Pvt. 20 Pur.	6914042		8-8-42
Jones, Gerald L. Cpl. 515 CAC	38031560		8-9-42
Howe, George C. Jr. 2/Lt. ac	0-378007		8-9-42
Lassor, John E. Pvt. 19 AB	6592616		8-9-42
Buis, Robert L. QMC	19053008		8-9-42
Stewart, Elmer J. T/Sgt. 48 Matl.	6343320		8-9-42
Grier, Joe R. S/Sgt. 27 Bomb	6926136		8-9-42
Stevens, Lester C. Pvt. 803 CE	7070272		8-9-42
Sedillo, Adam Pvt. 200 CAC	38012467		8-9-42
White, John H. Pvt. 194 Tank	20900759		8-9-42
Nolan, william P. Pvt. 454 Ord.	36027192		8-9-42
Kokitas, Albert J. Pfc. 7 CWS	13004748		8-9-42
Bernardy, Donald I. Pfc. 4 MC	280339		8-9-42
Ramirez, Juan Pvt. 515 CAC	38030019		8-9-42
Sutphin, Irving R. 2/Lt. Inf.	0-890391	Co. B.	8-9-42
Ward, Karl H. Pvt. 803 CE	33044917		8-10-42
Bailey, Gerald J. Cpl. 7 Matl.	19018331		8-10-42
Gunn, John G. Cpl. 31 Inf.	6978029	Co. E.	8-10-42
Hueston, Joe I. Pvt. 20 Pur.	6573215		8-10-42
Wilson, Woodrow W. S/Sgt. 17 Pur.	6032712		8-10-42
Weiner, Manuel J. Pfc. 27 Bomb	11024287		8-10-42
New, Donald B. Pvt. 192 Tank	36200864		8-10-42
Whipple, Lloyd L. Pfc. 7 Matl.	19018871		8-10-42
Rodriguez, Louis P. Pvt. 200 CAC	38012552		8-10-42
Boone, Delbert E. Pfc. 27 Matl.	13037076		8-10-42
Goldberg, Israel Pvt. 24 Pur.	11020323		8-11-42
Dawson, James W. 31 Inf.	16019359	Co. I. 2/Lt.	8-11-42

```
Schwartz, Adolph B. Pfc. 31 Inf.      16003892    Co. K.           8-11-42
Anderson, Ansgar R. Cpl. 440 Ord.     13000424                     8-11-42
Stevens, Raymond Pvt. 31 Inf.         14047720    Hq. Det. 3 Bn.   8-11-42
Morton, Howard T. 2/Lt. CE            0-890303                     8-11-42
McClure, Ross Capt. 803 CE            0-117935                     8-11-42
Johnston, Lyly Pvt. 59 CAC            17004120                     8-11-42
Muer, Harold A. S/Sgt. 3 Pur.         6725309                      8-11-42
Joskens, Charlds J. S/Sgt.            6668470                      8-11-42
Herring, Lester D. Cpl. 515 CAC       38029799                     8-11-42
Hartford, Oliver  2/Lt. 200 CAC       0-890145                     8-11-42
Holt, Elbert A. Pvt. 31 Inf.          18056415                     8-11-42
Milton, John D. Pvt. AC               18029873                     8-11-42
Von Bergen, William W. Sgt. 192 Tank20600043                       8-11-42
Davenport, Raymond M. Pfc. 454 Ord.  34148159                      8-12-42
Eye, Donald O. Cpl. 803 CE            7062197                      8-12-42
Briggs, Elton B. Pfc. 19 bomb         19015062                     8-12-42
Fugitt, Donald T. Pfc. 19 Bomb        18059206                     8-12-42
Boatfield, Robert J. Pvt. 19 AB       6982018                      8-12-42
Meuller, Alexander Pvt. 192 Tank      20600420                     8-12-42
Sell, Frederick, C. Pfc. 93 Bomb      19044964                     8-12-42
Baxley, William B. Pfc. 454 Ord.      14040603                     8-12-42
Morris, John G. M/Sgt. 91 Bomb        6354023                      8-12-42
Kukansky, Sam Pvt. 803 CE             6668023                      8-12-42
Eddleman, William H. Sgt. 31 Inf.     6823501    Co. E.            8-12-42
Sensing, Robert A. Sgt. 91 Bomb       6972974                      8-12-42
Martiez, Jerry G. Pvt. 200 CAC        38042204                     8-12-42
Mikula, John  Pvt. 17 Ord.            23032266                     8-12-42
Flores, Louis Pfc. 31 Inf.            19056645    Co. D.           8-13-42
Newman, Robert W. 2/Lt. AC            0-406579                     8-13-42
Coffindaffer, Rexall B. Pfc. 200 CAC 20843953                     8-13-42
Griffin, John F. Pfc. 17 Sig.         11020650                     8-13-42
Lucas, Perry A. T/Sgt. 59 CAC         R-1992478                    8-13-42
Carlson, Robert H. Pvt. 31 Inf.       6557335    Co. M.            8-13-42
Becotte, Paul A. Pvt. 803 CE          6153630                      8-14-42
Madison, Harold E. Pfc. 192 Tank      20645253                     8-14-42
Alexander, George M. Pvt. 7 Matl.     18029870                     8-14-42
Radel, Robert R. Pfc. 91 Bomb         1302808                      8-14-42
Forester, W.M. 1/Lt. SC               0-380349                     8-14-42
Humbarger, R.F. Cpl. 4 MC             286925                       8-14-42
Claussen, Manly J. S/Sgt. 20 Pur.     6944360                      8-15-42
Connelly, George F. Pfc. 31 Inf.      14628214    Co. D.           8-15-42
Pancitz, Arthur R. Pvt.808 MP         16005225                     8-15-42
Nicolas, Louis Sgt. 803 CE            6934474                      8-15-42
Poovey, Walter H. Sgt. 34 Pur.        6925997                      8-15-42
Sandburg, Carroll E. Pvt. 20 AB       6935250                      8-15-42
Kilduff, Wm. C. 2/Lt. 60 CAC          0-396747                     8-15-42
Miller, Guy O. Pvt. 194 Tank          37006330       .             8-15-42
Naska, Henry P. Pvt. 194 Tank         37025713                     8-15-42
Dujenski, John E. Sgt. 24 Pur.        6976638                      8-15-42
Prosser, Stanley M. Cpl. 20 Pur.      19030293                     8-15-42
Legg, John M. Pvt. AC                 15017607                     8-16-42
Binford, Lawrence E. Pfc. 27 bomb     14024239                     8-16-42
Ross, Ralph L. Pvt. 19 AB             6576936                      8-16-42
Bricker, Maurice R. Sgt. 21 Pur.      6938514                      8-16-42
Fischer, Jacob Pfc. QMC               12008354                     8-16-42
Connor, William R. S/Sgt. DFMI        17000679                     8-16-42
Thurlow, Ivan W. Pfc. 27 Bomb         14043639                     8-17-42
Miller, Lester O. Pvt. QMC            6728269                      8-17-42
Cook, Herman Civilian                                              8-17-42
Squires, Earl M. Pvt. 192 Tank        14017287                     8-17-42
```

Longnecker, Harry L. Pvt. 91 Bomb	15058750		8-17-42
Fuentes, Bruno G. Pvt. 200 CAC	38034244		8-17-42
Lehman, John H. Pvt. 3 Pur.	15059202		8-17-42
Murray, Talmadge L. Pvt. 24 Pur.	18029859		8-17-42
Hendry, James L. 1/Lt. 88 FA	0-350035		8-17-42
White, William W. S/Sgt. 31 Inf.	654404	Co. L.	8-17-42
Adams, Edwin B. Jr. Pfc. QMC	19028233		8-18-42
Silverwood, Robert E. Pvt. 19 Bomb	6632430		8-18-42
Mock, Paul O. 2/Lt. AC	0-448433		8-18-42
Russell, R.J. 2/Lt. CE	0-393353		8-18-42
Baldwin, Robert G. Pfc. QMC	20946387		8-19-42
Bovett, William C. Pvt. 7 CWS	34083080		8-19-42
Stonecifer, Francis H. Capt. Inf.	0-278432		8-19-42
Berlin, Robert C. Sgt. 19 Bomb	6281699		8-19-42
Kelly, Marshall F. Cpl. 200 CAC	20813495		8-19-42
McCardie, James H. Pfc. 698 Ord.	19002514		8-19-42
Buckley, Willis O. S/Sgt. 4 MC	264327		8-19-42
Cochran, Robert F. Pvt. 31 Inf.	19051616	Co. A.	8-19-42
Holland, Clayton L. Pfc. 4 MC	209553		8-19-42
Cederblom, Dean f. Pvt. 194 Tank	20900696		8-19-42
Chavez, Osie L. Pfc. 200 CAc	38011889		8-19-42
Scarborough, Frank C. S/Sgt. AC	6383178		8-19-42
Blumenthal, Robert R. Pvt. 48 Matl.	11010592		8-20-42
Overton, Glenn E. Sgt. AC	6931707		8-20-42
White, Guy F. Sgt. 31 Inf.	6862208	Svc. Co.	8-20-42
Ladley, John Pvt. SC AW	12009854		8-20-42
Antosiak, Alex J. Cpl. 515 CAC	360341122		8-21-42
Turturro, Augustine T. Cpl. 803 CE	32044121		8-21-42
Beardslee, Stuart A. Sgt. 17 Pur.	6916429		8-21-42
Hanson, Robeert II Pvt. 93 Ord.	17001811		8-21-42
Stump, James H. M/Sgt. DEML	6664318		8-21-42
McKnight, Melvin E. 2/Lt. AC	0-412694		8-21-42
Keevan, John Capt. CE	0-890056		8-21-42
Griffiths, Kenneth C. Capt. FA	0-21848		8-22-42
Angle, Henry Jr. Pvt. 31 Inf.	18043814	Co. A.	8-22-42
Conner, Malcolm L. Pvt. 7 Matl.	19050539		8-22-42
Ginnings, Vernon V. Cpl. 515 CAC	38012097		8-23-42
McCafferty, Brady E. Pfc. 7 Matl.	19040700		8-23-42
Hanks, Frank F. Pfc. 27 Bomb	6485852		8-23-42
DeViney, John S. Jr. Sgt. 3 Pur.	11011494		8-23-42
Hackley, Vernon T. Pvt. 31 Inf.	6880541	Svc. Co.	8-24-42
Bradley, harold K. Pvt. 803 CE	12009469		8-24-42
Robertson, James.A Pvt.	38055621		8-24-42
Whipple, Albert J. Pvt. 60 CAC	1108534		8-24-42
Ashton, Henry 1/Lt. FA	0-334549		8-24-42
Gniadek, John Pfc. 27 Bomb	11012157		8-24-42
Love, William E. Cpl. 200 CAC	20842461		8-24-42
Albusta, Leo A. Pfc. 803 CE	7024370		8-24-42
Elhers, Lawrence Pfc. 31 Inf.	6244414	Co. F.	8-24-42
Doughty, Henry M. Capt. FA	0-307008		8-24-42
Mull, Elwathan L. Pvt. 19 AB	6978280		8-25-42
Batson, Lewis M. Sgt. 20 Pur.	19048802		8-25-42
Gilman, William F. Cpl. 17 Pur.	11017555		8-25-42
Brayton, Olan K. Pfc. 409 SC	19002578		8-25-42
Verhagen, Elmer H. Pvt. 200 CAC	36203291		8-25-42
Ruminski, Robert A. Pfc. 192 Tank	35020286		8-25-42
Cameron, Graham B. Pvt.			8-26-42
Condos, James Pvt. 31 Inf.	17023570	Co. C.	8-26-42
Virgil, Trinidad Pvt. 525 CAC	38055754		8-26-42
Young, Peter M. Pvt. 28 Matl.	11014626		8-26-42

257

```
Huber, James O. S/Sgt. & Matl.        6575054              8-26-42
Tucker, Jack W. 194 Tank              20937841             8-26-42
Thompson, Randall A. Pvt. 3 Pur.      17010856             8-26-42
Pinkham, Arthur W. Sea-1c USN         58-055-38            8-26-42
Milton, Jackson T. Pfc. 31 Inf.       18038591   Co. K.    8-27-42
Duff, John F. Pfc. 803 CE             6975491              8-27-42
Hildensperger, James J. Pfc.          6920184              8-27-42
Jones, Jack E. 2/Lt. AC               0-409901             8-27-42
Davis, Raymond W. Pfc. 808 MP         19051350             8-27-42
Rogers, Willis L. Pvt. 200 CAC        36008552             8-27-42
Stevens, Hershel J. Pfc. 31 Inf.      17015783   Co. I.    8-28-42
Long, Thomas V. Pfc. 515 CAC          38011616             8-28-42
Leonard, Fred Pfc. 192 Tank           20523463             8-28-42
Major, Mitchell Capt. CE              0-890066             8-28-42
Pitsat, Richard G. Pfc. 200 CAC       20843973             8-28-42
Campbell, John J. EM USN              21-462-43            8-28-42
Merrill, Willard D. Pvt. OBS          11010150             8-28-42
Shumate, Harold M. Capt. CAC          0-266302             8-28-42
Reis, George H. Pfc. 192 Tank         35020366             8-29-42
Blythe, Howard O. Pvt. 515 CAC        20843006             8-29-42
Skee, Charles C. Pvt. 7 Matl.         19051487             8-29-42
Thompson, Wesley J. Pvt. 28 Matl.     11020790             8-30-42
Porter, George W. 2/Lt.  Inf.         0-890300   *         8-30-42
Johnson, Neil W. Capt. Inf.           0-282924             8-30-42
Stanton, John Pvt. 192 Tank           38020993             8-30-42
Cudworth, Frank G. Pvt. 409 SC        19019993             8-30-42
Kokoszka, Wlaoyslaw Pvt. 16 Bomb      11018884             8-30-42
Castillo, Filimon E. Pvt. 200 CAC     38012440             8-30-42
Nickerson, Jose B. Pfc. 200 CAC       38012179             8-30-42
Krauss, Charles W. 2/Lt. Ord.         0-                   8-30-42
Padgett, Thomas H. Civilian                                8-30-42
Ross, Roy L. Pfc. 454 Ord.            36027066             8-31-42
Maki, Tauno A. Pvt. 7 Matl.           19000665             8-31-42
Saiz, Renaldo Pvt. 200 CAC            38012389             8-31-42
Hickock, Clinton L. S/Sgt. 27 bomb    6828640              8-31-42
Welch, Alfred R. Pvt.                 18042244             8-31-42
Thomas, Wayne R. Pfc. 515 CAC         28043373             8-31-42
Jensen, Harry J. Pvt. 31 Inf.         36034218   Co. H.    8-31-42
Kennedy, Charles H. Pfc. 808 MP       6272405              8-31-42
Baird, Charles F. Pfc. FEAF           11013408             8-31-42
Muniz, Ignacio Pvt. 200 CAC           38011240             9-1-42
Fanning, Harold G. Pfc. 192 Tank      20645283             9-1-42
Carmack, Joseph D. Cpl/ 803 CE        6954227              9-1-42
Breuer, Rolf Pvt. 27 Matl.            11019686             9-1-42
Dovenberg, Dean Pfc 803 CE            39233545             9-1-42
Phillips, Robert T. Major M.C.        0-302031             9-1-42
Carpenter, Robert E. Cpl. 200 CAC     20843922             9-1-42
Mason, John S. Pvt. 803 CE            14011738             9-1-42
Harper, Floyd B. Pvt. 454 Ord.        36111524             9-2-42
Demaris, Richard C. Pvt. 17 Pur.      6132083              9-2-42
Wildharber, John E. Pfc. 27 Matl.     6569825              9-2-42
Talbott, Delbert Pvt. 194 Tank        39231797             9-2-42
Stamps, Scott A. Pfc. 27 Matl.        18001281             9-2-42
Kelly, Charles R. BMKR1c USN          22-423-22            9-2-42
Ennis, Robert Major QMC               0-462889             9-2-42
Butts, John J. Pvt. 59 CAC            19904256             9-2-42
Jennings, Jack E. Pvt. 93 Bomb        20305266             9-2-42
Lee, Ralph Jr. Pvt. 31 Inf.           6908083    Co. A.    9-2-42
Behre, William W. Pfc. 75 Ord.        19019509             9-2-42
Harris, Andrew E. Lt/Cmdr. USN                             9-2-42
```

```
Stickelmeyer, Lesley Pvt. CE        19054714                    9-3-42
Cone, Frank Capt. MC.               0-377316                    9-3-42
Symonds, Henyr H. S/Sgt. QMC        19028035                    9-3-42
Smith, Frank W. M/Sgt. AC            6225853                    9-4-42
Timberlake, Roscoe F. Pvt. 31 Inf.  11010686     Co. H.        9-4-42
Walker, Elwin G. Pvt. qmc           19024025                    9-4-42
Thorpe, Vernon G. Pvt. 31 Inf.      16046181     Co. G.        9-4-42
Quinlan, Thomas J. 2/Lt. Inf.       0-890293                    9-4-42
Allen, John N. Pvt. 60 CAC          16013470                    9-4-42
Grange, John V. Pfc. 200 CAC        20943796                    9-4-42
Gedrin, Stephen S. Pfc. 20 AB       11017187                    9-4-42
Muckey, Loren R. Pvt. 60 CAC        19016751                    9-4-42
Mann, Ralph C. 1/Lt. USMC                                       9-5-42
Morgensen, Stephen A. Pvt. QMC      39079568                    9-5-42
Levy, Melvin L. Sgt. 803 CE         34079568                    9-5-42
Hurtienne, Milton H. Pfc. 31 Inf.   19012809     Co. H.        9-5-42
Fletcher, Harry Sgt. 20 AB           6708952                    9-5-42
Henry, Ernest T. T/Sgt. 3 Pur.       6224943                    9-5-42
Cyr, Leonard E. T/Sgt. F.D.          6865080                    9-5-42
Todd, Roy A. M/Sgt. 27 Matl.         6281940                    9-5-42
Smith, John E. Pfc. 27 Bomb         14026215                    9-6-42
Hunold, Louis T. Capt. Inf.         0-330962     *             9-6-42
Haas, Charles W. Capt 57 Inf. PS    0-322128                    9-6-42
Horton, Thomas R. L/Col. Inf.       0-16515      *             9-6-42
Ourilla, George Sgt. 3 Pur.          6844179                    9-6-42
Fleener, James H. Pvt. 194 Tank     20900708                    9-6-42
Bieser, Merrill P. Pvt. 19 Bomb     19038078                    9-7-42
McGinnis, Joseph H. Pvt. 17 Ord.    32057982                    9-7-42
Bartik, Fred R. Pvt. M.D.           39228408                    9-7-42
Hackett, Ray Pvt. 17 Bomb           11016137                    9-7-42
Brown, Gillie E. Pfc. 194 Tank      20700221                    9-7-42
Gehl, Donald C. Pvt. 19 Bomb         6930598                    9-7-42
Jessee, Keith O. Cpl. 19 AB          6953564                    9-7-42
Minkler, Harry W. Pvt. QMC          19020914                    9-8-42
Bowles, Randolph E. Sgt. 48 Matl.    6399845                    9-8-42
Glassberg, Lawrence Pfc. 7 Matl.    19000265                    9-8-42
Dunn, William J. Pfc. SC            19028661                    9-8-42
Ritter, John W. Pvt. 680 Ord.       19017865                    9-8-42
Duff, David H. Sgt. 192 Tank        35001000                    9-8-42
MacDuffie, Arthur R. Sgt. M.D.       6147736                    9-9-42
Kipp, Ralph Sgt. 91 Bomb            11015737                    9-9-42
Friessell, Karl J. S/Sgt. 16 Bomb    6822154                    9-9-42
Whitten, Walter B. Pfc. 454 aord.   34084178                    9-9-42
Berry, William O. 2/Lt. 57 Inf. PS  0-890345                    9-9-42
Hester, Harry E. Sgt. 27 Bomb        7009206                    9-9-42
Doane, Archie Pfc. 2 OBS             6554746                    9-9-42
McCullough, Mallard E.Pfc. 48 Matl. 14027389                    9-10-42
Peters, Abraham E. Pfc. 680 Ord.    19054775                    9-10-42
McArthur, Albert C. T/Sgt. 192 Tank 20600465                    9-10-42
Deas, Norman Sgt. 31 Inf.            6276734     Co. I.        9-10-42
Golland, Daniel G. Pvt. CWS         16646196                    9-10-42
Kells, David E. 2/Lt. 515 CAC       0-890161                    9-10-42
Grobles, Clifton Pfc. 693 Ord.      19020345                    9-10-42
Powers, Clelon Pvt. 59 CAC          15065663                    9-10-42
DeCurtins, Albert Pfc. 192 Tank     35002395                    9-10-42
Ely, John W. Capt. Inf.             0-284846                    9-11-42
Heyrend, Cecil J. Pfc. 19 Bomb      19019671                    9-11-42
Flowers, John R. S/Sgt. 515 CAC     20842755                    9-11-42
Stoltzfus, Karl H. Pvt. 91 Bomb     13030333                    9-11-42
Hutchinson, William W. Sgt. DEML    19012545                    9-11-42
```

```
Courtney, James B. Jr. Pvt. 48 Matl. 6974522              9-11-42
Oldenettel, Arnold H. Pvt. 515 CAC   36050848             9-11-42
Simonson, Junior A. Pfc. 31 Inf.     19020965  Co. A.     9-11-42
Gercke, D.A. Sgt. AC                 6953613              9-11-42
Barnes, Donald H. Pfc. 34 Pur.       6584345              9-11-42
O'Connor, Eugene M. Pvt. 194 Tank    17026614             9-12-42
Cook, Edward H. Sgt. QMC             6921228              9-12-42
Judge, James R. Sgt. 20 AB           19046934             9-12-42
Ingebretson, Eldon L. Pfc. 194 Tank  39156780             9-12-42
Young, Warren Pvt. M.D.              17028787             9-12-42
Norman, Ernest R. Pvt. Ord.          18029976             9-12-42
Morris, Wallace R. S/Sgt. 91 Bomb    6249908              9-12-42
Martin, James H. Cpl 16 Bomb         6974092              9-12-42
Turrieta, Carlos T. Pvt. 200 CAC     20842534             9-12-42
Snelling, Herman L. WO USMC            155910             9-12-42
St.John Lewis M. Pfc. 2 OBS          19056773             9-12-42
St.Armour, Eugene K. Pvt 454 Ord.    32049273             9-13-42
Seavy, Emery M. Pvt. 27 Matl.        19049689             9-13-42
Mason, Chester T. Pvt. 59 CAC        6936246              9-13-42
Nelson, Cecil B. Pfc. QMC            18060006             9-13-42
Eachus, Robert L. Pvt. 19 Bomb       19044037             9-13-42
Roberts, John H. Pvt. 3 Pur.         17043461             9-13-42
Jenson, James Pvt. 31 Inf.           19056410  Co. D.     9-13-42
Nelson, Warren L. Pvt. 20 Pur.       12007429             9-13-42
Kerr, Kieth V. Pvt. 28 Matl.         29049446             9-13-42
Matthews, Edward Pfc. 91 Bomb        13032347             9-14-42
Adams, Vincenzo R. Sgt. 28 Bomb      R-2709804            9-14-42
Hecker, John E. Pfc. QMC             6840604              9-14-42
King, Ronald J. Sgt. 192 Tank        20645263             9-14-42
Merrill, Earton G. Pvt. 20 AB        14044342             9-14-42
McLaughlin, Jack H. Pvt. 31 Inf.     19013608  *          9-14-42
Zam, Joseph Cpl. 192 Tank            20500753             9-14-42
Williams, David A. Cpl. 4554 Ord.    14039457             9-14-42
Gloria, Andres Pvt. 200 CAC          38044840             9-14-42
Chester, James W. Pfc. 7 Matl.       19024081             9-15-42
Thomure, Harold C. Cpl. USMC           294979             9-15-42
McCrea, Joseph F. Pfc. 192 Tank      20645269             9-15-42
Pickens, James V. Pfc. 200 CAC       20842732             9-15-42
Yacob, George Pvt. 194 Tank          39076623             9-15-42
Stoltz, William H. 1/Lt. Inf.        0-392481             9-15-42
Graham, Charles G. Cpl. 803 CE       32048532             9-15-42
Lyons, Howard F. Pfc. 200 CAC        36050880             9-15-42
Jackson, James R. Sgt. QMC           6368401              9-15-42
Spradlin, Lord I. Cpl. QMC           6587256              9-15-42
Prather, Luther Pfc. 454 Ord.        14049203             9-16-42
Snead, Edward H. Pfc. 31 Inf.        13032814  Co. F.     9-16-42
Fenslaw, Edward S/Sgt. 20 Pur.       6840475              9-16-42
Haugh, John H. Pvt. 803 CE           32090627             9-16-42
Davies, Joseph L. Pfc. SC AW         13043460             9-16-42
Duncan, Robert T. RM1c USN           44-062-10            9-16-42
Bussert, Hubert M. Cpl. 7 Matl.      19038387             9-17-42
Adams, Joseph Capt. QMC              0-290240             9-17-42
Pope, Edward K. Cpl. 200 CAC         20843815             9-17-42
Packard, Henry H. Sgt. 803 CE        14045365             9-17-42
Querl, William C. Cpl. 31 Inf.       17027354  Co. G.     9-17-42
Mertz, Ralph W. Pfc. 75 Ord.         6814890              9-18-42
Shubert, Robert H. Sgt. 192 Tank     35002377             9-18-42
Clinkscale, Edgar H. Pvt. 4 CWS      19013525             9-18-42
Lucero, Gustavo Pvt. 200 CAC         20844166             9-18-42
LaRoque, Andrew Pvt. 31 Inf.         19019466  Co. I.     9-18-42
```

```
Porter, Virgil B. S/Sgt. 24 Pur.        6882226                      9-18-42
Wisniewski, Stephen M. Pfc. 31 Inf.      702568    Hq. Co.           9-18-42
Petee, Albert L. Pvt. CWS              19052705                      9-18-42
Clayton, Kermit Pvt. 515 CAC           38011877                      9-18-42
Cronk, Francis J. Pvt. 17 Bomb         14036508                      9-19-42
Rancke, Henry C. 2/Lt. AC              0-408846                      9-19-42
Turner, William C. Jr. Pvt. 27 Bomb    7009204                       9-19-42
Roberto, Rocco A. Pvt. 19 AB            6713688                      9-19-42
Seebourg, Arvid E. Pvt. 24 Pur.         6759796                      9-19-42
Clark, Freeland G. Pfc. 7 CWS           6575742                      9-19-42
Gray, William H. Pfc. 31 Inf.         10306788    Co. B.            9-20-42
Taylor, Dan Pvt. 31 Inf.                6076127    Svc. Co.          9-20-42
Smith, Oliver C. Pvt. SC AW            13027272                      9-20-42
Vallo, Peter D. Pvt. 515 CAC           38012203                      9-20-42
Dunlavy, Joe Martin WO 27 Bomb          6280691                      9-20-42
Carney, Everett J. 1/Lt. 803 CE        0-331381                      9-20-42
Dobson, Laurence E. Capt FA            0-364818                      9-20-42
Vonderheide, George F. M/Sgt. F.D.      6276390                      9-20-42
Woodson, LaMar A. Pvt. 192 Tank        39098887                      9-21-42
McAndrew, Harold J. Pfc. 200 CAC       36034175                      9-21-42
Oliver, Hurley Sgt. 75 Ord.           R-2367467                      9-21-42
Zamora, Zargosa C. Pvt. 200 CAC        38031208                      9-21-42
Tucker, James R. CWO AC                 1489619                      9-21-42
Reynolds, John E. Pvt. 19 AB           19054213                      9-21-42
Montoya, Pete A. Pvt. 515 CAC          38012068                      9-22-42
Prescott, John R. Pfc. 5 Inter.        11020705                      9-22-42
Young, Lou R. Pvt. M.D.                18003182                      9-22-42
Cornell, Emerson Pvt. 680 Ord.         19052624                      9-22-42
Miller, Edwin C. 2/Lt. AC              0-398760                      9-22-42
Prince, Sam A. Sgt. 200 CAC            20843481                      9-22-42
Thorne, Homer C. Pvt. 91 Bomb         14001183                      9-22-42
Batz, Rueben J. Pvt. 60 CAC           18000106                      9-22-42
Schweigert, Guy Sgt. 21 Pur.            6713446                      9-22-42
Wolfe, Frank J. S/Sgt. 91 Bomb         6375437                       9-23-42
Kerns, Francis Pfc. 3 Pur.              6998068                      9-23-42
Swartz, James W. Sgt. 17 Pur.           6913442                      9-23-42
Dawson, James D. Pvt 4 CWS            16019359    Co. I.Replacement  9-23-42
Bainbridge, James A. Sgt. 192 Tank     20600386                      9-23-42
Bryan, Carroll L. Cpl. 75 Ord.         19013209                      9-23-42
Dickmann, William H. Cpl. 24 Pur        6584505                      9-23-42
Parsons, Hugh Pvt. 28 Matl.           11013407                      9-23-42
Sisnerso, Jose G. Pvt. 200 CAC         38012394                      9-23-42
Gillespie, James W. Pvt. 192 Tank      35121630                      9-23-42
Davis, Kenneth E. Sgt. 200 CAC        20843793                       9-24-42
Meade, Lawrence K. Capt. CE            0-19182                       9-24-42
Reeves, Gerald D. Pvt. 31 Inf.        18033922    A-T Co.           9-24-42
Yaros, Steve F. Pfc. M.D.               6901283                      9-24-42
Floyd, Wyatt D. S/Sgt. QMC              6390327                      9-24-42
Cannady, Edward A. Cpl. 3 Pur.         19043363                      9-24-42
Radcliffe, William M. Pfc. 7 Matl.     19046012                      9-24-42
Hallock, Charles H. Cpl. 33 QMC         6039021                      9-24-42
Schlappich, Earl Pfc. 7 CWS           13009595                       9-24-42
Marshall, Anthony L. Sgt. 34 Pur.       6570808                      9-24-42
Winter, Benjamin F.Jr. Cpl. 21 Pur.    19054643                      9-25-42
George, Raymond W. Pvt. 803 CE         33082884                      9-25-42
Vetter, Theodore H. 2/Lt. Inf.         0-890189                      9-25-42
Dyer, Harold RM2c USN               26-232-09                        9-25-42
Ogerman, Emil F. Pvt. 33 QMC           39007351                      9-25-42
Cole, George H. Sgt. 680 Ord.           3900741                      9-25-42
Foster, Thomas Pfc. 31 Inf.             6651523    Hq. Co.           9-25-42
```

```
Peter, Charles A. Sgt. 31 Inf.          6983559  Co. C.          9-25-42
Sechrest, Lee H. Pfc. M.D.              6864561                  9-26-42
Sweeney, Edward Pfc. SC AW              6152263                  9-26-42
Elivas, Steve M. S/Sgt. 192 Tank       20500733                 9-26-42
Harvey, Raymond G. Pfc. 7 Matl.        19050293                 9-26-42
Williams, Dumont G. 1/Lt. 803 CE       0-890307                 9-26-42
Ward, John C. Pvt. 200 CAC             20842536                 9-26-42
Yeager, Fred R. Pvt. 194 Tank          20936422                 9-26-42
McNulty, John W. Pfc. M.D.             R-1409321                9-26-42
Williams, harry O. Sgt. 200 CAC        20843558                 9-26-42
Sinowitz, Raymond Pvt. 454 Ord.        32087314                 9-26-42
Apple, Nelson W. M/Sgt. 200 CAC        20842444                 9-26-42
Peterson, Dennis J. Pvt. 515 CAC       36008661                 9-27-24
Shuey, Cread E. Sgt. 60 CAC            6281587                  9-27-24
Gruber, William D. Pvt. 93 bomb        19018930                 9-27-42
Worrell, Morris R. Pvt. 31 Inf.        19051615  Co. F.         9-27-42
Connor, Howard B. 1/Lt. AC             0-339429                 9-27-42
Zinani, Joseph G. Jr. Cpl. 194 Tank    20900764                 9-27-42
Smisek, Lada CMM USN                   19-267-28                9-28-42
Martin, Phillips M. Pfc. AC            11016043                 9-28-42
Ball, Billy R. Pfc. DEML               17032792                 9-28-42
Rockwell, Charles W. T.T/Sgt. 194 T    20900764                 9-28-42
Gauske, Charles L. Pvt. 19 AB          16020840                 9-28-42
Haynes, Richard S. T/Sgt. 3 Pur.       6540313                  9-28-42
Butler, Gordon E. S/Sgt. 5 Inter.      6980708                  9-28-42
Brownlee, Raymond A. Cpl. 31 Inf.      19019214  Co. C.         9-28-42
Clark, Charles E. Pvt. 31 Inf.         19056610  Co. D.         9-28-42
Redden, James J. Pvt. 31 Inf.          17014224  Co. B.         9-28-42
Cornsilk, Jacob Pvt. 31 Inf.           19052984  Co. G.         9-28-42
Ferrell, John P. Pfc. 200  CAC         38012083                 9-28-42
Gripe, Donald J. CRMM USN              29-15-98                 9-29-42
Motter, Jesse H. Pvt. 680 Ord.         33013100                 9-29-42
Turner, Delbert D. Pvt 75 Ord.         19052599                 9-29-42
Cronin, Robert W. Cpl. 803 CE          36145038                 9-29-42
Rostedt, Joe W. Cpl.  3 Pur            17011348                 9-29-42
Gallegos, Adolfo Pfc. 200 CAC          38012171                 9-29-42
Cutsinger, Homer M. Cpl. 31 Inf.       19056765  Co. M.         9-29-42
Morris, Jeff W. Pfc. 200 CAC           20843723                 9-29-42
Roark, Roland R. Pfc. 31 Inf.          14037707  Co. E.         9-29-42
Solsbee, Wince Pfc. 194 Tank           20700257                 9-29-42
Miller, Roy E. Pfc. 200 CAC            2084271                  9-29-42
Crabtree, Alfred E. S/Sgt. 7 Matl.     6833888                  9-29-42
Pence, Robert K. Pfc. 515 CAC          38042277                 9-29-42
Scholl, John L. Sgt. 17 Pur.           6842008                  9-29-42
Zieman, Anthony M. T/Sgt. 21 Pur.      R-1013950                9-29-42
Hanell, John A. Sgt. 7 CWS             19054437                 9-29-42
Biggs, Lloyd W. L/Col. CAC             0-6607                   9-29-42
Breitung, Howard Edw. C. L/Col. CAC    0-15341                  9-29-42
Gilbert, Roydel Lt. (SR. Gr.) USN      82070                    9-29-42
Elliott, Rowland C. QM3c USN           26-583-02                9-29-42
Oja, Onnie A. Pvt. 200 CAC             36225663                 9-29-42
Rolls, Fred W. Pvt. 20 Pur.            19044320                 9-29-42
Pffeiffer, Edward Pfc. 28 Matl.        6980471                  9-29-42
Clark, Charles E. Pvt. 200 CAC         37054710                 9-30-42
Johnson, John A. Pvt. 24 Pur.          17027240                 9-30-42
Greer, Robert E. Pfc. 20 AB            6588834                  9-30-42
Dutelle, Joseph J. Cpl. 28 Matl.       6748303                  9-30-42
Pardue, Roy Cpl. 27 Bomb               6974081                  9-30-42
Devereux, Robert M. Pvt. Har. Def.     19020898                 9-30-42
Watson, Don Sgt. 515 CAC               38044933                 9-30-42
```

```
Sapp, James A. Pvt. 194 Tank        20937816                    9-30-42
Bryant, Francis E. Pvt. QMC         18024472                    9-30-42
Arnone, Arthur Pvt. 454 Ord.        33016872                    10-1-42
Golinski, Leo J. Sgt. 31 Inf.        6906060    Co. B.          10-1-42
Fuller, Harold A. M/Sgt. DEML       19046344                    10-1-42
Anderson, Walter Pfc. USMC                                      10-1-42
Youmans, Charlie A. Pfc. 27 Bomb    14011981                    10-1-42
Red, Gerald W. Pfc. 24 Pur.          6298725                    10-1-42
Jensen, Lars C. 1/Lt. Inf.          0-322145                    10-1-42
Nelson, Roland R. Pvt. 33 QMC       19013151                    10-1-42
Tully, Donald, J. Pvt. 17 Pur.      16000733                    10-2-42
Parsons, William H. Cpl. 803 CE      6584838                    10-2-42
Sheeran, William A. Pvt. 20 Pur.    13006857                    10-2-42
Roller, Gaines B. Pfc. 31 Inf.      13017054    *               10-2-42
Dancoe, Andrew Pfc. 24 Pur.          6751531                    10-2-42
Graves, James H. Pvt. 31 Inf.        6290701    Svc. Co.        10-2-42
Carter, Martin H. Pfc. 194 Tank     20950128                    10-2-42
Walburg, Arthur B. Cpl 31 Inf.       6930708    Co. D.          10-2-42
MacDonald, Sherman P. 1/Sgt. USMC     222750                    10-3-42
Johnson, Robert E. CMB USN          3651358                     10-3-42
Mabey, Rolf R. Pfc. 745 Ord.        39678698                    10-3-42
Davis, Jasper Jr. Pvt. 31 Inf.      14037623    Co. F.          10-3-42
Goodrich, Wallace Pvt. 194 Tank     20700233                    10-3-42
Wood, Neal D. Pvt. 27 Bomb          14060278                    10-3-42
Artis, Clayton Pvt. 16 Bomb         14060799                    10-3-42
Abbott, Carl F. S/Sgt. 194 Tank     20900646                    10-3-42
Bernd, Wellington W. Pfc. 7 CWS     33070093                    10-3-42
Redd, Talmadge W. Pvt. 200 CAC      38055543                    10-4-42
Cooke, Paul C. Capt. AGD            0-243073                    10-4-42
Amera, Alvin Pfc. 680 Ord.          19032413                    10-4-42
Molitor, Joseph M. S/Sgt. 5 Inter.   6911340                    10-4-42
Sanders, Lewis F. Sgt. 803 CE        6856705                    10-4-42
Tellez, Enrique, G. Pvt. 200 CAC    38030813                    10-4-42
Tock, John N. Pvtl 31 Inf.           6755883    Svc. Co.        10-4-42
Gesell, Oscar F. S/Sgt. QMC         R-325879                    10-4-42
Astorgano, Martin L. Pvt. 21 Pur.   19054921                    10-4-42
Dravis, Edwin D Pvt. 31 Inf.        7025703     Hq. Co.         10-4-42
Thomas, Bill J. Cpl. 200 CAC        20842598                    10-5-42
Giles, Conrad D. Pfc. M.D.          14042955                    10-5-42
Rooney, Paul E. M/Sgt. AC           R-48359                     10-5-42
Megown, Willard G. Pvt. 27 Bomb     34000666                    10-5-42
Lehman, Franklin P. Pvt. 454 Ord.   33000687                    10-5-42
McNeil, William H. 2/Lt. QMC        0-367430                    10-5-42
Walton, John Civilian                                          10-6-42
Wagner, Edward L.. Pvt 48 Matl.     11013693                    10-6-42
Ellis, Robert A. Pfc. 31 Inf.       19013629    Hq. Det. 3 Bn. 10-6-42
Mathews. Earl W. Cpl. 60 CAC        18043753                    10-6-42
Weimer, Earle R. 2/Lt. 33 Inf.      0-890267                    10-7-42
Davis, William K. S/Sgt. 48 Matl.    6394109                    10-7-42
White, Harry E. Capt. Inf.          0-354607    *               10-7-42
Goultney, William J. S/Sgt. 20 Pur.  6555913                    10-7-42
Thomas, Richard D. Pfc. 91 Bomb     13030274                    10-7-42
Hipp, Jessie P. Sgt. AC              6260606                    10-7-42
Burns, Dewey W. Pvt. 803 CE         69457648                    10-7-42
Smoot, Marion B. Pvr. 454 Ord.      14036528                    10-7-42
Williams, Fred Pvt. 31 Inf.          6662625    Hq. Co.         10-7-42
Miller, Karl E. Cpl. 31 Inf.        19052316    Co. G.          10-7-42
Malpass, Marion L. S/Sgt. 3 Pur.    1441556                     10-7-42
Mulford, Jesse R. CWT USN           1441556                     10-7-42
Wisnowski, Joseph L. Pvt 192 Tank   3601232                     10-7-42
```

263

```
Miller, Robert L. Pvt. 194 Tank        20900734              10-8-42
Rimmer, Hohn H. Pfc. 14 Bomb            7002428               10-8-42
Gonzales, Frankie D. Pvt. 200 CAC       20343960              10-8-42
Bradt, Audie Pvt. 754 Ord.              39080711              10-8-42
Raynes, Samuel L. Pvt. 192 Tank         14017456              10-8-42
Wagner, James S. Pfc. 808 MP            17019566              10-8-42
Deutscher, William G. Pvt. 34 Pur.      19013402              10-8-42
Donahue, Eugene A. Pfc. 31 Inf.         13004902    Co. D.    10-8-42
Griffin, Marion M. Cpl. 21 Pur.         18037825              10-8-42
Imperiale, Peter C. Cpl. 31 Inf.        6705790     Co. L.    10-8-42
Saarinen, Paul A. Sgt. 194 Tank         20700211              10-8-42
Locher, Joseph H. M/Sgt. 19 Bomb        R-742355              10-9-42
Maddux, Aubrey L. Sgt. 515 CAC          38011913              10-9-42
Sawyer, Reginald E. Sgt. 16 Bomb        6973568               10-9-42
Walker, Herbert J. Pvt. 91 Bomb         13028064              10-9-42
Corgan, Robert H. 1/Lt. FA              0-387030              10-9-42
Schlinglerman, Glenn G. Pvt. 192 T      36301335              10-9-42
Thomas, Howard G. BM1c USN              3756375               10-9-42
Miller, Robert J. Cpl. 31 Inf.          19056400    Co. C.    10-9-42
Bovee, James G. Pvt. 7 CWS              19021249              10-9-42
Hall, Wesley B. M/Sgt. QMC              R-2381538             10-9-42
Bak, Jospeh E. Sgt. 31 Inf.             6119664     Hq. Co.   10-9-42
Rawson, Eugene E. Pvt. 194 Tank         20900742              10-10-42
Collins, Jerome W. Pfc. 745 Ord.        39081178              10-10-42
Tapaszi, John G. Pfc. 194 Tank          39676178              10-10-42
Swift, william I 1/Sgt. 192 Tank        20600373              10-10-42
Olmstead, Barnes Sgt. 515 CAC.          38011833              10-10-42
Grimm, James S. Cpl. 803 CE             6226469               10-10-42
Hay, John F. 2/Lt. Tanks                0-432340              10-10-42
Lamb, Harry E. Pvt. 31 Inf.             19051498    Co. E.    10-10-42
Cates, Marvin Cpl. 200 CAC              38011920              10-10-42
Gibb, Lawrence Jr. EM2c USN             3370898               10-11-42
McMurdo, Hew B. Jr. Pvt. 31 Inf.        19000784    Co. B.    10-11-42
Holt, Elbert A. Pfc. 31 Inf.            18056415    Co. F.    10-11-42
Owens, William B. T/Sgt. 93 Bomb        6259451               10-11-42
Bostedt, Glen C. Cpl. 3 Pur.            17011361              10-11-42
Miller, Harold J. Pfc. M.D.             6893688               10-11-42
White, Patrick J. T/Sgt. 808 MP         R-347373              10-11-42
Den, Oscar Sgt. 194 Tank                20523475              10-11-42
Clark, Ashward J. Pfc. QMC              6744273               10-11-42
Cronin, Francis Sgt. 409 SC             11020667              10-11-42
Ashborn, Walter L. 1/Lt. QMC            0-890084              10-11-42
Johnson, Harold 2/Lt. AC                0-427816              10-11-42
Barnes, William S. Pvt. 803 CE          18033784              10-12-42
McCone, Jean Pvt. 192 Tank              36200714              10-12-42
Lambert, Richard Sgt. FEAF              6998536               10-12-42
Watt, Richard G. S/Sgt. 20 Pur.         19010253              10-12-42
Gauck, Ernest W. Pvt. 12 QMC            6706935               10-12-42
Boardman, Jack A. Pfc. 7 Matl.          19038520              10-12-42
Lyle, Carl W. Capt. 45 Inf PS           0-352915              10-12-42
Slinter, Richard C. Sgt. 27 Bomb        7003837               10-12-42
Crews, Stanley A. Pvt. 27 Bomb          38002887              10-13-42
Blakely, Eugene L. Pfc. 12 MP           19051294              10-13-42
Richitelli, Charles A. Pvt. 48 Matl.11024453                 10-13-42
Wheeler, Ernest E. 60 CAC               16013653              10-13-42
Mooney, Ewell R. Pfc. 31 Inf.           12008388    Co. C.    10-13-42
Howe. Wallace A. M/Sgt. 515 CAC         20842479              10-13-42
Friel, James E. S/Sgt. 808 MP           6573839               10-14-42
Priest, Lowell Pvt. 200 CAC             38012049              10-14-42
Fuller, Leigh A. Maj. Inf.              0-17239     *         10-14-42
```

```
Jannisch, Fred A Cpl. 192 Tank          20600451                    10-14-42
Scott, Lee R. Pvt. 17 Ord.              36003248                    10-14-42
Holbrook, Walter E. Pvt. 19 AB          19010577                    10-14-42
Witt, Lawrence Pvt. 19 Ab               16006633                    10-15-42
Farnham Gerald A. Sgt. 31 Inf.           6983443    Co. C.          10-15-42
Nisnevits, Oscar Pfc. 803 CE            32074402                    10-15-42
Markett, CArl L. 803 CE                 32074151                    10-15-42
Lindley, Eugene W. Pvt. 4 CWS           18660098                    10-15-42
Bagwell, John M. Cpl. 24 Pur.           19013512                    10-15-42
Welch, John M. Pfc. 803 CE (MD)         35030729                    10-15-42
Thomas, Charles W. T/Sgt. 27 Matl.       6813585                    10-15-42
Ek, Karl L. 1/Lt. 88 FA                 0-320782                    10-15-42
Shurtleff, Reid P. 1/Lt. 24 FA          0-416430                    10-15-42
Wallace, Ernest L. Pfc. FEAF             6560212                    10-15-42
Mason, John B. Pfc. USMC                  286313                    10-16-42
Clemans. Charles R. T/Sgt. 91 Bomb       6278760                    10-16-42
Evans, Guilford E. 2/Lt.                0-427316                    10-16-42
Ellis, James D. Capt. FA                0-298228                    10-16-42
Stanton, Raymond G. Pvt. 27 Matl.       19016028                    10-16-42
Monroe, Emery O. Pfc. 194 Tank          20720309                    10-16-42
Dukatnik, Robert Sgt. 21 Pur.            6299751                    10-16-42
Updike, Richard H. Cpl. 200 CAC         20848599                    10-16-42
Lockhart, Max D. Pfc. 31 Inf.           17018699    Svc. Co.        10-16-42
Terry, Mack V. Jr. Sgt. 27 Bomb          7001086                    10-17-42
McKee, Arthur CMM USN                    1336232                    10-17-42
Grimes, Rudyard K. Capt. 57 Inf.        0-22031                     10-17-42
Jones, Richard L. Pfc. 31 Inf.           6573716    Co. C.          10-17-42
Bullard, Raymond V. Pfc. 28 Matl.       19019492                    10-17-42
Bickford, Vernon A. Sgt. 28 Matl.        6078173                    10-17-42
Tade, Ray E. Cpl. 20 Pur.               19046179                    10-17-42
Perry, George L. Jr. Sgt. 17 SC          6953622                    10-17-42
Carlon, Fredrick Pvt. 31 Inf.            6139469    Co. D.          10-17-42
Baggett, Paul R. Sea1c USN               3600868                    10-18-42
Hopper, Joseph E. Pvt. 75 Ord.          19038800                    10-18-42
Nance, Hugh B. Pvt. 200 CAC             38012362                    10-18-42
Twomby, William C. 2/Lt. 31 Inf.        0-890379    Co. B.          10-18-42
Gibson, Clifford L. Pfc. 192 Tank       35002428                    10-18-42
Zurline, Philip F. Pvt. 21 Pur.         18002667                    10-18-42
Dailey, Frank H. Sgt. 3 Pur.             6576428                    10-18-42
Poratoski, Walter Sgt. 31 Inf.          R-1030910   Co. I.          10-18-42
Cavett, Clarence E. Sgt. 34 Pur.        18014612                    10-18-42
O'Donovan, James J. Maj. 31 Inf.        0-294421    Hq. Det. 3 Bn.  10-18-42
Keve, Ohn M. Pvt. M.D.                  17002287                    10-18-42
Matkins, Creighton H. Cpl. 21 Pur.       6862194                    10-19-42
Fishel, John M. S/Sgt. FEAF              6860937                    10-19-42
Parr, George W. 1/Sgt. DEML              1902043                    10-19-42
Buckett, Reavers B. Cpl. QMC             6529561                    10-19-42
Norfleet, Allen M. Pfc. 91 QMC           6937034                    10-19-42
Boyd, Harmon E. Cpl. 515 CAC            38012305                    10-19-42
Whiteside, Beford Jr. Pfc. 17 Bomb       7002913                    10-19-42
Holland, William C. 1/Sgt. 200 CAC      20842982                    10-19-42
Allen, James D. MM1c USN                 2814517                    10-20-42
Bordner, Henry D. Pvt 194 Tank          39601669                    10-20-42
Bourne, Thomas S. Pfc. 20 AB            14013309                    10-20-42
Brown, James C. Pfc. Co. K. 31st.        6532983    *               10-20-42
Brown, William E. Pvt. 192 Tank         14010327                    10-20-42
Gavda, Kusti N. Pvt. 27 Bomb.           11049897                    10-20-42
Guinn, Thorton 2/Lt. Inf.               0-890292    *               10-20-42
Harrington, Roy E. Pfc. 27 Matl.         6913861                    10-20-42
Jones, Richard M. S/Sgt. 93 Bomb         6398070                    10-20-42
```

```
McBride, J.B. Pfc. 31 Inf.            18033923   Co. F.       10-20-42
McClellan, James. A. Pvt. 803 CE       6898335                10-20-42
Mears, Wyman F. Maj. 71 FA            0-242661                 10-20-42
Stevens, Leland R. Pfc. AC             6935971                 10-20-42
Sweet, Bernard F. Pfc. 24 Pur.         6977380                 10-20-42
Hall, Nilus L. Sgt. 515 CAC           38011899                 10-21-42
Trotter. Elmer L. Sgt. 91 Bomb         7000462                 10-21-42
Nanny, Clyde Pvt. QMC                  6244140                 10-21-42
Tubb, James E. Pvt. 31 Inf.            6210845   Co. K.        10-21-42
Hughes, James A. Pvt. 454 Ord.        34084162                 10-21-42
Morgan, George E. Pfc. 31 Inf. MD     37033580   Med. Det.     10-21-42
Iooney, Virgil L. Pvt. 200 CAC        38012349                 10-21-42
Lafromboise, Frank Pvt. 60 CAC        19054323                 10-21-42
Wiggins, Elwood L. Pfc. 7 Matl.       19050241                 10-21-42
Sims, James A. Cpl. 200 CAC           38011992                 10-21-42
Walsh, Patrick H. Pvt. 60 CAC         15061805                 10-21-42
Paul, Clifford A. Sgt. 803 CE          6722467                 10-21-42
Masson, Richard B. Pfc. USMC                                   10-21-42
Rice, Leonard B. Pfc. USMC             229926                  10-21-42
Spensley, Homer V. Pfc. 200 CAC       20842999                 10-21-42
Hicks, Gerald L. Pfc. 31 Inf.         16041179   Co. E.        10-22-42
Pronchick, Fred C. Pvt. 803 CE        33070127                 10-22-42
Clark, James P. Pvt. 454 Ord.         14040621                 10-22-42
Becktow, George W. Sgt. 17 Pur.        6911560                 10-22-42
Morse, Robert J. Pvt. 803 CE          32046303                 10-23-42
Cunningham, John O. Pfc. 194 Tank     35100564                 10-23-42
Zoberbier, Roy 2/Lt. 31 Inf.         0-890238   Co. M.         10-23-42
Reimen, John W. AGMM USN               1830108                 10-24-42
Williams, Howard R. Pvt. 194 Tank     39676506                 10-24-42
Drake, Henry A. Cpl. 200 CAC          20843587                 10-24-42
Oie, Casper J. S/Sgt. 21 Pur.          6937581                 10-24-42
Bush, Thomas O. 1/Lt. 31 Inf.        0-375811   Co. A.         10-24-42
Sullivan, Robert E. 1/Sgt. 31 Inf.     6763372   Co. H.        10-24-42
Youmans, Elwyn Pvt. AC                12016296                 10-24-42
Berrier, William L. Cpl. AC           18007819                 10-24-42
Smallwood, James E. AOM3c USn          3602244                 10-25-42
Clinton, Edward J. Pvt. 803 CE         6978526                 10-26-42
Jones, Stanley P. Cpl 31 Inf.          6574621   Co. G.        10-26-42
Hickman, Daimer, F. Pvt. 31 Inf.      19044382   Hq. Co.       10-26-42
Stephenson, Lonnie D. Cpl 31 Inf.      6584384   Co. H.        10-26-42
Reid, Melvin L. Pvt. 200 CAC          38012051                 10-26-42
Snyder, Eugene A. Pvt. 693 Ord.       12002994                 10-27-42
Wilson, Robert H. Pvt. 19 Bomb        19049067                 10-27-42
Bickmore, Floyd W. M/Sgt. 194 Tank    20900643                 10-27-42
Sneckus, Stanley A. Pvt. QMC           6951801                 10-27-42
Shorts, Howard B. Pvt. 28 Matl.        6949917                 10-27-42
White, Clyde L. 2/Lt. 31 Inf.        0-890268   A-T Co.        10-27-42
Bachelier, Leo S. Cpl. 31 Inf.        17016388   Co. C.        10-27-42
Murphy, Joseph C. Pfc. 31 Inf.        14042476   Co. I.        10-28-44
Lanier, Charles S. Pfc. 31 Inf.        6384960   Co. I.        10-28-42
Berendt, Louis F. Sgt. 31 Inf.         6832240   A-T Co.       10-28-42
Dunbar, Layton W. S/Sgt. 34 Pur.       6272791                 10-28-42
Urich, Harold G. Pfc. 21 Pur.         19049448                 10-28-42
Sanchez, Alfonzo B. Cpl. 515 CAC      38011997                 10-28-42
Nelson, Arvid K. Pvt. M.D.            19054295                 10-28-42
Lemelin, Albert  L. Pvt. 803 CE       14014724                 10-29-42
Chugg, George W. Pvt.24 Pur.          19006075                 10-29-42
Elings, John 2/Lt. 31 Inf.           0-890406   Co. A.         10-29-42
Avitabile, Frume J. Pvt. 803 CE       32081920                 10-29-42
Thompson, Samuel H. Pvt AC            13003316                 10-29-42
```

```
Malarky, Daniel J. British Civilian                            10-29-42
Osborn, Leroy L. Pvt. QMC              6581760                  10-30-42
Reese, Abraham R. Pvt. 200 CAC        38012094                  10-30-42
LaRoque, Joseph S/Sgt. AC             R-612904                  10-30-42
Langdon, Eugene H. Pvt. 28 Matl.       6999533                  10-30-42
McHugh, John T. Cpl. 803 CE           32092724                  10-30-42
Fisher, Louis R. Pfc. 19 Bomb         13025078                  10-30-42
Myers, Arrol L. Corp. 31 Inf.          6260315   Co. I.         10-30-42
Kaspari, Robert V. Pvt. QMC           19004372                  10-30-42
Davis, Victor S. Pvt. 14 Bomb         11019036                  10-30-42
Stump, Melvin E. Pvt. 19 Bomb         13035020                  10-30-42
Fulton, Jess E. G/Sgt. USMC             102525                  10-30-42
Holman, Elliott, Cpl. 28 SC           19030456                  10-31-42
Williams, Wallace B. Pvt. 60 CAC      18050063                  10-31-42
Smith, Richard C. Sgt. 17 Bomb         6913957                  10-31-42
Snyder, James F. Pfc. 31 Inf.         14037841   Co. C.         10-31-42
Gates, Leonard D. Sgt. 200 CAC        20842390                  10-31-42
Jackson, Leonard Pvt. 60 CAC          19054317                  10-31-42
Adams, Charles K. Cpl. 31 Inf.         6931201   Co. C.         10-31-42
Price, Western Sgt/ 31 Inf.            6852945   Co. G.         10-31-42
Brewer, Harlow I. Capt. D.C.          0-346913                  10-31-42
Mulvaney, Robert F. Pfc. 803 CE       32033470                  10-31-42
Foltin, William J. Pvt. 31 Inf.        6229856   Co. C.         10-31-42
Lhoest, Edmond Pvt. 19 Bomb           13037308                  10-31-42
Dzubezynski, John T. Cpl 803 CE       33082173                  10-31-42
Dickerson, Ozro S/Sgt. CE             19024422                  10-31-42
Harris, Louis H. Cpl. 31 Inf.          6923769   Co. G.         10-31-42
Gordon, Robert F. Pfc. 7 Mat.         20916790                  10-31-42
Bloho, Paul Cpl. 409 SC                7022718                  11-1-42
Winters, Charles B. Pfc. 808 MP        6664117                  11-1-42
Calkins, William E. Pvt. QMC          19020993                  11-1-42
Bruntmyer, Lloyd R. Pfc. 7 Matl.      19048914                  11-1-42
Erwin, Kenneth G. Cpl. 59 CAC         18049796                  11-1-42
O'Hara, Thomas W. Pvt. 680 Ord.       32115031                  11-1-42
Clark, Walter Cpl. QMC                19053642                  11-1-42
Doyash, Harold W. 4 USMC                                       11-1-42
Smith, Henry J. Pvt. 59 CAC            6671009                  11-1-42
Hennessy, Harland Pvt. 803 CE         32092573                  11-1-42
Myers, Melvin J. Pvt. 31 Inf.         20938906   Co. K.         11-2-42
Bolin, William F. Cpl. 31 Inf.         6864788   Co. M.         11-2-42
Combs, Richard A. Pvt. 17 Ord.        15016369                  11-2-42
Johnson, Floyd E. 1/Lt. CE            0-362072                  11-2-42
O'Neil, Bob N. 2/Lt. 92 INf PA        0-890380                  11-2-42
Stouter, Raymond E. S/Sgt. 2 OBS      6925030                   11-2-42
Penan, Morris P. Pvt. 16 Bomb         11024363                  11-2-42
Arrighi, Leo A. Pvt. 27 Bomb          11011361                  11-2-42
Heller, William H. CWO 24 Pur.                                 11-2-42
Keck, Bertram, M. Pfc. 31 Inf.        17013699   Co. H.         11-2-42
Vitelli, Pasqual Sgt. 808 MP           7622067                  11-2-42
Harris, Henry C. SM2c USN              3765416                  11-2-42
Colon, Edwin F. Pvt. 31 Inf.          19054282   Co. H.         11-3-42
Casperson, Worley L. Pvt. 194 Tank    20900695                  11-3-42
Relihan, Charles K. Sgt. HPD           6706320                  11-3-42
Richardson, John M. Cpl. 21 Pur.      19049097                  11-3-42
Sloop, Gilbert L. Pvt. 60 CAC         17023848                  11-3-42
Smith, James E. 1/Lt. 31 Inf.         0-365850   Co. E.         11-4-42
Garelicke, Simon Sgt. DEML            17026405                  11-4-42
Engesser, Marens A. Pfc. 31 Inf.       6581604   Co. L.         11-4-42
Clark, Raymond V. Pfc. 808 MP          6895243                  11-4-42
Phillips, Lewis R. Pfc. 192 Tank      20645237                  11-4-42
```

```
Beard, Lawrence r. Pfc. 803 CE          33003794                    11-4-42
Walsh, John J. Pvt. 59 CAC              R-1018888                   11-4-42
Procter, Daniel 1/Sgt. 31 Inf.          R-1016736   Co. G.          11-4-42
Watson, Miad I. Sea1c USN                                           11-4-42
Merritt, Thomas A. Pvt. 200 CAC         38031075                    11-4-42
Savage, Herbert N. Pvt. QMC             20930296                    11-5-42
Crevier, Wesley J. Sgt. 2 Obs.          19019969                    11-5-42
O'Brien, William J. Ensign USN                                     11-5-42
McCarthy, Roy E. Pfc. 27 Matl.          6937864                     11-5-42
Russo, Damuel A. Pvt. 27 Bomb           11019919                    11-5-42
Traylor, Larkin B. S/Sgt. 31 Inf.       6246957     Hq. Co.         11-5-42
Steagall, Irwin W. Cpl. 200 CAC         18012034                    11-5-42
Durbin, Charles A. Cpl. 7 Matl.         6289351                     11-5-42
Harris, John A. Pvt. 28 Matl.           6884562                     11-6-42
Rittel, Willie Pfc. QMC.                13025659                    11-6-42
Waltenbaugh, Arthur L. Pfc. M.D.        7022778                     11-6-42
Anderson, Grubbs Sgt. 803 CE            6230676                     11-6-42
Walsh, Stanley J. Sgt. 192 Tank         20645226                    11-6-42
Grimes, Allen B. 1/Lt. 45 Inf. PS       0-398785                    11-6-42
Ahlberg, David A. Sgt. 28 Bomb          6584381                     11-6-42
Hathaway, Albet E. CQMc USN             3106390                     11-6-42
Merrill, Donald W. 1/Lt. CAC            0-315774                    11-6-42
Christianson, John E. Capt. SC          0-890029                    11-6-42
Norris, William M. Sgt. 200 CAC         20842349                    11-6-42
Cornell, Arthur R. 2/Lt. 698 Ord.       0-392984                    11-7-42
Waller, William Sgt. QMC                R-422032                    11-7-42
Preckel, Michael A. Pfc. V.D.           6591395                     11-7-42
Trogstad, William E. 1/Lt. CE           0-890220                    11-7-42
Cobia, Sant P. Pfc. 31 Inf.             6389050     Svc. Co.        11-7-42
Willis, Durward L. Pfc. 16 bomb         7001269                     11-7-42
Regalado,Tony M. Pvt. 200 CAC           38012565                    11-8-42
Padgett, Thadius H. Sgt. 31 Inf.        6802967     Co. F.          11-8-42
Morton, Howard G. Pvt. 59 CAC           36116904                    11-8-42
Scott, Wesley W. Pfc. V.D.              6911614                     11-8-42
Tunks, Fred Jr. Pvt. 31 Inf.            18001617    Co. M.          11-8-42
Peart, Bill Pvt. 194 Tamk               29301975                    11-8-42
Gordon, Ernest M. Pvt. 194 Tank         20700234                    11-9-42
Heart, William W. Pvt. 7 CWS            16004868                    11-9-42
Goff, Alton K. Pvt. 192 Tank            20645258                    11-9-42
Thorstead, Darrell K. Cpl. 31 Inf.      6559729     Hq. Det. 1 Bn.  11-9-42
Kucskar, Joseph J. Pvt. 803 CE          32045420                    11-9-42
Burns, Joe Pvt. 808 MP                  19056308                    11-9-42
Drake, Richard F. Pvt. 3 CWS            32092830                    11-9-42
Harper, James W. Pvt. 93 Bomb           19019043                    11-9-42
Robinette, John E. Pfc. 192 Tank        35001446                    11-10-42
West, Hugh C. Pvt. 83 Bomb              19014635                    11-10-42
Yuranko, Joseph R. Pfc. M.D.            3501426                     11-10-42
Taipale, Walter W. Pvt. 192 Tank        36201042                    11-10-42
Van Alst, Willard F. Pfc. USMC          280796                      11-10-42
Jesser, Robert F. Pvt. 194 Tank         20949691                    11-10-42
Gould, Robert H. Pvt. 27 Matl.          11013460                    11-10-42
Day, Eugene L. S/Sgt. 17 Bomb           6251014                     11-10-42
Mahoney, William G. 2/Lt. 93 Bomb       0-418045                    11-10-42
Chapin, Ora. E. Pfc. USMC               290871                      11-10-42
Halpin, Joseph A. CM1c USN              3412428                     11-10-42
Dunn, Robert A. Sgt. 27 Matl.           6976699                     11-10-42
Rees, Arthur Pfc. 27 Matl.              11017169                    11-11-42
Field, James R. 2/Lt. 3 Pur.            0-406728                    11-11-42
Pillings, William D. Cpl. 200 CAC       38012006                    11-11-42
Villarreal, Elias Pvt. 200 CAC          38029861                    11-11-42
```

```
Dorhn, Dorrance P. Pfc. QMC                              11-11-42
Murphy, William J. Pfc. 20 AB        19018442           11-11-42
Looman, Richard H. Cpl. 59 CAC       19038682           11-11-42
Ross, Raymond L. Pvt. 31 Inf.         6833229  Hq. Co.  11-12-42
Dagon, John T. T/Sgt. CWS             6897724           11-12-42
Dunagon, Thomas S. S/Sgt. 7 Matl.    R-421030           11-12-42
Gilman, Earl W. RM2c USN              3720071           11-12-42
Carroll, Kenneth H. Pvt. 27 Mat.     11011343           11-12-42
Cooke, Jerald W. Pvt. 17 Pur.        11016030           11-12-42
McClendon, James H. S/Sgt. AC         6398015           11-12-42
Paine, Donald H. Sgt. 194 Tank       20700204           11-13-42
Steinfelt, Pat A. Pvt. 803 CE        33013314           11-13-42
Riley, Richard M. Maj. M.C.          0-348988           11-13-42
Shantley, Harry B. 2/Lt. Inf.        0-890242  *        11-13-42
Mitchell, Don E. Pvt. 31 Inf.        17014175  Co. C.   11-13-42
Waldroff, Kenneth B. Cpl. 59 CAC     17025000           11-13-42
Oluschak, Peter Pfc. 31 Inf.          6948029  Co. G.   11-13-42
Robertson, John M. Pfc. 24 Pur.      16027710           11-13-42
Ouzounian, Gregory Pvt. 93 Bomb      19050448           11-13-42
Alexander, Bruce F. Sgt. 31 Inf.      6544700  Co. A.   11-13-42
Forsythe, James M. Pfc. 803 CE        6580873           11-13-42
Rogers, Elmo L. Seals USN             3560700           11-13-42
McCulley, Jake E. 2/Lt. 2 Obs.       0-413533           11-13-42
Aram, Francis E. Cpl 194 Tank        20900656           11-13-42
Gregg, Donald A. Pfc. 60 CAC         15061710           11-13-42
Byron, John C. Pfc. 27 Matl.         15046200           11-13-42
Freeburg, James P. 1/Lt. AC          0-342678           11-14-42
Gallaway, Seymoure Sgt. 7 Matl.       6711415           11-14-42
Hommerson, Gerrit K. Pvt. SC AW      12027849           11-14-42
Akers, Lowell C. Pvt. 680 Ord.        6561680           11-14-42
Harris, John C. Cpl. 3 Pur.          18001283           11-14-42
Lowery, Eldon L. Pfc. 429 SC         14057664           11-14-42
Kingman, Stanley H. Pfc. FEAF        11020662           11-14-42
Jaramillo, Tranquilino Pvt. 200 CAC  38012011           11-14-42
Cunningham, Raymond W. Pvt. 31 Inf.   6284091  Co. H.   11-14-42
Larson, Gordon N. Pfc. 59 CAC        19030403           11-14-42
Mohead, George W. Pvt. QMC            6966213           11-14-42
Twomey, Francis WO(Jg) AGD            1100859           11-14-42
Curran, Bernard J. Pvt. 17 Pur.      11017039           11-14-42
Bizzell, Richard H. Pvt. 27 Bomb     34144636           11-14-42
Seiff, Harry M. Pfc. 20 Pur.         19046304           11-14-42
Bradner, William W. T/Sgt. 28 Matl.   6936284           11-15-42
Yanover, George Pvt. 27 Bomb         11024231           11-15-42
Blonien, Elmer F. Pvt. 192 Tank      36206285           11-15-42
Alstott, Raymond A. Pvt. 20 AB        6581615           11-15-42
McKinney, Richard E. G/Sgt. USMC       196259           11-15-42
Newton, Martin Sgt. 803 CE            6065154           11-15-42
Slenker, LeRoy M. Pvt. 31 Inf.       19004368  *        11-15-42
Causey, Truman G. S/Sgt. AC           6350976           11-15-42
DeCloss, Raymond N. Pvt. M.D.        20900700           11-15-42
MacDonald, Joseph C. Pvt. 60 CAC     19012604           11-15-42
Legett, Ernest R. S/Sgt. 454 Ord.     6374760           11-15-42
Laniauskas, Petrer Pvt. 803 CE        6150019           11-16-42
O'Brien, Francis M. Pfc. 27 Bomb     11024305           11-15-42
Conlon, Joseph L. Pvt. 27 Matl.      11031319           11-15-42
Brown, John I. S/Sgt. AC              6383974           11-15-42
Loesche, Karl R. Sgt. 3 Pur.          6909314           11-16-42
Frey, Vernon J. Pfc. 93 Bomb         19012821           11-16-42
O'Gorman, William G. T/Sgt. DEML     17929919           11-16-42
Crette, Albert L. Sgt. 3 Pur.        R-1082932          11-16-42
```

```
Gonzales. Joseph M. Pvt. 808 MP      6580583                  11-16-42
Bell, Robert O. Pvt. M.D.            19017765                 11-16-42
Johnson, Earl E. Pvt. CAC            6587357                  11-16-42
Cuda, Raymond T. Pvt. 680 Ord.       19015217                 11-16-42
Taylor, Ralph N. Cpl. 192 Tank       35002510                 11-17-42
Bruce, Edward A. 1/Sgt. 20 AB        6650012                  11-17-42
Roe, Marion Pvt. 200 CAC             38031328                 11-17-42
Marback, Fred Pfc. 194 Tank          20900729                 11-17-42
Quande, Kenneth M. Stkpr3c USN       3162904                  11-17-42
Monteith, Charles F. 1/Lt. 92 CAC    0-350587                 11-18-42
Alinell, Mike Cpl. AC                6785934                  11-18-42
Comm, Lawrence A. CMM USN            2792697                  11-18-42
LeGrand, Carl W. Pfc. 34 Pur.        1108263                  11-18-42
Thomas, Evert S. Maj. AGD            0-109097                 11-19-42
York, George Sr. Civilian                                    11-19-42
Hanscomb, Lawrence K. Sgt. 31 Inf.   6137280   Co. E.        11-19-42
Ruarkm John W. Cpl. USMC             278681                   11-19-42
Simmons, George G. Cpl. 60 CAC       19019886                 11-19-42
Collins, Frederick G. Cpl. QMC       6578818                  11-19-42
Bain, Daniel C. Pfc. 803 CE          33035131                 11-19-42
Gutierrez, Juan E. Pfc. 200 CAC      20843125                 11-19-42
Lobdell, Lloyd J. Pfc. 192 Tank      20645267                 11-19-42
Nichols, Harvey A. Pfc. 33QMC        7009171                  11-19-42
Waid, Charles M. Pvt. M.D.           19049058                 11-19-42
Kelder, Arthur H. Pvt. M.D.          36016623                 11-19-42
Kovach, John Pvt. 192 Tank           20500764                 11-19-42
Hirschi, Harold S. Pvt. 19 Bomb      19028407                 11-19-42
Overby, Evans E. Pvt. 19 Bomb        13035026                 11-19-42
Rogers, Henry A. Pvt. 17 Bomb        11013703                 11-20-42
Meyer, Raymond D. S/Sgt. 31 Inf.     17018655   Hq. Det. 1 Bn.  11-20-42
Reagan, Jack H. S/Sgt 93 Bomb        6561153                  11-20-42
Mayfield, Leland D. Sgt. 3 Pur.      18019761                 11-20-42
Moore, Harold M. SF2c USN            3751929                  11-20-42
Cotton, Clarence J. WT2c USN         3051727                  11-20-42
Burks, John C. Pfc. 31 Inf.          6274321   Co. H.        11-20-42
Simoni, Tony P. Pfc. 200 CAC         38011839                 11-20-42
Snow, Roy B. Pfc. 24 Pur.            19010634                 11-20-42
Clapp, Harold C. Pvt. SC             11029035                 11-20-42
Spriesterbach, Wayne L. Pvt. 2 Obs.  18043879                 11-20-42
Hicks, Gilbert J. Pfc. 750 Ord.      6993875                  11-20-42
Madden, Elwood K. Cpl. USMC          213023                   11-20-42
Russell, Donald Kent Pvt. 31 Inf.    6864947   Co. I.        11-21-42
Bach, Paul L. Capt. Inf.             0-311373   *            11-21-42
Schantz, Lloyd H. MM2c USN           2385632                  11-21-42
Smith, Austin J. Pvt. 515 CAC        36225756                 11-21-42
Briggs, Peter D. Pvt. 4 CWS          39011385                 11-21-42
Harrie, Robert M. Pfc. 192 Tank      20645293                 11-21-42
Striplin, John L. Pfc. 194 Tank      39234489                 11-21-42
Sayles, Oliver D. Jr. S/Sgt. 17 Pur. 6755413                 11-21-42
Moody, D.L. Craig S/Sgt. 803 CE      6856703                  11-21-42
Westbrook, Seth L. S/Sgt. 60 CAC     R-1099876               11-21-42
Burchfield, Robert E. S/Sgt. 5 Inter.6946473                 11-21-42
Elishoff, James K. Cpl. USMC         266058                   11-22-42
Martin, Alex Cpl. 19 Bomb            6571837                  11-22-42
Crouse, David D. 1/Sgt. 808 MP       R-740489                 11-22-42
Hasselkus, Howard L. Sgt. 192 Tank   35015891                 11-22-42
Pierce, Robert C. Sgt. 7 Matl.       6825221                  11-22-42
Ulrich, Ernest H. Pvt. M.D.          38055475                 11-22-42
Lane, Lyman L. Pfc. USMC                                      11-22-42
Thorne. Gale H. Pfc. 31 Inf.         6565951   Co. D.        11-22-42
```

```
Walsh, John E. Cpl. 31 Inf.            6983544  Co. H.           11-22-42
Penny, Bruce H. Pvt. 7 CWS            14039411                   11-22-42
Schermerhorn, Carl V. Capt. 57 Inf.  0-307776                    11-22-42
Settergren, Robert A. Pfc. 60 CAC    19017435                    11-22-42
Huffman, Harold F. S/Sgt. 60 CAC     R-2286380                   11-22-42
Havens, Robert G. M/Sgt. 192 Tank    20645204                    11-23-42
Dammrow, Stanley A. Cpl. FEAF        17030323                    11-23-42
Lawrence, Albert J. Cpl. CWS         11019656                    11-23-42
Gillis, Joe Pfc. 194 Tank            20900714                    11-23-42
Grill, Leo M. Pfc. CE                19054590                    11-23-42
Nehrbass, Henry W. Pvt. 808 MP       16003474                    11-23-42
Groseclose, Robert D. Pvt. 59 CAC    19032159                    11-23-42
Burtz, John A. Pvt. 48 Matl.         14002111                    11-23-42
Harden, Allen G. Pvt. 17 Ord.        35021188                    11-23-42
Miller, David I. Pvt. 27 Bomb        11018833                    11-24-42
Newman, Harry J. M/Sgt. 59 CAC        6544622                    11-24-42
Wolfe, Joseph W. Sgt. 59 CAC         R-562986                    11-24-42
Huber, Charles J. S/Sgt. SC          19056748                    11-24-42
Clark, LaMonte T. Capt. CE           0-890078                    11-24-42
Mattox, Samuel E. Pvt. 34 Pur.       15066235                    11-24-42
Scanlon, Raymond G. Pfc. 200 CAC     36204818                    11-24-42
Hoyt. Frank W. Pvt. 19 Bomb          11019905                    11-24-42
Cox, Richard Pvt. 19 Bomb             6556975                    11-24-42
Shields, John S. Sgt. 200 CAC        20843601                    11-24-42
Grui, George Pvt. 194 Tank           37026117                    11-24-42
Vaughn, Walter Sgt. 17 Ord.          15061420                    11-25-42
Howell, Fredrick C. Sealc USN          334953                    11-25-42
Nelson, Lloyd Pvt. 803 CE            37037644                    11-25-42
Beasley, James B. Cpl. 59 CAC        R-3284522                   11-25-42
Stoughton, John A. Sgt. 803 CE       32092238                    11-25-42
O'Rourke, Vincent C. S/Sgt. 200 CAC  20842727                    11-25-42
Lawler, Lee E. Pfc. 31 Inf.          19020675  Co. H.           11-25-42
Slchoenwolf, Fred Lt. Sr.Gr. USn        62218                    11-25-42
Simpson, Ben W. Sgt. 60 CAC           6287417                    11-25-42
Woodman, Edward B. Pvt. 27 Bomb      11013467                    11-25-42
Matteson, James E. Cpl USMC            269284                    11-25-42
Eldridge, Carliee Pvt. 454 Ord.      34140025                    11-25-42
Carey, Edward P. Pvt. 803 CE         32073966                    11-25-42
Lloyd, Edward J. SM1c USN              228356                    11-26-42
Anson, William F. Sgt. 194 Tank      20900690                    11-26-42
Kiser, Que Pfc. M.D.                 19012362                    11-26-42
Bard, George H. Pfc. 31 Inf.          6086481  Co. M.           11-26-42
Erwin, Delmer W. Pfc. 31 Inf.        17014221  Hq. Det. 2 Bn.   11-26-42
Blurton, Ralph A. Pfc. 31 Inf.       16017957  Co. A.           11-26-42
Frazier, Homer W. Pfc. 48 Matl.       6394959                    11-26-42
Richards, Gurnia J. Pfc. 17 Bomb     14014962                    11-26-42
Hefler, Paul E. Pvt. 59 CAC          15017099                    11-26-42
Dudley, Ernest H. Pvt. 19 Bomb       19014459                    11-26-42
Frasher, Cleo J. Pvt. 20 AB           6668013                    11-26-42
Pagel, Nelson A. Pvt 454 Ord.        32022047                    11-26-42
Cairns, Charles N. 1/Lt. SC          0-315350                    11-27-42
Bennett, Chester O. 1/Lt. Inf.       0-890007  *                11-27-42
Miller, George H. Capt. CE           0-890109                    11-27-42
Carter, James H. QMC                 18052467                    11-27-42
Hals, Galland L. Pvt. 803 CE         13016412                    11-27-42
Magalesfzky, David Pvt. 91 Bomb      13028043                    11-27-42
McHale, Ellis K. Pvt. 75 Ord.        36052726                    11-27-42
Johnson, L. Pfc. USMC                  272642                    11-27-42
Albee, Liqias H. M/Sgt. TC           R-2365596                   11-27-42
Griffith, Charlie Pvt. 60 CAC        14043785                    11-27-42
```

```
Lovett, Thomas S. Civilian                                                  11-28-42
Zimmer, George E. Sgt. 200  CAC        38012592                             11-28-42
Fulton, Leonard Jr. Pvt. 200 CAC       3803974                              11-28-42
Bassett, Harvey K. Pfc. 31 Inf.        19021117    Co. D.                   11-28-42
Aycock, Charles H. Pfc. 200 CAC        38911867                             11-28-42
Steinke, Ernest E. Pvt. AC             37047258                             11-28-42
Seeman, Emil Pvt. 60 CAC               16008541                             11-28-42
Wells, William Pfc. 200 CAC            36204774                             11-28-42
Ward, Donald R. Pvt. 803 CE            32028106                             11-29-42
Copeland, Elton Pvt. 31 Inf.           17014495    Hq. Co.                  11-29-42
McGough, Robert E. Pfc. 803 CE         6853940                              11-29-42
Allen, Clarence L. Pvt. 194 Tank       35100651                             11-29-42
Wyatt, Dudley D. Sealc USN             3212616                              11-29-42
Shatto, Alva E. M/Sgt. CAC             R-348522                             11-29-42
Tafoya, Gilbert G.  Pfc. 200 CAC       38012624                             11-29-42
Reynolds, John B. Sgt. 429 SC          6562455                              11-29-42
Furby, John T. 1/Lt. 194 Tank          0-372101                            11-30-42
Bonds, Henry H. T/Sgt. 31 Inf.         R-55506     Hq. Co.                  11-30-42
Tebrinke, Robert E. Sgt. 91 Bomb       6915753                             11-30-42
Massey, Sigmund F. Pvt. 7 Mat.         18010732                            11-30-42
Freeland, Charles E. Cpl. 17 Ord.      31401646                            11-30-42
Owen, Carl C. Pvt. 59 CAC              18021312                            11-30-42
Jennings, Harvey A. 2/Lt. Tank         0-890433                             12-1-42
Rusch, Henry H. 1/Sgt. HPD             R-3271468                            12-1-42
Spencer, Norman F. Sgt. 192 Tank       20200272                            12-1-42
Dean, Fred E. Cpl. 31 Inf.             6285997     Co. H.                   12-1-42
Keech, Carl H. S/Sgt. Ac               6679942                             12-1-42
Eaton, Lewis Cpl. USMC                 191772                              12-1-42
Miller, John A. Pfc. 28 Matl.          6977636                             12-1-42
Birch, Dall C. Pfc. M.D.               1905448                             12-1-42
Hayes, Lewis E. Pfc. 59 CAC            19056745                            12-1-42
Wyatt, John H. Pfc. 803 CE             6398417                             12-1-42
Butler, Edward W. Pfc. 803 CE          18049241                            12-1-42
Hall, George W. Pvt. 20 Pur.           11014679                            12-1-42
McClung, Dale W. Pvt. 31st. Svc. Co.19017273-Bro. David Co. E. 12-1-42
Houser, James M. 2/Lt. Inf.            0-890022    *                       12-2-42
Bostrom, Clarence 1/Lt. M.A.C.         0-890049                            12-2-42
Tamony, Edward F. 1/Sgt. 200 CAC       20843357                            12-2-42
Cade, Max A. Pfc. M.D.                 19000492                            12-2-42
Shariff, Marvin R. Pvt. 200 CAC        38012560                            12-2-42
Hall.  Pvt. 18 Bomb                    38060403                            12-2-42
Pearsal, Cpl. 17 Pur.                  731359                              12-3-42
Hammer,  Cpl.  27 Matl.                6984172                             12-3-42
Hall, Edward L. Capt Inf. M.P.         0-319575    *                       12-7-42
Carlson, Arthur W. M/Sgt. 7 Matl.      6641180                             12-7-42
Mixson, Ralph H. Pfc. 17 Bomb          14027304                            12-7-42
Avery, Earl E. Pvt. 2 Obs.             19018324                            12-7-42
Gallagher, Henry C. Pvt. QMC           646795  ·                           12-7-42
Ash, Wesley C. Pvt. 60 CAC             11023657                            12-8-42
Karrer, Roy N. 194 Tank                20934905                            12-8-42
McLean Clair C. Pfc. 31 Inf.           6526317     Svc. Co.                12-8-42
Moseley, Corville Cpl. CE              12010163                            12-9-42
Lamb. Robert E. Pfc. 24 Pur.           6980086                             12-9-42
Anderson, Maxwell G. Pfc. 515 CAC      8012572                             12-9-42
Rabuzzi, Gene E. Pvt. 19 AB            6667825                             12-9-42
Honstein, Louis C. Jr. Pvt. 409 SC     19000591                            12-9-42
Thompson, Ross H. T/Sgt. F.S.          R-333157                           12-10-42
James, Richard R. T/Sgt. 724 Ord.      6544711                            12-10-42
Gisner, Robert J. TM2c USN                                                12-10-42
Bailey, John C. T/Sgt. 31 Inf.         17011905    Svc. Co.               12-10-42
```

```
Northcutt, Milton M. Pvt. 200 CAC      38012007                      12-10-42
Marks, Corbett H. Pvt. 93 Bomb         13037417                      12-10-42
Brooks, Thomas F. Pvt. 194 Tank        37100389                      12-10-42
Goetz, Russell A. Pfc. 17 Pur.          6920215                      12-10-42
Ferguson, John L. Pfc. 28 Matl.         7033071                      12-10-42
Thomany, Rupert C. Pfc. 16 Bomb         6277430                      12-11-42
Butz,   Joe O. Pfc. USMC                                             12-11-42
Bond, William F. Pvt. 724 Ord.          6418055                      12-11-42
Fetzer, Leo F. Pvt. 31 Inf.            13002533   Co. K.            12-11-42
Schmidt, Elmer S. S/Sgt. 7 Matl.        6570074                      12-11-42
Kenney, Bernard J. RM1c USN              795222                      12-12-42
Busbee, George Pvt. 31 Inf.            16019352   Co. D.            12-12-42
Elrod, Henry F. Sgt. 454 Ord.            000757                      12-12-42
Wolfington, Thomas C. Sgt. QMC         13004875                      12-12-42
Wallace, Leon H. Pfc. 31 Inf.           6251622   Co. F.            12-12-42
Malamont, John Pfc. 803 CE             32109570                      12-12-42
Sanchez,    Pvt. 200 CAC                                             12-19-42
Hudson,   Sgt. 93 Bomb                  6915995                      12-20-42
Mussell, Ronald T. T/Sgt. 228 SC        6029588                      12-20-42
Gonsolin, Edward M. Capt. Inf.         0-307640   *                 12-20-42
Sparling, Daniel J. Pvt 17 Ord.         3930061                      12-21-42
Harrera, Lorenzo R. Pvt. 200 CAC        3801223                      12-21-42
Lee. Walter L. Cpl. 200 CAC             2084348                      12-21-42
Hoxie, Leon Q. Pfc. 16 Bomb             7002751                      12-23-42
LaManga. Salvador G. Pfc. 31 Inf.      12008379   Hq. Det. 1 Bn.    12-23-42
Lopez. David Pvt. 200 CAC               3801192                      12-23-42
Trisler, Edward V. Pvt. 194 Tank         205234                      12-23-42
Stehr, Frank J. Jr. 1/Lt. 88 FA         0-3787                       12-24-42
Pettibone, Raymond S. 1/Lt. 454 Ord.0-3625                          12-24-42
Foster, Charles H. Civilian                                         12-24-42
Preston, Lee A. Sgt. USMC                238081                      12-24-42
Wendroff, Robert D. Pfc. M.D. 194      37026129                      12-24-42
Locke, Lonzo P. Pfc. 31 Inf.            6921891   Co. D.            12-24-42
Millard, Cleophas Sgt. 515 CAC         37054346                      12-25-42
Gurnsey, Robert L. Pvt 7 Matl.          6298052                      12-25-42
Nash, James O. Pvt. 7 Matl.            16027165                      12-25-42
Stephens, Harry R. Pvt. 59 CAC         15017128                      12-25-42
Barlow, Woos R. Sealc USN                                           12-26-42
Hohlfeld, Jack P. Sgt. 24 Pur           6557683                      12-26-42
Shampine, Craig L. Sgt. 21 Pur.         6567364                      12-26-42
Kros, Donald E. Pvt. 200 CAC           20842455                      12-26-42
Wright, D.E. Pvt. M.D.                 18060020                      12-26-42
Mercado, Fred F. Pvt. 4 CWS            18043897                       1-3-43
Tiernan, John V. Pvt. 7 CWS            32092937                       1-3-43
Milet, John D. Sgt. USMC                 246756                       1-4-43
Cullen, Michael T. Pfc. 59 CAC         R-152      ?                  1-4-43
Purvis, Harold E. Pvt. 31 Inf.          6296875   Co. H.             1-5-43
Heath, Nealis C. Cpl. 19 Bomb           6978535                       1-6-43
Meister, Louis Pvt. 60 CAC             13024566                       1-6-43
Stanfill, Emmitt D. Pvt. 60 CAC        19054306                       1-6-43
May, Emil R. Sgt. 27 Bomb               6971449                       1-6-43
Murray, James H. Sgt. 93 Bomb           6564899                       1-7-43
Mitchell, James S. Pvt. 31 Inf.        19013612   Co. B.             1-7-43
Snow, William K. CPO USN                                             1-7-43
Manel, Frank J. Pfc. USMC                268231                       1-7-43
Floor, Peter Jr. Pvt. 17 Ord.          39002017                       1-8-43
Pulliam, William E. Pvt. CAC           37014208                       1-8-43
Tweed, Raymond Pvt. 803 CE              6900135                        1-8-43
Daniels. Elmer Pfc. 59 CAC             1501735                        1-9-43
Acamando, John J. S/Sgt. CAC            6981597                       1-9-43
```

```
Combest, Wayne V. Cpl. 24 Pur.        19015587              1-10-43
Caton, Norman B. Pfc. 28 Matl.        19020048              1-10-43
Foley, Calvin W. Pfc. 409 SC          19044458              1-10-43
Shane, George E. Pvt. 59 CAC          17016402              1-10-43
Kally, Thomas A. Pvt. 91 Bomb         13028021              1-10-43
Knipe, Edward Sgt. QMC                R-2365235             1-12-43
Evans, Vincent E. Pfc. 60 CAC         16008576              1-13-43
Liden,   S/Sgt. 5 Inter.              6879956               1-31-43
Burnette   Pfc. AC                    6580867               1-31-43
McIntire,   CTM USN                   2085907               2-2-43
Honeycutt, Roy P. Jr. Pvt. 808 MP     19052503              2-3-43
Chavez, Laudento Cpl. 200 CAC         38012289              2-4-43
Tracey, Dellart, C. CRM USN           3281404               2-13-43
Nelson, Orlando C. S/Sgt. 21 Pur.     6937733               2-13-43
Schlosser, Gerald W. Sgt. 194 Tank    20900667              2-13-43
Pavia, Fred C. Jr. Cpl. 12 MP         6873640               2-14-43
Lawrence, Raymond P. Pfc. M.D.        6794076               2-18-43
Haynes, Ira, F. S/Sgt. 31 Inf.        6740800   Co. A.      2-21-43
Williams, Robert W. s/Sgt. 7 CWS      6906704               2-23-43
Cannon, William F. Pvt. 27 Bomb       11024133              3-3-43
Roebuck, George B. GM3c USN           2660220               3-3-43
Brown, Chester E. Pvt. 24 Pur.        11011298              3-4-43
Mason, Jessie K. Pvt CWS              13017808              3-9-43
Coulter, Walter L. 1/Lt. 31 Inf.      0-890091   *          3-10-43
Ericson, Paul S. Civilian                                   3-12-43
Schrader Herbert A. Pfc. USMC         293509                3-16-43
Wortman, Harry G. Pvt. 194 Tank       39525547              3-24-43
Baker, Ernest E. Pvt. M.D.            33050086              3-27-43
Trujillo, John B. Pvt. 200 CAC        38011925              4-14-43
Llewellyn, John A. Cpl. 59 CAC        19020669              4-16-43
Lester, Robert B. Civilian                                  5-15-43
Leffler, Fay F. Pvt. 59 CAC           18049915              6-5-43
Mansker, Charles R. Pfc. 4 USMC                             6-13-43
Allison, Elroy A. Pfc. 192 Tank       6972937               6-21-43
Payne, Ralph G. Pvt. 31 Inf.          18043796   Hq. Co.    6-23-43
Browning, Robert J. Pvt. 31 Inf.      14038443   Co. C.     7-8-43
Connell, Walter R. Pvt. 34 Pur.       19015417              7-11-43
Guilfoyle, Lucien M/Sgt. M.D.         R-351564              8-8-43
Brown, Calvin L. M/Sgt.   CAC         6134001               8-17-43
Yeager, Taylor J. Pvt. 12 M.P.        14046231              9-24-43
Shove, Robert G. FM2c USN             3214308               10-27-43
McCord, Jilian C. Pvt. 698 Ord.       14054973              10-29-43
Irwin, Wilburn M. Civilian                                  11-30-43
Carey, Chester A. Pfc. QMC            6503782               12-22-43
Best, Henry C. Civilian                                     2-18-44
Bell, William Pfc. QMC                6460529               3-12-44
```

The End

Made in the USA
Charleston, SC
20 August 2010